# GROWTH GROWTH GROWTH

JULIAN COBBING

Human History and the Planetary Catastrophe

Published by Catalyst Books LLC
701 La Chapa Unit B El Paso TX 79912 USA
www.catalystpress.org


First published in 2023 by Mvusi Books, Makhanda, South Africa

ISBN Print 978-1-967673-00-1
ISBN Ebook 978-1-967673-86-5
Library of Congress Control Number: 2025944089



Distributed worldwide by Consortium Book Sales & Distribution, a division of Ingram, with the exception of the South African Development Community (SADC) territory, where it is published and distributed by Mvusi Books.

Consortium Book Sales & Distribution
Phone: 612/746-2600
cbsdinfo@ingramcontent.com
www.cbsd.com

Editor: Robert Berold
Cover design: Brian Garman
Text design and layout: Liz Gowans

Revised edition, first printing
10 9 8 7 6 5 4 3 2 1

Printed in the United States of America

# Contents

# 1. Growth and the Human Crisis

*Homo sapiens,* humans – us, our species, you and me – are in trouble. Our economic system ('capitalism') that dominates the planet is dependent on growth at all costs. If that growth were to stop, the system would collapse. At the same time, the resources of the Earth that our economic system consumes are finite. This obvious contradiction means our economic system is unsustainable.

Everyone, at some level, knows this. Yet the people in charge, who make the decisions, keep on growing the economy. Some don't seem to care about the consequences, others hope that yet-to-be-discovered technical means will allow the planet to cope indefinitely. But there is no 'world government' that could survey the whole crisis or have the power to bring about the changes that might lead to a sustainable future.

Every environmental index shows the path we have taken is unsustainable. Climate has become more capricious and extreme. Forests (both tropical and non-tropical) are being cut down for farmland. The carbon and methane we pump into the atmosphere has caused a planetary rise in temperature which will reach 1.5 °C by the early 2030s, if not earlier. The melting of land ice in Antarctica and Greenland is already raising sea levels. By the 2040s, irreversible runaway global heating will be underway.

At the same time, the resources which our economies are consuming are running out. Oil, on which so much depends, is forecast to last only into the 2040s. And our population growth, together with our battering of the environment to make way for cities, fields and roads, is killing off other species – a massacre which is already amounting to the seventh, and quickest, extinction in the history of life on Earth.

As an historian, I have since 1970 been teaching 'normal' history, with a focus on Africa, most of those years at a small university at the southern tip of Africa. The need to link the teaching of history to our planetary crisis became clear to me during 1995, sparked by relentless news of environmental crisis alongside the Rwandan genocide of 1994. I wanted with some urgency to design a course on 'world crisis' that, given its importance to young people's lives, I felt should be taught to first year students. I was lucky to have the support of the head of our department and encouragement from other staff.

I started teaching the course in 1997, to students aged 18 or 19 who knew practically nothing about history. To our surprise the number of students enrolling in the course far exceeded our expectations. Young people were clearly only too aware of the ominous trends facing them, and wanted to know more. I ran the course for 16 years, from 1997 till after my retirement.

This book is a written and somewhat distilled version of the lecture course. It focuses on historical developments which have generated crises, or accelerated existing human crises. The beginning of agriculture was the first of these: from a species perspective, it hurled us into permanent crisis. Other such developments were the invention of firearms, the printed book, and the clock, all of which led us directly to imperialism and industrialisation.

For some tastes my emphasis may appear skewed, too preoccupied with Europe. But whether we like it or not, much of today's world is rooted in what happened in Europe after the 1400s, particularly the way Europe's emerging nation states and their rivalries initiated industrialisation and the development of capitalism. The nineteenth century saw huge further steps in this direction, with the development of the steam engine, factories and railways, electric lighting, and the increasing control of governments by a voracious capitalism.

This enormous momentum led to what historian Eric Hobsbawm called the 'age of catastrophe': the wars of 1914-45; Stalinism; the Nazi massacres of 1939-45; and the nuclear bombs dropped on Japanese cities by the United States in 1945. Then followed the 'golden age' of capitalism, and its collapse into the post-1980 decades of neoliberalism, the weakening of democracy, and the financial crash of 2008.

Concurrent with this chronology are four themes. The first is our population growth and its impact on the environment. Our current eight billion population is increasing by around eighty to ninety million a year: it will reach ten billion by the 2050s. Food output per person is declining; water aquifers are being depleted; the oil on which much of our industry and food depends will be gone by 2050. And there will be no large animals left in the wild by the 2080s.

Secondly, our financial and political-corporate systems are founded on continuous growth of output and consumption. If economic growth ceased, there would be deflation, unemployment, and the collapse of corporations and small businesses. Large corporations simply cannot contemplate the end of growth. Those with money and power are preoccupied with growth, even when they pay lip service to reducing pressures on the environment. Environmental activist groups have little influence on them.

Thirdly, we are in a moral, spiritual, psychological and educational crisis. Our older religious and moral constraints have been weakened and are being replaced with consumerism. We live in a psychological world fixed in the present tense, cut off from the past and future. Human qualities such as love, decency, and empathy have been eroded by our competitive social environment and the amorality of social media. Despite the overwhelming reality of climate change, the fact is that in practice little can be done about it. This leaves our societies stricken with a paralysed despair, self-destructive attitudes, and a growing fear of what awaits us in the future.

The fourth theme is the human compulsion to self-massacre. Population pressure and contemporary weaponry have ensured that war and genocide take place continuously and increasingly. Since 1900 we have experienced a hundred million dead in two world wars, while genocides have become more hideous in scale. Genocides, I argue, are not aberrant events, but a central feature of who we are. We can be certain that mass killing will continue into the future. It can only increase in frequency and intensity as environments are destroyed and a killer species puts itself under intense evolutionary stress.

So, a cheerful book! It has no original ideas. Its originality, if any, is its bringing together of the vectors and themes most relevant to our present crisis.[1] I write with the conviction that we humans, despite our delusions to the contrary, are an unimportant, recent, and even irrelevant component of a much wider life system. From the planetary perspective, the solution to the problems we have created is the extinction of our species. And we have indeed created the conditions for that to happen. From our own perspective, our only hope is to correct our behaviour. But this, as we shall see, is going to be very difficult.[2]

## 2. Our Relationship with Everything Else

Where did we come from? How old is the Earth? How long have we been around? How do we relate to other life forms? Why are we superior to other animals? *Are* we superior? Is there any purpose to our existence? Only humans experience these puzzles: everything else, alive or not alive, simply *is*, and does not think about it.

Until the past century we knew very little about the age of the Earth, our age as a species, and details of the emergence of life. The cosmologies of many 'primitive' humans saw us, and in places still see us, as having emerged from the Earth, the mother. Any number of 'gods' or 'spirits' were imagined in cosmologies across the planet in countless small societies. But, for reasons that we will see, Christianity came to dominate the rapacious, 'successful' part of the world centred on Europe, and Christianity saw us created specially by God in *his* own image, above, outside of, and in charge of nature, with the female relegated to an assistant. Variants of this idea, spreading out from Europe after about 1500, were an animating image of capitalist man: 'nature the horse and man the rider', as the seventeenth-century English entrepreneur, Francis Bacon, put it.

The ideas about evolution put forward by Alfred Russel Wallace and Charles Darwin in the 1850s modified this self-image and shocked the literate classes of the nineteenth century. Man, it seemed, had evolved over thousands if not millions of years from more primitive animals, and had not been specially created by God. The shock to the Christian church was great and priests and bishops denounced evolution in innumerable sermons. Evolutionary theories were, however, strengthened by Gregor Mendel's research on the gene in the 1860s, which, although not taken up until the early twentieth century, provided the first plausible mechanism for the driving of the evolutionary process. The Darwin-Mendel theories had by the 1950s been generally accepted by the world of science in what became known as the neo-Darwinist consensus.[3] The objections of the church gradually softened as it became clear that the scientific notion evolution was, if anything, strengthening the exceptionality of the human species. We had fought our way to the top over millennia and occupied the position of top dog in nature, in charge, and able to do whatever we wished.

Is it a pure coincidence that Darwin's ideas of evolution coincided with the outburst of ultra-competitive capitalism of the mid-nineteenth century? Theodore Roszak in his *The Voice of the Earth* notes plausibly: 'All the harsh competitive assumptions of the Manchester School [a nineteenth-century version of today's neoliberalism] got mixed into the foundations of Darwinian biology. Far from reading the ethos of the jungle into civilized society, Darwin read the ethos of industrial capitalism into the jungle, concluding that all life had to be what it had become in the early mill towns: a vicious "struggle for existence".' This thought is echoed by the evolutionary scientist Stephen Jay Gould, who wrote 'Charles Darwin derived natural selection more by wondering how he might transfer the *laissez-faire* principle of Adam Smith's economics into nature than by observing tortoises on the Galapagos Islands.' Despite Darwin's own misgivings, evolutionary Darwinism became a central ingredient in later nineteenth century 'social Darwinism' where the focus was on struggle, the survival of the fittest, and the right of the strongest to take what they wished. These ideas were adopted enthusiastically by the fascist and ultra-capitalist movements of the twentieth century.[4]

Even if, formally, scientists do not credit the evolutionary process with 'progress', and will, if pushed, deny that humans are a special animal, in practice the bulk of scientific thought takes the same position as Francis Bacon: man is separate from and outside of nature, in charge of things, and effectively in the role of God. Most scientists have little time for the admonition of the nineteenth-century Native American chief Seattle: 'Man did not weave the web of life, he is merely a strand in it. Whatever he does to the web he does to himself.'[5]

The support given to the Darwinian theory of evolution by Gregor Mendel's discovery of the gene led to more questions. If evolution happened when an organism was acted on by the environment so that only 'good' variations survived and passed on their genetic material, what was the mechanism by which the information was passed from one generation to the next? Studies of disease-causing bacteria and viruses by Oswald Avery and other geneticists in the 1930s and 1940s led to the discovery of the central role of nucleic acid in the process, or deoxyribonucleic acid to give it its full name: DNA for short. This was followed in 1953 by the unravelling of the complex structure of DNA by Francis Crick, Rosalind Franklin, and James Watson. In sexual reproduction of plants and animals a single chain of DNA splits into two, each half re-forming into a new cell. In the process very occasionally there is a molecular error, leading to the variation necessary for the environment to 'work on'.

Further support for Darwin's theory was provided in 1956 by the American Clair Patterson's accurate calculation of the age of the Earth. Darwin had stressed that evolutionary changes could only happen over an extremely long time scale, and the presumption in the 1860s that the Earth was only around a few million years old did not provide enough time for the animal and plant kingdoms to have evolved by the slow processes Darwin imagined. Patterson – by using the rate at which uranium decays into lead – was able to demonstrate that the Earth is 4.55 billion years old. This was plenty of time for evolution to have happened. With the discoveries of genes, DNA, and the much older age of the Earth, the neo-Darwinist consensus hardened. By the 1960s it had become the orthodoxy that we humans had evolved as the pinnacle of the evolutionary process.

Other discoveries of the 1950s and 1960s, however, led to doubts that we were kings of the planet. New dating techniques of geologists demonstrated that humans had only evolved around a quarter of a million years ago: a long time ago, but insignificant in the context of a planet 4.55 billion years old, let alone a universe over 12 billion years old. The work of Elso Barghoorn on ancient rocks in Swaziland showed that the first primitive living cells on Earth appeared in the oceans about 3.8 billion years ago. Multicellular life had to wait until about 700 million years ago, and the plants only began to evolve on land around 450 million years ago. The first mammals appeared about 70 million years before the present era (BP, as we shall term it from now on), and the earliest hominids around 2.5 million years BP. *Homo sapiens* emerges a quarter of a million years ago. Even the olive thrush in my garden evolved about 9 million years BP.

If we compress the 4.55 billion years of the Earth's age into a single year: the first life form appears some time in early May, the dinosaurs get going in mid-December, whilst *Homo sapiens* makes an appearance at 11p.m. on 31 December. In that hour, as we will see, we have got up to a lot of mischief.[6]

Neo-Darwinism as a framework for situating humans in the system of life had become generally accepted in schools and universities by the 1960s, with natural selection, competitive struggle between life forms, and progress being its central themes. But just then an alternative framework began to appear: the Gaia hypothesis (later promoted to a 'theory'). Its first promoters were the British scientist James Lovelock and the American biologist Lynn Margulis. They demonstrated that all life on our planet is deeply implicated in modulating the chemical composition of the atmosphere, the land and the oceans, and that all life effectively constitutes a single, alive system.

Lovelock (who, like Darwin, was born in Wiltshire, England) was in 1965 working on the US space programme in Pasadena, Texas. At that time the first space probes were about to be sent to Mars: one of the objectives being to determine whether there was life on Mars. Lovelock was an expert in the composition of gases, and knew that, since his gasometers showed that the atmosphere on Mars was about 95% carbon dioxide, life could not exist there. Better to spend the dollars on other things. One day, wondering why, unlike Mars, Earth has a chemically very unstable atmosphere that has nevertheless persisted for eons, it occurred to Lovelock that the maintenance of the atmosphere depended on life itself. Without life, the Earth's atmosphere would be about 98% carbon dioxide, and the Earth, like Mars, would be a dead planet. Perhaps, he speculated, the many species of life on the planet were collectively cooperating to stabilise this instability so as to maintain optimum conditions for life itself? Lovelock's neighbour, the novelist William Golding, suggested the name Gaia, the ancient Greek Goddess of the Earth, for Lovelock's hypothetical collective of life. The name turned out to be unpopular as scientists tend not to like any suggestion of supernatural or mother images. Nevertheless work carried out by Lovelock, joined by Lynn Margulis after 1969, fleshed out the 'Gaia hypothesis' into a serious proposition.[7] In crucial ways it cuts across Darwin's evolutionary theory, and even today there has been no satisfactory amalgamation of the two macro-theories.

The Gaian theory undermines a lot of the basic assumptions of biological science as it stood in the 1960s. It proposes that the larger organisms on the planet, including ourselves, are dependent on the trillions of microscopically small bacteria that inhabit every nook and cranny of the Earth, and would not exist without them. Margulis and her son, Dorian Sagan, tell the story in their book *Microcosmos.* When the Earth condensed out of the original explosion, it was a planet circling the sun that had no life on it. This situation lasted for over 500 million years until the first life began. How this happened is still the big mystery. The first living things were single cell bacteria, with an outer membrane containing cytoplasm, particles of protein, and pieces of DNA. The extraordinary complexity of even one strand of DNA makes it difficult to visualise how it could have self-assembled out of the necessary chemical constituents: nitrogen, oxygen, sulphur, hydrogen and carbon. Most experts pass over the problem with a vague paragraph or two, suggesting that given enough time the self-assembly of life was an accident or coincidence that was inevitable. Other scientists, including the astronomer Fred Hoyle, disagree. In Hoyle's view, for life to have spontaneously appeared is as feasible as a Boeing 707 self-assembling out of a junkyard. He suggests that life was seeded on to Earth from outer space. Even if that is correct, the question of how life could have appeared in outer space remains.[8]

Once the first bacteria were alive in the oceans that were still forming, they spent two billion or so years getting up to mischief. They replicated either by subdividing their cells or by borrowing material from other bacteria. This borrowing of other bacteria's DNA, and the sharing of life information globally, invites the idea that we are really looking at one planetary life species. Some bacteria invented spirochaetae, which enabled them to move. Others learnt the process of fermentation, which created molecules of the basic life energy source called adenosine triphosphate, or ATP. A key breakthrough was the evolution of bacteria that used ATP to 'fix' nitrogen, whereby nitrogen is taken from the atmosphere into the oceans and converted into amino acids, necessary for life. 'All organisms depend for their existence on nitrogen-fixing bacteria', Margulis and Sagan write, and without nitrogen fixation life would have died out very quickly.[9]

Even more critical were those bacteria that developed photosynthesis, whereby, in combination with the energy from the sun, hydrogen and carbon are turned into carbohydrates. The first versions of photosynthesis used hydrogen from deep sea sources and from volcanoes. An improved version by other bacteria developed the high energy capacity to break apart the water molecule, $H_2O$, and use the hydrogen atoms for photosynthesis whilst excreting the oxygen. Margulis and Sagan conclude: 'The evolution of photosynthesis is undoubtedly the most important metabolic innovation in the history of life on the planet.'[10] Without it we would not exist. (Humans still cannot artificially create photosynthesis, though after the development of electricity in the later nineteenth century, we became capable of fixing nitrogen.)

The problem with photosynthesis using water is that the oxygen that is discarded is, or was, poisonous for all bacteria. At first the oxygen given off fused with other elements and was kept out of the air. At the time this was happening, the atmosphere contained less than 1% of oxygen, and bacteria could cope with it. But as time went by the build-up of oxygen in the atmosphere reached 10%, and around 2.5 billion years BP, life was faced with what is known as the oxygen poisoning crisis. Over the next half a billion years, however, bacteria evolved a method to coexist with the oxygen build-up, and some actually came to depend on oxygen, opening up the path to the evolution of multi-celled species.[11]

By 1.5 billion years BP, the combined efforts of bacteria had created the planet much as it is today. Instead of the evaporation of water and the build-up of carbon dioxide to over 90%, as had happened on Mars and Venus, planet Earth's bacteria had created a highly unstable atmosphere that was 'just right' for life. And this atmosphere, although chemically unstable, has been maintained to this day at about 21% oxygen, about 79% nitrogen and traces of other gases, including less than 1% methane. The trillions of bacteria, which brought about this beautiful planet as seen from space, inhabit the thin skin of the planet's surface down to several miles in depth. Margulis and Sagan write: 'The environment is so interwoven with bacteria, and their influence is so pervasive, that there is no really convincing way to point your finger and say this is where life ends and this is where the inorganic realm of non-life begins.'[12] Fritjof Capra emphasises that 'life is much less a competitive struggle for survival than a triumph of cooperation and creativity.' He concludes: 'all bacteria are part of a single microcosmic web of life.'[13] In which, he might have added, humans are irrelevant.

Around 2.2 billion years ago a new type of cell made its appearance, much larger and more complex than the bacterial cell. Inside, it contained a nucleus, in which DNA coils of great complexity were intertwined. These cells are termed eukaryotes, in contrast to the simpler bacterial cells which are termed prokaryotes. In some variations of this new nucleated cell there are several other 'bits and pieces' including mitochondria, which play a vital role in creating cell energy. (All this was unknown to Darwin in the 1850s. When he wrote *The Origin of Species* it was thought that all life was 'big', and that the oldest species were about half a billion years old.) Neo-Darwinists assumed that the mitochondria evolved in the normal evolutionary competitive struggle, whereas Margulis and Sagan show that the mitochondria were previously independent bacteria that had 'moved in' and settled down in a symbiotic rather than competitive process. They stress: 'The view of evolution as a chronic bloody competition among individuals and species [...] dissolves before a new view of continual cooperation, strong interaction, and mutual dependence among life forms. Life did not take over the globe by combat, but by networking.'[14]

The new eukaryotic cells evolved, and within a billion years had developed into multi-cellular creatures, which, within a further 300 million years, had given rise to fish, plants and animals. All these 'higher' forms of life had emerged out of bacterial cells; had had their conditions for existence created by bacteria; and were still teeming structurally with bacteria which co-inhabited them. Margulis and Sagan write: 'Our own bodies are composed of one thousand billion ($10^{12}$) animal cells, and another *ten* thousand billion ($10^{13}$) bacterial cells...The microcosm is still evolving around us and within us. You could even say...that the microcosm is evolving *as* us.'[15]

Margulis emphasises that Gaia is 'not an organism but an emergent property of interaction among organisms'.[16] If we take together the ideas that bacteria are the key life form, that the basic theme of bacterial life is cooperation rather than competitive struggle, and that bacteria operate at a planetary level almost as a single life system in which it is difficult if not impossible to discern individuals, we get what is known as the 'weak' version of the Gaia hypothesis.

The 'stronger' version, the one Lovelock prefers, is the view that planet Earth is inhabited by a single being, which may be likened to the goddess Gaia.[17] 'How does "Gaia" make "her" decisions?' conventional biologists enquire sarcastically: 'Does she hold weekly committee meetings?' Fortunately for Gaia there is no need for committee meetings or clumsy forms of human management. Instead, it has been shown that vastly complex interplays within systems can achieve their own stable existence, even when conditions are 'far from equilibrium', by a process termed 'autopoiesis'. Provoked by Gaian theory, much work has been done in this field in the past fifty years. Fritjof Capra in his *The Web of Life* refers to the work done on autopoietic systems by Humberto Maturana and Francisco Varela. Capra describes autopoiesis as 'a network of production processes in which the function of each component is to participate in the production or transformation of other components of the network. In this way the entire network continually makes itself'.[18] In other words, the 'life system' can, as a totality, interact or cooperate to bring about balances 'far from equilibrium' in the atmosphere, the oceans, and in the soils. The idea of autopoiesis is not conceptually remarkable.

Ongoing research into details of life on Earth as an autopoietic system make it an exciting field of study. The findings, either conclusive or likely, include the following:

1. Methane, which is vital for life, reacts with oxygen and disappears, but life replenishes it at a rate of around 500 million tons a year to keep its proportion in the atmosphere at exactly 0.7%. (Today we are raising this level considerably since methane is given off by cattle.)
2. Carbon dioxide: originally the atmosphere contained upwards of 10%, but, as the sun over 4 billion years got hotter, life reduced levels down to around 0.25% (250 parts per million), stabilising temperatures over eons at around 22°C (degrees centigrade), a level favourable to life (now interfered with by human activity). The basic mechanism here is the interplay between photosynthesising bacteria, which take carbon from the atmosphere, thus cooling it, and methane-producing bacteria, which adjust atmospheric temperatures upwards as necessary. Temperatures are further adjusted when carbon is taken in by the sea and used by ocean

organisms to make their shells, which are eventually compressed below the ocean surface into huge beds of carboniferous rocks. Carbon is also breathed in by trees and plants, and later buried under the ground, forming the coal, oil and gas deposits that humans are busy returning to the atmosphere today.

3. Sodium chloride is absorbed in the oceans, and is kept more or less exactly at 3.4% of the seawater volume. Should salt levels rise above 5%, marine life would become impossible. Yet salt runs off from land all the time. It is thought that to counteract this salt run-off, algae form vast deposits of salt in coastal areas which later become buried underground so as to maintain levels viable for marine life. (In the 1950s Soviet cotton fields using irrigation brought one such buried salt deposit to the surface adjacent to the Aral Sea.)
4. Sulphur, needed for life on land, is washed into the oceans in river run-off. Without some mechanism for returning it to the land, organisms would soon be starved of essential sulphur. Microscopic sea organisms, for example *Emiliania huxleyi*, give off dimethyl sulphide when they die, a form of sulphur which is blown onto land by winds, where it decomposes into sulphur that is useable by plants.
5. Oxygen, once a poison to bacteria, has its present-day levels, of around 21% of the atmosphere, kept stable by trees and plants which produce oxygen. As soon as levels increase to about 25%, forests burn, making life impossible, and below 15% life pushes concentrations up.
6. Nitrogen, which is essential for life, is the most abundant gas in the atmosphere at about 79%. The two major problems with nitrogen levels are both solved by bacteria. Firstly, by a process of nitrogen fixation, bacteria break down nitrogen gas into forms of the element useable by life. Secondly, nitrogen dissolves in the oceans, and over hundreds of millions of years it would have disappeared altogether if not returned to the atmosphere. This is done by bacteria and eukaryotic species in the oceans which, by a complicated chain, absorb fixed nitrogen for their growth, and then recycle it back as free nitrogen, which rises to the ocean surface and then moves back into the atmosphere.[19]

Without these fine tunings devised by living systems, the extremely unstable atmosphere of Earth would have settled at over 90% carbon dioxide. Margulis and Sagan sum up: 'With teams of growing and dying bacteria inhabiting every possible locale on Earth's surface and continually selecting the best local solutions to the problem of maintaining life at any given time, the surface is kept in a stable and hospitable state. Consisting of life, the environment is continually regulated by life, for life...Moreover in their alliance with animals and plants, which could not live or evolve without them, the Earth's bacteria form a complete planetary regulatory system.'[20]

And all this without a single committee meeting.

Every few hundred million years this Gaian life system, the fossil records demonstrate, experienced a catastrophic extinction shock, each of which wiped out a large proportion of species. Recovery from these mass extinction events always took many millions of years, and usually resulted in a different mixture of species. The great oxygen poisoning crisis of 2.5 billion BP, mentioned above, was one such catastrophe. There have been at least five others since the Cambrian geological era began about 600 million years ago. The worst extinction event happened approximately 250 million years ago when over half of all biological families and an astonishing 93% of individual species disappeared, thus ending the Permian era. This was when the trilobites became extinct. About 65 million years BP, in a catastrophe that ended the Cretaceous era, about 75% of species disappeared, including the dinosaurs.

The causes of these catastrophes are much debated by geologists. The 'Permian-Triassic' event is variously attributed to global warming or cooling, a major lowering of ocean levels, volcanic eruptions, disruptions to the major ocean currents, and the 'clathrate gun' hypothesis, whereby methane trapped under the oceans explodes upwards following a major warming event, thus compounding the warming situation (methane being a potent warming gas). The event that ended the Cretaceous and caused the dinosaur extinction, has since the early 1980s been attributed to a large planetesimal colliding with the Earth.[21]

Nowadays scientists are talking about a sixth mass extinction since the Cambrian era began, and the first one to be caused by the activities of a single species in the system – humans, ourselves. Our exponential increase in population, combined with our economic fixation with growth and competition, make us a very dangerous species. Since the 1970s, 69% of all land animals have become extinct as a consequence of human killing activities. Lovelock writes: 'Sometimes in anguish, concerned environmentalists ask if humans have become a leukaemia of the Earth.'[22] Jean Baudrillard echoes Lovelock: 'Ours is a society founded on proliferation, on growth which continues even though it cannot be measured against any clear goals. An excrescential society whose development is uncontrollable... There is no better analogy here than in the metastatic process in cancer.'[23] This cancerous attack on the life system has occurred within an extremely short time in the context of Gaian chronology. And as a relatively insignificant component of the system, we are vulnerable to elimination. Lovelock warns: 'If we lose our habitat, the system of life and its environment on Earth, Gaia, will go on. But humankind will no longer be part of it...the rules of Gaia are such that organisms that harm their environment do not long survive. We would do well to understand this rule, which may have fatal consequences for our species.'[24]

Neither do we pose a threat to the system overall, whatever our short term impact. Lynn Margulis sums up: 'No planetoid collisions or nuclear explosions have ever threatened Gaia as a whole. So far the only way in which we humans prove our dominance is by expansion. We remain brazen, crass, and recent, even as we become more numerous. Our toughness is a delusion. Have we the intelligence and discipline to resist our tendency to grow without limit? The planet will not permit our populations to continue to expand. Runaway populations of bacteria, locusts, roaches, mice and grass always collapse...We cannot put an end to nature; we can only pose a threat to ourselves.'[25]

Bear in mind our precarious position as we proceed. Conventional history (what I call 'history-history') tends to focus on human progress, and thus is a form of species self-congratulation. As this book unfolds we will switch between human events and our vulnerable position within the Gaian system, whilst admitting – to quote Stephen Jay Gould – that as yet 'we do not even know how to conceptualise, much less to draw, the world view that would place *Homo sapiens* into a proper relationship with the history of life.'[26]

## 3. Humans Emerge within the Gaian System

Our self-fascination ensures that much research has gone into the emergence of us humans, *Homo sapiens.*[27] But despite the academic careers devoted to our origins, it is surprising how little we know about how, or indeed when, we emerged within the Gaian system. What we do know is that the first humans appeared, almost certainly in Africa, about a quarter of a million years ago. It is not agreed when 'we' became 'we', but it was about then that we succeeded *Homo erectus* as the planet's key hominid. Debate still continues about the extent to which the early 'archaic' forms of *H. sapiens* were different from us; for example in their 'cognitive' abilities. It is not clear when we evolved into unambiguously intelligent humans with whom we could hold a conversation. This could have been any time between 40,000 and 300,000 years ago. Either way, if the duration of life on Earth of 3.8 billion years is compressed into a single year, we have been around 0.01% of that time, or 52 minutes.

In this chapter we examine briefly some of the questions regarding our emergence, followed by a brief discussion of some of our singular traits. It has to be stressed that there is still no accepted, agreed-upon paradigm regarding our emergence. There is no shortage of evolutionary theories, and new unexpected evidence is regularly dug up by paleo-anthropologists.

It is true that we are very closely related to chimpanzees, with whom we share about 97% of our genetic structure. Chimps evolved in Africa around 10 million years BP, and the first hominid, *Homo habilis*, appeared in Africa at about 2.5 million years BP. Interconnecting the two species there have been various transition species, which have included several species of *Australopithecus*. The anatomical and mental kinship of *Homo habilis* with chimpanzees is sufficiently close to warrant some specialists to say they should be put into the same genus. *Homo habilis* did, however, have an upright walking gait, and a redesigned pelvis, and took the manufacture of crude tools way beyond what chimps can do.

By around 2 million years ago *Homo habilis* had given way to *Homo erectus*, with more modern skeletal features, and a much larger brain capacity. *Homo erectus* is, or was, a fascinating animal. It was still around

500,000 years BP, and perhaps even later, and is thus chronologically by far the most successful of the hominids, being in existence for between one and two million years. *Homo erectus* is African in origin, though, by around 1.5 million years BP, it had spread into Asia and parts of Europe. It is virtually certain that by a million years BP *Homo erectus* had mastered the deliberate use of fire for cooking and heating. It is assumed that meat eating led to the enlargement of *erectus's* brain capacity, so that by half a million years ago it had doubled in size from approximately 600 to 1200 cubic centimetres, not far short of our own brain size. Were they conscious as we are, even if at a more primitive level? Could we have conversed with them? They did not write things down: all we have are their bones. The structure of the lower part of the skull gives us clues as to the relative position of their larynx and pharynx. Interpreted one way, this meant they could verbalise roughly as we do; but interpreted the other way they could not, and thus could not have been conscious in quite the same way as we are.

From about 300,000 years BP *Homo erectus* developed into 'archaic' forms of us, *Homo sapiens*. Experts tend these days to defer granting the full badge of modern humanness until further developments had taken place by about 150,000 years BP. There is a grouping of interlocking academic debates about this. The possible permutations of interpretation are many, and difficult to be certain about, views changing as new evidence is unearthed and academic trends change.

For example, did modern forms of *Homo sapiens*, us, evolve simultaneously out of *Homo erectus* over Africa, Asia and Europe? Or did modern humans appear first in Africa 100,000 to 50,000 years BP, and migrate out of Africa some time in those 50,000 years? If the latter, did the new arrivals in Asia and Europe massacre earlier forms of *Homo sapiens*, or merge with them over many thousands of years of interbreeding? These questions interfuse with another question. By about 150,000 years ago a form of *Homo sapiens*, named *Neanderthalensis* (after the valley in Germany where it was first discovered in the 1850s), had emerged over much of the Middle East and Europe. Are they, are we, subspecies: *Homo sapiens sapiens* (us) and *Homo sapiens neanderthalensis* (them); or are we separate species, *Homo sapiens* and *Homo neanderthalensis*? Did we, *sapiens*, outcompete and massacre *neanderthalensis*; or did we interbreed with them, and merge our genetic structures?

The neanderthals could hunt with sophisticated tools, like us, and buried their dead and obviously had a concept of death, like us, and lived much as we did. On the other hand their eyebrow ridges were prominent, and their legs on average on the short side; they also tended to live in colder regions. Are these anatomical differences sufficient to warrant separate species status? Or are they close enough for a neanderthal not to be noticeable if seen suitably dressed on the London underground? Recent analysis of DNA traces is tending to view them as separate species, which supports the 'out of Africa' hypothesis. On the other hand science has shown that we have a proportion of our genetic structure that is neanderthal, suggesting that *sapiens* interbred with *neanderthalensis,* and did not massacre them. The last full-boned neanderthals are thought to have been pushed into the far south-western corner of Europe, where they disappeared about thirty thousand years ago. By then *H. sapiens* was painting on walls and had become an artist. But beware: the self-praise of our intelligence and artistic talents is rooted in nineteenth-century social-Darwinism and may not correspond with any actual superiority of our evolutionary past.

Another strand in the tangle of debates concerns 'cognition'. Our design of tools and weapons took a leap forward between about 100,000 and 50,000 years BP. Art discovered on cave walls in France and other parts of Europe seems to have been 'better' about 40,000 years ago than 100,000 years earlier. Some paleo-anthropologists like to reserve the full badge of humanness to the products of this supposed 'cognitive revolution'. This would imply that either we were the same species with different cognitive versions, or that full humanness did not materialise until a very short time ago. It seems clear, though, that we were artists and 'cognitively' very capable, well before 40,000 years ago, so the late cognition hypothesis is unlikely to be correct. Much earlier humans were for example already burying their dead and indicating their preoccupation with the mysteries of death.

The current theory is that there was a series of cognitively capable human migrations out of the African savannas southwards into today's South Africa and northwards into Europe and Asia in the 50,000 or so years either side of 100,000 BP. The 100,000 years before agriculture were interspersed with periods of ice advance when sea levels dropped sharply, allowing migration movements that are not possible today. Modern humans reached Australia about 70,000 years ago, via Indonesia and New Guinea. Skills at making clothes led to migrations into the colder parts of Siberia and Europe. Between 16,000 and 11,000 years ago, and possibly earlier, *Homo sapiens* crossed what is today the Bering Straits, at that time periodically above sea level, into North America, and over the next couple of thousand years southwards throughout the Americas.

Although it is true that we are intelligent, hence 'sapiens' (Latin for 'intelligent'), an observer from space might be more struck by the fact that we use this intelligence to kill other animals and each other. Apparently animals of the African savannah, having evolved with us over thousands of years, were the most skilled at surviving *Homo sapiens*. But the larger animals of Europe and Asia, such as the mammoths, woolly rhinoceros and sabre-toothed tigers, were massacred. In parts of Ukraine and southern Russia early humans used tusks from mammoths they had killed to construct the frameworks of their dwellings. The evidence for the massacre of larger animals by *Homo sapiens* as we moved into new territory is also seen in Australia and the Americas. Many of the larger species there did not survive the arrival of humans very long. In Australia animals that were driven to extinction in the 30,000 years after our arrival included many genera of marsupials, for example a two metre high wombat called the diprotodon. In the Americas animals we killed off included horses, bison, elephants, giant armadillos and sloths – anything that was too slow or too trusting. This pattern persisted throughout history, until, as we shall see later, we have become the perpetrators of the sixth mass extinction currently being carried out (seventh if we include the oxygen poisoning extinction). Wherever humans have migrated in the past several thousand years, larger animals and birds have been driven to extinction. As Thomas Berry wrote in 1988: 'If there were a parliament of creatures, its first decision might well be to vote the humans out of the community, too deadly a presence to tolerate any further. We are the affliction of the world, its demonic presence. We are the violation of the Earth's most sacred aspects.'[28]

Anthropologists have long debated whether humans' skill at killing included self-killing on a large scale (genocide) from the beginning of our history as a species, or whether our skill at mass murder is a consequence of post-agriculture overcrowding and other abnormal pressures. One school of thought sees us as being naturally peaceably inclined; only resorting to killing when under stress.[29] The other – surely more realistic – school sees us as formidable self-killers from day one, as evidence in the early history of Australia bears out. The chapters ahead will reveal all too many episodes of self mass-killing.

Let us set an imaginary scene in Africa in some human encampment near a river around 50,000 years ago. The women are resting from collecting firewood, and the men are discussing the hunting expedition planned for the next day. The children are playing. Maybe seventy or eighty individuals all told. They have similar mental facility as you or me – in other words they are what we call conscious. Consciousness is, though, not so easy to define. We presume we are more conscious than other intelligent animals, but cannot be certain exactly where the difference lies. It implies intelligence, to be able to imagine the future, and to be able to mull over possibilities. Psychologist Stuart Sutherland, in *The Macmillan Dictionary of Psychology*, describes it as: 'Consciousness: the having of perceptions, thoughts and feelings; awareness. The term is impossible to define except in terms that are unintelligible without a grasp of what consciousness means. Many fall into the trap of equating consciousness with self-consciousness – to be conscious it is only necessary to be aware of the external world. Consciousness is a fascinating but elusive phenomenon: it is impossible to specify what it is, what it does, or why it has evolved. Nothing worth reading has been written on it.'[30]

Be that as it may, the conscious Stone Age group that we are observing speak their own language, but cannot write, so the stories they tell get altered over time, overlaid by others, and even the great ones get forgotten from one generation to another. The vocabulary is sufficiently large to permit complex group organization, and to lay down rules of behaviour encoded in practices guarded by older members of the group.

Compared to chimpanzees and monkeys, we humans have broken free, if that is the appropriate phrase, from instinctive behaviour. We have an imagination that can lead us to act in a very large range of ways in any given situation. Our brain capacity gives us omnipossibility, which means we can make a decision to do one action, beneficial to the group, or another action, harmful to the group. An individual may innocently, or, worse, deliberately, i.e. consciously, behave so as to harm the interests of the group. We may assume that groups that did not evolve a moral code of behaviour and an ability to enforce penalties against transgressors would have been at an evolutionary disadvantage. Behaviours that harmed the group had to be clearly separated off from those that were beneficial, or at least not harmful. It is to be stressed that the distinction between harmful and beneficial, that is between evil and good, was not something written in the sky, and probably varied from one *sapiens* group to another. What the elders had evolved as their moral code did, though, tend to be attributed to instructions from spirits or gods who watched each individual closely.

Over the generations, the moral code of a surviving/successful group would have needed to be hammered home in the education of the children. Children's education centred on practical skills for survival on the one hand, and behavioural obedience on the other. Those groups that were not, over the generations, able to enforce 'good' behaviour would have been out-survived by those that did. Long-established, successful bands must have had agreed on sanctions for 'evil' actions by individuals, and group acquiescence in necessary controls. This implies the group recognition of 'elders' for their experience and knowledge, and group unity where younger members acknowledged the authority of the older ones. The permutations of situations experienced by a group were potentially infinite, good times giving way to bad, unpredictably. Both individually and as groups, humans are highly variable, capricious, and cannot be pinned down. These are aspects of our consciousness and mark us off from all other animals.

As *Homo sapiens* we differ as well from other animals in our sexuality. Whereas the female of our closest relatives – chimpanzees, vervet monkeys, gibbons etc. – come into season at specific times of the year when they are fertile and exhibit their availability to be mated with, adult human females are fertile throughout the year, and show no clear indication of when they can be fertilized. There is a very high sex drive, and it is permanent, and not restricted to a fertility window. The relevant specialists do not agree why this should be so. The permanent sex drive can be used for its purpose of fertilization, or it can be redirected as 'libido' into other pursuits, for example hunting, war, sport or writing novels.

Why we are naked is by no means obvious. Was it because we started to make our own clothes, and could dispense with hair? And in hot climates? The only original suggestion I shall make in this book is that our nakedness is somehow associated with the necessity for a high sex drive in our species. One example of our omni-possibilities is that we can decline to have sex, and can refuse to create children. However, any brake on the decision to procreate in societies where child death rates would have been high would have threatened the existence of the group and put it at an evolutionary disadvantage. Consciousness and the ability for couples to say no to children (as for example in 1930s Soviet Union) needed therefore to be counterbalanced by a compelling sex drive, permanently switched on, hence the boosted epigamic sex features such as the male penis, the female breast and the nakedness. The ability of a conscious being to say no to sex had to be outmanoeuvred. Otherwise we would not be here. In turn, the possibility of sublimating sexual energy in other activities became one of our most dangerous features, and a fuel for history.

The features of *Homo sapiens* evolved slowly over hundreds of thousands of years, out of *Homo erectus* and in turn out of *Homo habilis*, then out of *Australopithecus*. Not much is known about these forebears' group behaviour, intergroup relationships, or propensity for violence between groups. All that we know has to be inferred from evidence left in camp and burial sites. Apart from the sun and the stars, they had no clocks. Time was circular, repeating from season to season, year to year. Either the intelligence or cultural drive ensured that innovations were infrequent, and as likely to be forgotten as embraced. The right angle and straight line were rare until agriculture. 'In a hunting and gathering society,' writes Gary Snyder, 'you learn the landscape as a field, multidimensionally, rather than a straight line...In a society in which everything comes from the field...the landscape with all its wrinkles and dimensions is memorised. You know that over there is milkweed from which comes glue or string, over the hill beyond that is where the antelopes water.'[31]

Peter Matthiessen wrote on the state of mind of humans who are not ruled by clock time: 'Such concepts as Karma and circular time are taken for granted by almost all native American traditions; time as space and death as becoming are implicit in the earth view of the Hopi, who avoid all linear constructions, knowing as well as any Buddhist that Everything is Right Here Now. As in the great religions of the East, the Native American makes small distinction between religious activity and the acts of every day: the religious ceremony is life itself. Like the Atman of the Vedas, like the Buddhist Mind, like Tao, the Great Spirit of the American Indian is everywhere and in all things unchanging. Even the Australian aborigines – considered to be the most ancient race on Earth – distinguish between linear time and a "Great Time" of dreams and myths, and heroes in which all is present in this moment. It stirs me that this primordial intuition has been perpetuated by voice and act across countless horizons, and the early Indo-European civilizations... And it is a profound consolation, perhaps the only one, to this haunted animal that wastes most of a long and ghostly life wandering the future and the past on its hind legs, looking for meaning, only to see in the eyes of others of its kind that it must die.'[32]

When time was repeating itself circularly over eons, such societies could have had very little idea of progress. With no means of writing they could not have been able to compare happenings in the present with different happenings of the past, except over the briefest of time-spans. In other words they had no history in the double sense of not having a written record and of little changing over the generations. This was to change when agriculture ushered in our ability to produce food surpluses, and live in permanent settlements. Fields and villages introduce the life focussed on straight lines, which are deadly: the trout fishing line, spears, arrows, trajectories, lines of soldiers, furrows, rectangular buildings, mental ideas of progress, the pursuit of paradise in the future. The more straight lines, the more we move in the direction of history, progress and disaster.

It is easy to fall into the temptation of romanticising pre-agricultural societies. Early *Homo sapiens* had from day one a propensity towards violence and mutual killing, and everywhere *Homo sapiens* migrated, large numbers of animals were massacred. By 10,000 years ago humans in widely separated parts of the world were each, in their own separate environments, moving towards organizing the production of foods: beginning agriculture. With agriculture, population expands, events accelerate, and the means are developed to write down stories as well as the edicts of rulers. Thus history begins, and we embark on our tragic destiny.

# 4. Agriculture

Around 11-10,000 years BP, humans began for the first time systematically growing their own food. One of the early areas was today's Syria, Iraq and Turkey, where the main crops were wheat and barley. Villages arose, static settlements became common and these early farmers worked in fields, and herded cattle. Over several thousand years improved varieties of wheat were developed, and grain surpluses in good years led to population increases. Specialist professions, for example potters, could be fed by group surpluses, and other divisions of labour evolved. By between 8,000 and 6,000 years BP similar centres of grain production had emerged in India, China and the Americas based on locally suitable crops, such as rice and maize. With cattle and other possessions came chattels and capital, both words deriving from 'cattle'. Food surpluses permitted the emergence of classes of chiefs and specialists, along with divergences in consumption and social class. There was a switch towards masculine control and the subordination of girls and women as compared to hunter-gatherer societies. Societies became more vulnerable to years of drought and famines were common. For some 5,000 years such societies evolved systems of chiefly rule over village settlements. The means of enforcing their rule over wider areas did not yet exist, nor did the requisite food surpluses.

This was to change around 5,000 BP with the development of two critical technologies: bronze weapons and pictogram writing, which, in combination, were to lead to larger political structures and the first cities. The bronze weapons, controlled by elites, led to armies of soldiers armed with bronze swords and axes, and equipped with bronze protective armour and helmets. Pictogram writing evolved through various methods of chiselling into stone: stories could be recorded, and law codes were devised, along with a new class of judges and soldiers to operate them. The first cities were established in fertile regions, such as the valleys of the Tigris and Euphrates in Mesopotamia, in today's Iraq. Other cities emerged in the river valleys of the Nile (ancient Egypt), the Indus and the Yellow. The key requirements were access to water and soils of suitable fertility.

Bronze weapons maximised surplus extraction and enabled the rise of ruling aristocracies who imposed taxes on 'free' citizens, and forced labour on slaves. This opened up the emergence of often brutal class systems. Conflict between wealthy families over who was to control the tax pot produced civil wars and clashes between competing city states. Priests, scholars, or experts were charged with finding out the parameters of any context, vetting them for their advantage to the rulers, censoring them where necessary, arguing away alternative viewpoints, and giving psychic support to those in power. They posited the existence of gods who invariably bore an uncanny resemblance to the kings. Most of the early stone records in museums are either lists of taxes owed to the rulers, or religious glorification of the kings, and praises for their military talents. One example in the British Museum is a 'List of Ashurbanipal's Court Scholars' during the years 668-627 BCE. It illustrates the sort of experts of the time, not very dissimilar to the kinds we have today: 'The document [chiselled into stone!] names forty-five individuals who were on hand to advise the king. There were seven astrologers, nine exorcists, five experts on liver omens, nine physicians, six chanters, three experts on foretelling the future through the movement of birds, three interpreters of dreams, and three Egyptians.'[33] Ashurbanipal doubtless had his share of disasters.

Other specialists devised mathematics and calendars. The royal administrations required the measuring of everything, not just taxes to be exacted. A major function of the measurements was to coordinate labour. In Mesopotamia some of the measuring systems that were developed are still universal, such as the practice of dividing the day into twenty-four hourly units. A system of sixties subdivided into twelves became standard, with the circle subdivided into 360 degrees, and time into hours, days, months and years. It was not until the 1790s that French revolutionaries replaced some of the sixties with their hundreds, and the twelves with their tens; with the metre and the franc divided into hundreds. The British only switched from the twelve-based system of pounds, shillings and pence to the hundred 'ps' in a pound system in 1971.

The coming of cities and the growth of populations in them, based on coordinated labour systems and military raids on neighbours, made the Sumerian city states vulnerable to famine, epidemics, incapable rulers, attacks by other groups, and changes in the environment. Many lasted for hundreds of years, but all eventually collapsed, often suddenly, as the exhibits in the museums reveal. One of the more common causes of a civilization's collapse was the beginning of permanent drought and the running out of water.

The turbulence of events compared to pre-agricultural times gives rise to 'History', our term for what is in effect a permanent species crisis: progressive cycles of population expansion, overreach, collapse, new technologies and energy extraction, and the emergence of a new though temporary equilibrium. This has been expressed as 'White's Law': 'Culture evolves as the amount of energy harnessed per capita per year is increased, or as the efficiency of the instrumental means of putting the energy to work is increased.'[34] In each cycle there is more 'success', but also more vulnerability: population scale is increased, extraction of resources is extended, living standards are on average improved, but the environment is further attacked and degraded.

Civilizations based on bronze and pictogram scripts reached their peak in the two or three thousand years of the Egyptian states in the Nile valley (c.5,000-2,500 BP). Bronze was not available in abundance, however, and comprehension of pictograms carved into stone was restricted to a small number of scholars, and not available for large readerships. This limited the maximum size of the political unit. Two critical developments of around 1,500-1,000 BCE (3,500-3,000 BP) were to change this: the harnessing of iron, and the devising of the alphabet. Combined with the first use of paper, these two developments were to permit the emergence of much larger imperial units.

Iron revolutionized both agriculture and warfare and in turn the potential size of states. Because iron is available in far greater quantities than copper-bronze, once refining techniques had been developed, larger, better-armed armies were possible. The result was the rise of the Greek city states, and within a thousand years, the development of the Roman Empire. Iron ploughs gradually replaced wooden ones, and soils could be dug deeper with less energy. Food supply expanded as in turn did populations.

The alphabet was to have an even more profound impact. It first appeared around three thousand years ago on what today is the coast of

Syria, then known as Assyria. Two forms evolved from the first version: that of the Greek (and Russian) script, and that of the Western Latin script, which you are reading. Instead of hundreds if not thousands of pictograms, about twenty-five symbols, in themselves meaningless, could be combined into a virtually infinite number of words, with meaning. Combined with the use of papyrus from the Nile valley, which gave us the first forms of paper, instructions and information could be shared amongst a much larger number of people, over a wide area. The combination of the iron spear, and thousands of armed men reachable by written orders from a political centre, led to the potential for empire and imperialism.

The critical importance of the alphabet tends to go unnoticed by historians. But as Marshall McLuhan writes: 'The alphabet meant power and authority and control of military structures at a distance.' [35] The scale of human organization was hugely increased. McLuhan notes as well its critical psychological impacts: 'Literate man, once having accepted an analytic technology of fragmentation, is not nearly so accessible to cosmic patterns as tribal man...Indifference to the cosmic, however, fosters intense concentration on minute segments and specialist tasks, which is the unique strength of Western man.'[36] That is to say, we habitually examine everything in minute detail, with narrower and narrower specializations, but fail to understand the wider picture, what it is all about, or where we are going. As McLuhan puts it: 'Only alphabetic cultures have ever mastered lineal sequences as pervasive forms of psychic and social organization. The breaking up of every kind of experience into uniform units in order to produce faster action and change of form (applied knowledge) has been the secret of Western power over man and nature alike.'[37] The alphabet underlay the rise to power of the Greek states and their successor the Roman Empire, which in turn explains the beginning of Europe's rise to power. (The psychic boldness of European imperialists horrified African societies in the nineteenth century.)

The alphabet, slowly at first, led to an explosion of texts and literacy. From about 1,250 BCE to the time of Christ (the year zero in our modern calendar) plays and epic poems were not only created but also recorded. Today's universities and schools still study Greek and Roman writers. The first story I was confronted with by my teachers in the 1950s when

I was six was a version of Homer's *Odyssey* (alternating with *Babar the Elephant*!) Iron weapons and written orders on paper sent to widely spread military units led to the Greek empire of Alexander the Great. The political and scientific works of Plato, Socrates and Aristotle still underpin Western thinking. By the third century BCE Greek was being replaced by Latin as the dominant imperial language. By the time of Christ Roman power extended over much of the Mediterranean region and southern and central western Europe.

Nowhere was the power of the written text more evident than in religion. Widely distributed written teachings were essential to today's great global religions: Judaism, Buddhism, Confucianism, Christianity and Islam. Some readers of this book will believe that the particular religion to which they adhere is God-inspired, and the only one that is true. If so they should forgive me for my 'neutrality' in this realm. Since 100,000 years BP humans, both *sapiens* and *neanderthalensis*, had been burying their dead in such a way as to indicate a belief in the afterlife. Most of the beliefs and teachings of human mystics, holy leaders, and cult leaders in the millennia before written texts have disappeared. It was only after texts could be replicated and distributed after about 1,250 BCE – whether in China, India, the Middle East or Europe – that religious texts could be handed down from one generation of priests and disciples to the next.

Invariably systems of religious belief were used to place the rulers on pedestals and make them inter-confusable with gods, hence the great religions were accepted by ruling groups, even if not always straight away. Religions thus became tools of the powerful as well as serving as moral codes. Some were formally peaceful (Buddhism), and others more militant (Christianity and Islam). Each had a mystic dimension, with beliefs about the afterlife. Bringing people together, they served as synchronised human families, offering escapes from isolation and loneliness. They could also be political organizations, strong enough to survive the breakup of the state they had emerged within, as was the case with Christianity after the fall of the Roman Empire.

The successful religions, by cementing their institutional structures and sacred texts, crowded out newer competitors. This helps explain why all the major religions on the planet today – Judaism, Buddhism,

Confucianism, Christianity and Islam – were founded in roughly the same 2000-year segment of historical time, 1,000 BCE to 800 CE. The greater the age of their texts, the more god-given they seemed to be. Young people drilled in the content of a religion by parents or priests found it a mental challenge to reject the teachings, and in many societies, such as medieval Europe, to do so was dangerous. The great religions remain effectively unchallenged to this day.

The political rise and fall of Rome lasted over a thousand years. Three hundred years of a republic were followed by several hundred years of empire. Iron weapons, written texts and long, straight roads underlay its success. The success of the Roman empire, however, could not endure forever, and, as it expanded in area, there came a time when its administrative capability became overstretched. Joseph Tainter describes the sequence: 'The establishment of the Roman Empire produced an extraordinary return on investment, as the accumulated surpluses of the Mediterranean and adjacent lands were appropriated by the conquerors. Yet as the booty of new conquests ceased, Rome had to undertake administrative and garrisoning costs that lasted centuries. As the marginal return on investment in empire declined, major stress surges appeared that could scarcely be contained with yearly Imperial budgets. The Roman Empire made itself attractive to barbarian invasions merely by the fact of its existence. Dealing with stress surges required taxation...so heavy that the productive capacity of the support population deteriorated...In the later Empire the marginal return on investment in complexity was so low that the barbarian kingdoms began to seem preferable.'[38] Within a few hundred years Rome had collapsed and disappeared as an empire, with the core city of Rome reduced from a population of over a million to about 40,000.

The first imperial Roman emperor to convert to Christianity was Constantine, in the early fourth century CE (CE meaning the Common Era, formerly expressed as AD). Temples to a variety of gods all over the imperial state began to give way to Christian churches. Between the seventh and tenth centuries CE, the organizational sub-units of the Catholic church survived after the imperial structures collapsed, with Christian bishoprics established as far away as Britain and northern Germany. As the Roman governmental structures went into decline, and

Rome itself, the centre, collapsed, the structures of the Catholic Church remained, and were to provide a unifying presence in medieval Europe. Christian Catholic popes based in Rome held sway over a wider political area than even the most powerful king or emperor, and conflict between the Roman Catholic church and various states is a central theme of medieval and early modern European history.

The history of India and China parallels that of the western and central European region in the fifteen hundred years after the death of Christ – with cities, kingdoms, forms of slave or serf labour, and expanding scales of population. Throughout the world technological innovations slowed, and political structures remained variants on the same themes. As Rome collapsed, Europe went into relative economic and political decline, even as the population expanded. Although the image of Europe entering a period of 'dark ages' after the decline of Rome is more a reflection of the sparseness of historical documentation than of a regression in living standards, there was little to indicate that the modern world would be conceived in Europe rather than India or China.

# 5. Why Europe?

The modern nation state and modern industrial capitalism emerge explosively out of Europe after the late 1400s. This chapter investigates the technical breakthroughs that made this possible.

Around 400 CE the European sector of the Roman Empire had a small population of about 25 million people. Europe was more or less entirely covered in oak, ash, elm and beech forests, with human settlements in clearings. The forests contained dangers, and the howls of wolves triggered fears that still inhabit the European mind. Over the next half a millennium, as the Roman administrative centres collapsed, local ruling groups applied force via horse-mounted, iron-armoured soldiers (knights), and established 'manors', on which peasants were brought into a system of forced labour (serfdom). Peasant surplus produce was seized by the local lords, and recycled into the feeding of their policing armies. Given the difficulties of communication over wider areas, power was locally centred. Local lords or barons held the real day-to-day power, and the 'big' lord, or 'king', was a *primus inter pares*. Although he (seldom a she) was usually succeeded by his eldest son, the lineage could be overthrown and replaced by a new one if its capacity to attract the support of the barons weakened.

By around 1,000 CE a system of feudalism had evolved over much of Europe (only reaching England in 1066). This was a system where the big man/king with his large military retinue legally owned all the land, and gave it out to big lords as 'fiefs', or 'manors'. In return the lords had to pay allegiance to the feudal monarch, periodically prove their fealty, provide military support to the king when needed, and usually make a token payment. The big lords in turn imposed the same process on 'gentry', who owed them allegiance. At the lowest level were labourers who had no rights to land, were compelled to work on their superiors' land, and had no right of movement. This was the institution of serfdom, not fully abandoned in eastern Europe and Russia until the communists took over in 1917 (to be replaced under Stalin in the 1930s by a variant form of forced labour). Towns emerged as commercial and trade centres, with the urban elites wresting what rights they could from the monarchies, and starting the first parliaments.

The main crop in Europe was wheat, and, in a climate of regular rains and excellent soils, wheat surpluses led to rising populations. The use of iron tools, such as hoes and ox-drawn ploughs, permitted regular good yields. A hard-work ethic was encouraged by the Christian church whose priests and bishops (answerable to the pope in Rome) allied with the ruling land owners. Vast amounts of forest were cut down for new fields, dwellings, tools and fuel. Advances were made in windmills and watermills, enabling the processing of more grain with less energy. Local towns grew in size, as they could be fed, becoming hubs where specialists such as blacksmiths and butchers were available. The rising populations due to increased wheat production led to tensions and clashes between feudal groups, with civil conflict frequent. Richard Manning remarks: 'Wheat was the empire builder; its bare botanical facts dictated the motion and violence we know as imperialism.'[39] Feudal monarchs fought each other, or combined to raid into the Middle East (the Crusades). Records of these conflicts in Latin provide historians of this era with their raw material.

As populations grew, periodic famines became more frequent, and by the 1300s CE a renewed phase of crisis was reached throughout much of Europe. The Black Death (a form of bubonic plague spread by fleas) drastically cut back Europe's population in the 1340s and 1350s, and also in subsequent epidemic outbreaks. Labour shortages and peasant uprisings increased tensions.

There was nothing to indicate that the next grouping of solutions lay just ahead, and that it lay in Europe. China and India were as far advanced as the European political units (not yet nations), but were to be left behind by Europe over the next 600 years. Why was that? Three new developments intermeshed to give a dramatic boost to European power relative to the other human power centres: firearms; the printing press; and clocks. The result of these three technological breakthroughs was to be the world's first nation states.

Let us take guns first.[40] The first use of gunpowder in primitive cannons was in the German Rhineland in the 1320s. Early cannons were used during the hundred years war between England and France (the 1340s to 1440s) but were not very efficient and were almost as dangerous to their users: they did not immediately replace the central importance of archers and horse-mounted knights. From the mid-1400s, however, smaller firearms were being manufactured, primitive early muskets called arquebuses. This was a new killing machine, constantly being improved. By the early 1500s its bullets could penetrate armour and kill knights. Larger, improved cannons were able to destroy feudal castles. A temporary arms race between mounted horsemen with thicker and heavier armour, and arquebus-armed foot soldiers, was soon decided in favour of the latter. (The knights' horses became too big and heavy to move quickly.) The implications were to be profound. Knights and feudal castles were suddenly obsolescent, and the feudal era ended.

Between about 1450 and 1550 powerful barons fought it out to see who were able to establish centralised kingdoms in widespread civil wars in which firearms became widespread. Loser barons tended to be reduced to regional rulers owing allegiance to a more powerful central monarch, such as Charles VIII in France and Henry VII in England. Ferdinand and Isabella similarly were able to fuse the separate provinces on the Spanish peninsula into a united Spanish kingdom (Portugal finally asserting its independence in the 1640s). Fights over internal power hierarchies were, by the 1500s, evolving into wars over national boundaries, and to the gelling of the European structure of rival nations. 'Modern' European history begins. The clashes and wars between the new monarchical states were to provide the material for conventional European history over the next several hundred years in an era extending from the 1480s until 1945. Sequences of warfare, revision of national boundaries in peace treaties, and interval periods of recovery, are familiar to students of European history.[41]

Successful centralising monarchs based their power on large standing armies, often of mercenaries. These consisted of the employment of many thousands of troops, who had to be clothed in uniforms. The better they were able to operate in coordination, the more victories were possible. The parade ground is the symbol of the new era. The mass manufacture of firearms, cannons and uniforms in factories formed an early root of the industrialisation to come. Firearms and trained troops enabled relatively small numbers of troops from competing European proto-nations to conquer 'native' groups overseas, and it is the firearm that permits the initiation of European imperialism in the 1500s. This is symbolised by the mnemonic we learned as English schoolchildren: 'In 1492 Columbus sailed the ocean blue.' Yes, certainly improvements in sailing vessels were important, and it is true that viruses and bacteria played a role in the European conquest of most of the planet: but without firearms the Europeans would easily have been thrown back by local military forces. In turn the information and raw materials Europeans brought back from imperial areas turbo-charged industrialisation.

The manufacture of firearms involved precision engineering that was to be adapted into making different forms of 'tubes'. The telescope, for example, was to provide a basis for modern physics, as was the microscope for biology. And later came the steam engine. All of them were forms of proboscises to extract energy and knowledge and suck it back for home use.

The second technology that underpinned, indeed necessitated, the nation state was the printing press, using moveable type.[42] As with guns, the first printing press was developed in western Germany, with Gutenberg's printing press of 1452. The age of Gutenberg had begun, and was to last unchallenged until the electronic computers of the 1970s. The printing press was the most dramatic improvement in human communication since the alphabet. The result was the book and the mass production of printed documents that, combined with the firearm, underlay centralised monarchical power. The first consequence was the enlargement of bureaucracies. Uniform systems of administration could be established to the far corners of the emerging national boundaries. Single national systems of spelling and written speech were necessary, hence the rapid evolution of national languages in the sixteenth century. The mass production of books provided an additional impetus to industrialisation. Libraries proliferated, underlying the scientific revolution that now began. There could be a synchronization of thoughts and genius which had barely been possible before. Ideas flowed across the new national boundaries. Intellectual breakthroughs in one region could rapidly spread over the whole continent, which further stimulated scientific advances.

The accompanying psychological changes are stressed by Marshall McLuhan. The *content* of a medium, that is the message or information it contains, is not as important as the invisible *effects* a new medium has on the way our minds work. McLuhan remarks: 'Our conventional response to all media, namely that it is how they are used that counts, is the dumb stance of the technological idiot. For the "contents" of a medium is like the juicy piece of meat carried by the burglar to distract the watchdog of the mind.'[43] Or as he puts it in his famous, though frequently misunderstood, aphorism: 'The medium is the message.'[44]

What McLuhan meant by this is that the particular content or message carried from one person to another by a medium, say a book or the TV, is less important than the way in which the very use of that particular medium affects the way we think and behave, invariably in an unconscious way. Thus printing allowed knowledge content to be communicated: but more important were the effects on the European psyche. McLuhan reflects on 'that most potent gift bestowed on Western man by literacy and typography: his power to act without reaction or involvement. It is the kind of specialization by disassociation that has created Western power and efficiency. Without this disassociation of action from feeling and emotion people are hampered and hesitant. Print taught men to say, "Damn the torpedoes. Full speed ahead."'[45]

The book also contributed to the creation of the adult-child relationship that was to last until the age of computers. As industrialisation advanced and more schooling was required for young people, the more children's access to relevant knowledge could be controlled by adults. Secrets, for example about the 'facts of life', could be withheld from the child. This separation was to last until television after the 1940s made it no longer possible.

The third of the key inventions that underlay European power was the clock. Early clocks were used by Benedictine monks to wake themselves up for prayer at ungodly times like 3 a.m. They had no intention of using this time-reminding machine to synchronise the industrial world and make the factory possible. Neil Postman writes: 'what the monks did not realise is that the clock is not merely a means of keeping track of the hours but also of synchronising and controlling the actions of men.' He continues: 'And so by the middle of the 14th century, the clock had brought a new and precise regularity to the life of workman and merchant. It made possible the idea of regular production, regular working hours, and a standardised product. Without the clock, capitalism would have been impossible. And so, here is the great paradox: the clock was invented by men who wanted to devote themselves more rigorously to God; and it ended as the technology of greatest use to men who wished to devote themselves to the accumulation of money.'[46]

The clock was first operational in Paris in the early 1400s. It was without a minute hand until sufficiently improved in accuracy in the 1650s. The clock produces the human fixation on duration and speed, and intensifies the combined application of human energy. In McLuhan's words: 'Clocks are mechanical media that transform tasks and create new work and wealth by accelerating the pace of human association. By coordinating and accelerating human meetings and goings on, clocks increase the sheer quantity of human exchange.'[47] It was to be the primary instrument, not only of capitalism, but of the scientific revolution. Lewis Mumford notes: 'The clock not the steam engine is the key medium of the modern industrial age.'[48] It was the machine that regulated machines, and regulated the human labour that operated them. The clock gave rise to the timetable, which from the 1830s was to permit the railway system. The obsession with time, and timing, underlies the factory system. By the 1990s one and a half billion watches were being made in a year. (Today the smartphone ties its human owner yet more closely to a speeded up global coordination of time and action.)

The clock was also to play a vital role in European navigation of the oceans. Sailors could already tell where they were on the high seas in so far as latitude was concerned by measuring the angle of the stars. But for them to be able to accurately determine longitude, the precision measuring of time was necessary. A prize was offered by the British government for the first person to devise a clock accurate enough to do this, and was won by the Englishman John Harrison in 1759 with his T4 chronometer. Ships could now be directed around the world with absolute precision. It took only a few short years from the T4 chronometer for Europeans to be accurately searching the Pacific Ocean for land and resources. And after a few more years the colonization of Australia began.[49]

None of these technologies were developed in the same way in China.[50] The three breakthroughs of the firearm, the printed book, and the clock were, in their combined, inter-potentiating impacts, to drive half a millennium of European power over most of the rest of the planet, before China and India caught up. They brought us to the nation state, the scientific revolution, imperialism, industrial capitalism, the demographic explosion, five centuries of European global domination, and endless war between rival European powers, until the atom bomb compelled them to desist. They also fuelled a relentless attack by humans on the planetary Gaian system and were a disaster for other animals.

## 6. Imperialism

Before the late 1400s, Europe's capacity to imperialize the world was non-existent.[51] But in the 1500s and 1600s the transformations brought about by the nation state (based on guns, books, clocks and also better designed ships) enabled Europe's nations, in competition with each other, to begin the extraction of energy from other parts of the planet. The most successful nations in the earlier phases were those on the western fringes of Europe: France, Spain, Portugal, the Dutch Republic and England. Conflicts over imperial access spilled over into warfare in Europe itself, beginning with Charles VIII of France's invasion of the Italian peninsula in 1494, and lasting until the German attack on the Soviet Union in June 1941. The resources brought back to Europe as a result of imperialism were an important base for the industrialization that followed. In addition, there was colonialism in which European settlers formed colonies in the Americas, India and the Pacific, most of which eventually became independent.[52]

The first competing thrusts of imperialism were led by the Portuguese and Spanish after the 1480s. The islands off the north-west shores of Africa were divided up between them: the Canaries to Spain, Madeira to Portugal. In 1488 the Portuguese Bartolomeu Dias rounded the southern cape of Africa, and his successor Vasco da Gama crossed the Indian Ocean and landed in India (setting up the Portuguese colony of Goa). After Columbus's 'discovery' of the Caribbean islands in 1492, central and South America were similarly divided up: Brazil to Portugal and most of the rest to Spain. Spanish adventurers 'discovered' the Pacific Ocean in the early sixteenth century, and Spanish settlers began to move into Mexico and Colombia. Accompanying them were priests of the Catholic Church whose task was to force the 'natives' to change their religious beliefs and accept European rule. The work ethic was encouraged and indigenous labour was organised in near-slavery conditions. Other Spanish 'conquistadores' advanced along the west coast of South America into what later were called Ecuador, Bolivia, Peru and Chile. All eyes were ever alert for raw materials, minerals and cultivatable land. Silver and diamonds were in particular demand. By the mid-1500s the silver so extracted had given Spain, the 'mother country', previously unimagined wealth, and produced the first major inflation in the European economy.

Plants were exchanged. Potatoes migrated from Peru to Spain, and cotton and tobacco plantations were established in the Americas. Alfred Crosby speaks of 'the empire of the dandelion' as Europe's 'weeds' took a lift on ships crossing the Atlantic. He writes: 'The seams of Pangaea were closing, drawn together by the sailmaker's needle. Chickens met kiwis, cattle met kangaroos, Irish met potatoes, Incas met smallpox – all for the first time.'[53] Smallpox was exported from Europe to the Americas, while syphilis was sent from the Americas to Europe.[54]

European sailors mastered the planet's wind systems. Improvements were made in ship design. In 1519 Magellan led Spanish ships around the tip of South America, only to be killed when he arrived in the Philippines. Magellan's deputy, Elcano, and his sailors were probably the first men to circumnavigate the planet when they arrived back in Seville in 1522. By the eighteenth century Europe's ships were sailing the oceans of the world with increasing accuracy, helped by the telescope, first invented by the Dutchman Hans Lippershey in 1608, and John Harrison's T4 chronometer of 1759.

An energy extraction process ensued, as Europeans plundered the world for its resources, taking over land in regions where coveted crops could be grown. Indigenous peoples were compelled to work for European enterprises. Africans were captured mostly from the west coast of Africa, shipped across to the Americas, and put to work as slaves on the new sugar and cotton plantations being developed there. Developing European industries exported their wares to Africa, especially alcohol and obsolete guns. Crops grown and minerals mined in the Americas were then shipped back to Europe, completing the so-called triangular trade. Owen Lattimore wrote of this early era of imperialism: 'Big territories were conquered with small forces. Income, first of all from plunder, then from direct taxes and lastly from trade, capital investments and long-term exploitation, covered with incredible speed the expenditure for military operations. This arithmetic represented a great temptation to strong countries.'[55] European administrations are still 'apologising' for the slave trade.

Between the 1500s and the 1800s European diets were transformed by the changed economic order. Slave-grown sugar was consumed in Europe. The first chocolate factories opened in Britain in the early 1800s, using cocoa brought in from west Africa. Coffee and tea changed Europe's drinking habits. The first coffee houses opened in London in the 1690s, linked to the new stock market where shares in the new export-import and insurance companies were quoted. The English became addicted to tea. It allowed them to keep awake longer, and be more productive. Tobacco was first smoked in pipes in the late 1500s; with the development of cigarettes in the nineteenth century it became a very widely used addictive substance. Large companies evolved to produce, sell and import these new commodities. A global intermesh of trades developed that could get quite complicated. For example: after the English had, by the early 1800s, taken over much of India and begun trading from there with the Chinese, British manufactured goods were exported to India in exchange for the Indian tea crop; in turn opium grown in India was traded with China for a different sort of tea, which was then sent back to India, and from there back to Britain. By the 1840s the British were going to war against China to force its rulers to accept opium as an import. Until the 1850s the monopoly British East India Company was ruling India, saving the British government the expenses of administration. It was only in 1857, when the poor administration of the Company provoked an uprising against its rule, that India was taken over directly by the British crown. Queen Victoria became 'Empress of India', a title the British monarchy was to retain until 1947.

Cotton, hitherto rarely obtainable in Europe, was grown on huge plantations in Brazil, the West Indies and the southern part of British north America (after 1783 the United States). Exported back to Britain, the new cotton and weaving enterprises linked up with the steam engine to establish the world's first factories. Cotton clothes, compared to the wool clothes, improved health.

Perhaps most important of all, a root crop, the potato, found in Peru, was genetically improved, and from the 1600s slowly crept into the European diet. By the 1700s the potato had become a major European food crop.[56] Maize from Latin America was also imported. Together these crops improved European fertility rates. The people of Ireland, for example, became increasingly dependent on the potato, with bad results after the potato blight of the mid-1840s: in Ireland a deadly famine occurred in 1847 when the potato crop failed.

In 1865 William Stanley Jevons, a prominent nineteenth-century coal economist, defined 'imperialism' for the English (without using the word): 'The plains of North America and Russia are our cornfields; Chicago and Odessa our granaries; Canada and the Baltic are our timber forests; Australasia contains our sheep farms, and in Argentina and on the western prairies of North America are our herds of oxen; Peru sends her silver, and the gold of South Africa and Australia flows to London; the Hindus and the Chinese grow tea for us, and our coffee, sugar and spice plantations are all in the Indies. Spain and France are our vineyards and the Mediterranean our fruit garden, and our cotton grounds, which for long have occupied the southern United States, are now being extended everywhere in the warm regions of the earth.'[57]

In the 400 years after Columbus the extraction of energy from the new colonial areas, boosted by slave labour, led to a dramatic rise in Europe's population. Population statistics were only kept from the nineteenth century, but estimates can be made. In the early 1500s Europe's population (including Russia) was approximately 60 million people, around 12% of a total global population of about 500 million. By the time of the first steam-powered factories in the 1830s, Europe's population had nearly quadrupled to about 230 million, about 23% of a global population that had just reached a billion. By the time of the First World War in 1914 Europe's population had further expanded to about 450 million, 27% of the world's population of 1.7 billion. Put another way, Europe's population increased nearly eightfold in the 400 years between Columbus and the First World War, whereas the global population had increased by just under three and a half times.

Books and the standardisation of national languages led to more efficient accumulation of knowledge and quicker and wider knowledge-sharing across Europe. An idea broached in Moscow could be in Paris or London less than a month later. Dramatic breakthroughs in science were made in all the sciences. Just a few examples. In the 1520s a Pole, Kopernik (Copernicus), proved that the Earth circled the sun – not the other way round as had previously been believed. In the 1680s an Englishman, Newton, defined gravity and explained how this force kept the Earth in orbit. That orbit was described with increasing precision (only to be adjusted by Einstein in the early twentieth century). The other planets accompanying the Earth in revolving around the sun were discovered and given names. In the early 1600s an Englishman, Harvey, described the circulation of the blood and the function of the heart in pumping it around the body. Breakthroughs in the science of chemistry were pioneered by Priestley in the 1790s. Travellers from Europe around the world brought back evidence on a host of subjects that could be rapidly shared around the continent. Animal collectors brought back thousands of slaughtered species that in the 1730s enabled a Swede, Linnaeus, to originate a system that subdivided the world's living species into orders, families, genera and species.

A superabundance of new specializations came into being. The 'specialist' on any subject would know everything, or at least all there was to know at that point. He (or, as time went on, she) posed their dangers. 'For the specialist,' as McLuhan remarks, 'is one who never makes small mistakes while moving towards the grand fallacy'.[58] The European and United States education systems were subdivided into disciplines that were increasingly sealed off from each other. As information became nearly infinite, it became impossible for a single human to have an overview of the whole, and narrower specialisation became unavoidable. The inability to see the 'big picture' has contributed to the political paralysis we are in today.

The new nations that came into being with books, guns, and clocks evolved government systems in which the interests of the landed feudal classes were brought into alliance with other classes, such as families that had acquired new wealth in the trade linked to imperialism, and the emergent industrial class. The clashes and eventual compromises between these groups underlie each nation's history. For example, serfdom was abolished in the more economically developed areas, and replaced with a 'free' labour market. Labour could more easily be redirected to where it was most useful, so enhancing economic growth. This happened first in western Europe, and then more slowly in eastern Europe. In Russia, serfdom was only formally abolished in 1863, a major cause of the country's slow move towards capitalism.

The competition between Europe's nations over colonies and imperial plunder interfused with the previous preoccupation of Europe's 'feudal' classes with struggles over land. The result was a new era of warfare. The sixteenth century was the era of Spanish power. Religious conflicts between Catholics and the newly arising Protestants were central to the wars of the next 150 years. A German, Luther, and a Swiss, Calvin, used the new printing potential to spread their Protestant challenges to the papacy far and wide. Catholic Spanish power was challenged in the then Spanish Netherlands by Dutch Protestants in the 1570s – and between the 1570s and the 1650s, Europe erupted into a series of wars, of which the Thirty Years War from 1618 to 1648 was the most brutal. Spanish power was replaced by that of Louis XIV's France in the latter half of the 1600s. In Germany, Prussia emerged as the dominant power in northern Germany, vying with Habsburg Austria to the south. Conflicts in Germany and Italy led to the so-called War of Spanish Succession in the early 1700s, the War of Austrian Succession in the 1740s, and Seven Years War from 1756 to 1763. Prussian hegemony in north Germany was established by Frederick the Great, though only after Berlin had been occupied by the Russian army in 1760.

These wars, for Germany and Italy, were inextricably connected with wars between an increasingly powerful England and France for territory and trade in North America and India. England's successes[59] saw it establish English-speaking dominance in the eastern regions of north America, and Canada. England's bid to continue parasitising off their American colonists led to the latter rebelling in 1776, and the establishment of the English-speaking United States. France's aid to the American rebels, notwithstanding the French gloating and schadenfreude at England's discomfort, led to its own bankruptcy. The French Revolution, provoked by the French monarchy's attempt to suck more money from its population to pay for its wars, began in 1789. The revolution, successful by 1793, unleashed formidable new French energies which saw a French civil war transform into France's invasion of much of the rest of Europe under Napoleon (1797-1815). Britain's manipulation of the continental alliances against France, in combination with its continuing naval power, imperial profits and industrialising strength, led to a British supremacy in Europe after 1815 that lasted nearly a century.

## 7. Steam Engines and City Pox

The cargoes of goods carried by Europe's ships as they sailed the ocean blue were monetized by new banks that were established as early capitalism began.[60] The Dutch Bank of Amsterdam was one of the first, in 1609. Europe's monarchies gave some investment groups monopoly rights of trade in this or that area of the globe; from these the private company, the basic building block of the capitalist economy, emerged. Ships and their cargoes needed to be insured against loss, and the first insurance companies were established. People with money invested in the new trading companies and were given, in return, the promise of a proportionate share of the profits (assuming profits were made: often they weren't). An exchange system for such shares developed, and the first stock market was established in 1609 in the Dutch Republic. The Bank of England followed in 1694, and the London Stock Exchange in 1698.

As population increased and more land was needed for the cultivation of food, more trees were cut down for fuel, and for building houses and ships. The smelting of iron to manufacture ploughs and guns was done with charcoal, a form of wood. Heating of homes was done with wood. England[61] in particular, being a comparatively small island, began to run out of wood as its forests were cut down. By the 1600s the English had to turn to coal, of which they had plenty, for home heating. As more coal was dug, deposits on or near the surface disappeared. Mines had to be dug deeper, and before long they became prone to flooding. To pump water out of the mines by human hand was backbreaking work, and the quest was on for a mechanical pump. In 1698, Thomas Savery built the first steam engine. Savery's steam pump was not efficient enough, but in 1709 Thomas Newcomen invented the Newcomen steam pump, which can be regarded as the first machine of the industrial age. One of Newcomen's huge early engines can be seen in London's Science Museum, adjacent to a reconstruction of the filthy conditions of an early coal mine. It is difficult to see Newcomen's engine as the iron father of the industrial revolution. But the design was improved, and by the 1770s hundreds were in operation in the British mines. What was now needed was to turn Newcomen's vertical motion machine into one with a more efficient rotary motion.

The race amongst inventors for a rotary motion steam engine was won by James Watt in 1782 (just as Britain was losing its American colonies). The first factory to build these engines was established at Soho near Birmingham by Watt's partner Matthew Boulton. The Watt-Boulton steam engine was a spectacular success: technical developments rapidly allowed the rotary motion engine to drive spinning jennies to spin cotton cloth. By the early 1800s Richard Trevithick had married Watt's engine to a 'carriage' which ran on rails that could be used, instead of horses, to carry freshly mined coal from the minehead to the nearest canal or port.

The ramifications of these early steam engines were revolutionary. They were to permit the building of the world's first factories and the world's first railways, which revolutionized the structures of society. Theodore Roszak describes the overall transformation: 'It begins in the Midlands of Britain, a tiny island off the western edge of the Eurasian land mass. Gray and black dots issuing smoke like strange, smouldering sores break out on the surface of the planet. The dots spread across western Europe, leap the ocean to North America, then to other continents...Focussing in more closely, we can see heaps of slag and rubble forming around them like weltering flesh. We see the smoke thicken into man-made clouds that block out the sky. Rivulets of oily waste and noxious fluids issue from these fuming sites into nearby lakes and streams. We are watching the rise and spread of the first industrial towns...Gaia had been stricken by City Pox.'[62]

The first railway line to carry coal and passengers was opened in September 1825 with a steam-powered locomotive designed by George Stevenson. A speed of 15 miles per hour was achieved. By the 1830s railways were spreading throughout Europe and the United States. Both the word and the concept of *speed* appear. By the 1840s speeds of 40 mph were common (by 1936 the world's fastest steam engine, the Mallard, could do 126 mph). The power of the steam engine was symbolised by a painting I remember (I don't recall the artist) of horses in a field running in terror from a passing train.

The speed of the steam engine led to two problems. First, how do you prevent trains from colliding? Or, if the track is a single track, how do you make sure they wait their turn? The invention of the electrical telegraph solved this problem. Signals could be sent more quickly than trains could travel, and so the signal box was born. The second problem was ensuring that signalmen knew where trains were, and letting passengers know exactly when the train would depart or arrive. The railway timetable was born. Today we are all slaves to someone else's timetables, and it is difficult to imagine a world when there weren't any.

Railways revolutionised communication systems in Britain, then Europe, then throughout the world. Hitherto a letter carried by stage coach might take a week or two to arrive from a distant part of Britain. Now the passenger trains carried post in special mail vans. A national standardised system of postal and parcel charges began in 1840 when the Penny Black, the world's first postage stamp, was issued. Speedier and cheaper letters gave a huge boost to the organisation of the industrial system.

The building of the railway network that spanned the British Isles, and later Europe, North America, and the rest of the world, was the largest industrial undertaking in history. Railway companies made fortunes for the early investors of the 1830s and 1840s, but often made heavy losses for later investors. Huge pools of labour were required; many people were drafted in from rural areas suffering from overpopulation – including young people without access to land as a result of the British government's policy of enclosing the commons. Railways brought entire countries into a single unified transport system. The journey between London and Bristol, for example, ran into the problem that Bristol clock time was 30 minutes behind London time. So a unified national time structure was legislated: Greenwich Mean Time became the national time in 1847.[63] By the 1890s a unified global time was agreed between the nations, with hourly zones extending from zero degrees longitude running through Greenwich.

The speed of transport now made it possible to have national football leagues, the first one being set up in Britain during the early 1860s. The Saturday football results soon became a key event in the week, and, after the radio was invented, were discussed in the pubs. National football teams began to be selected, and international games first took place in the 1880s. Seaside holidays became feasible, giving a boost to the national addiction to fish and chips. An efficient railway system meant that one could travel good distances to work in city centres. To get away from the grubby, working class regions of the city centres, the wealthier people migrated out to new suburbs. Towns expanded into cities, and cities grew ever larger in size. The railway termini in the city centres throughout Europe were feats of engineering and industrial design, some of them as fabulous as medieval cathedrals.

Quite apart from the railway revolution, the steam engine revolutionised production, mechanising it, and leading to the first factories in the 1820s and 1830s. The steam engine was adapted first to power cotton spinning, and later to power factories for the weaving of woollen cloth. Economies of scale, hence larger profits for the factory owners, were only achievable by having large numbers of looms run by one engine. Hence the factory replaced the isolated workshop. Factories were grouped together. Several of the small villages in the midlands and north of England, which lay close to the coal mines, grew into colossal cities, and the countryside began to blacken. Fogs, as described in some of Dickens's novels, were common. The Clean Air Act would have to wait until 1956.

The new working class had zero political rights. They had to work long hours for extremely low wages, and if they were women, for even lower wages. Exhaustion and malnutrition were everywhere. Trade unions were set up, but in the first decades of industrialisation were banned, with strikers often being deported to Australia. The fact that all the profits went to the owners of the factories (the capitalists) and none to the workers, who barely subsisted, led to the first defining of the concept of 'capitalism' during the early nineteenth century. By 1850 Louis Blanc was defining capitalism as 'the appropriation of capital by some to the exclusion of others'. This was the beginning of radical writing pushing for political reforms, culminating in the writings of Karl Marx, calling for revolution and the overthrow of the capitalist class. Factories spread into other industries. Overproduction of this or that product was commonplace, and when sales collapsed, workers were laid off. This new, sometimes mass, unemployment created revolutionary tensions, as seen in Britain and France during the 1840s. The concept of 'socialism' was born in France in the 1830s, and revolutionary tensions from Europe's workers were one of the fuels of the 1848 revolutions across the continent.[64]

The industrial revolution started by the steam engine had changed the population and wealth patterns of society, and at a rapid rate. However in most European countries political rights were still confined to the wealthy landowners. The new factory owners, the capitalists, had as yet no political voice. This tempted them to ally with their own discontented workers. In Britain the land owners understood that they would have to buy off the capitalists by giving them the vote and a part in government. A series of parliamentary 'reform acts' realigned the interests of the capitalists and landowners, who, intermarrying, as money fused with money, had by the early twentieth century formed a single, hybrid 'ruling class'. In France, revolutionary tensions in the late 1840s were, after 1851, brought under control by Napoleon III, sometimes seen as a proto-fascist dictator. Capitalists and landowners in France continued their alliance after the overthrow of Napoleon III in 1870 during the Third Republic (1871-1940). In Germany, on the other hand, the capitalist groups never obtained proper control over the levers of government, which were held on to by the landed Junker class. Throughout Europe, however, the potentially revolutionary nature of the workers was diluted as the railway construction boom took off, and the economy expanded, reducing unemployment. To help matters along, the capitalists and landowners were mostly able to buy off a section of the workers with higher wages and greater supervisory authority. This change helped defuse political tensions, giving even the lowest paid workers something to work towards.

Throughout western Europe the new political alliances between capitalists and the owners of landed estates ushered in a new ethos of government. The capitalists wanted as little intervention in their affairs as possible. This non-interference in capitalist affairs was given the name 'liberalism'. In Britain the governments of Gladstone and Disraeli had in practice to do a lot of interfering in the operations of factories to keep the working class from getting out of hand. Nineteenth-century Britain was beset with endless Factory Acts and Public Health Acts.[65] Urban authorities were compelled to put in proper sewage systems to deal with the cholera that had become common in the insanitary industrial towns since the 1830s. Working hours in factories were regulated, and in the early 1900s the eight-hour day was brought in. Unemployment benefits were introduced, and annual holidays made mandatory.

The increasing demands placed on worker skills – in factories, government structures and the military – meant government was forced to set up a single national education system. Learning the so-called three Rs was every child's experience after the 1860s – reading, 'riting, and 'rithmatic. The idea was to provide just enough education to enable the child to operate in an industrial setting, but not too much to set them thinking. It remained difficult for a talented child from the working class to rise into the middle class, but not altogether impossible. These dramatic expansions in government expenses had to be paid for. In Britain it necessitated the reintroduction of the income tax in 1845, and higher taxes on trade. In all these matters the non-interference of 'liberalism' had to retreat. It re-emerged as the dominant ethos of government only in the 1980s with Reagan and Thatcher.

All this is what McLuhan would describe as the 'message' of the steam engine: Penny Black stamps, factories and smog, railways, football teams, Education Acts, income tax, seaside holidays, improved roads, sewage systems, suburbs. It also enabled the Nazi and Stalinist atrocities of the twentieth century, as steam locomotives carried people to the Russian slave camps in Siberia and to the German gas chambers in Poland.

# 8. Electricity and Oil

Two key moments in the human crisis came in 1859, with the discovery of oil in the United States, and in 1884 with the first steam turbine to generate electricity.[66] Let's look at electricity first. The British physicists Michael Faraday and James Clerk Maxwell discovered and refined the concept of electromagnetism, opening up many practical applications. By the late 1830s the electric telegraph using the Morse code was being used in the early railways to operate signalling systems. The telegraph system spread rapidly throughout Europe and the United States: the age of the telegram began. By the late 1860s, telegraph wires had been laid under the Atlantic Ocean to provide instant communication between England and the United States and the Cape Colony in southern Africa. Letters between London and Cape Town, which had taken three or four weeks to arrive by ship, were superseded by instant telegrams. In 1865 the German, Werner von Siemens, invented the electric motor, and in 1884 the Englishman, Charles Parsons, invented the first steam turbine, driven by coal-fired boilers in the method which still generates about 37% of the world's electricity. With the steam turbine and electric motor we enter the age of electric trams and the London Underground railway system.

Electricity from the burning of coal was to transform human lives. In 1876 the American, Thomas Edison, manufactured the first electric light bulbs. In 1879 came Alexander Bell's telephone. In 1895 the first cinema opened in Paris, though until the early 1930s without sound. The cinema gradually replaced the music hall as the primary urban source of entertainment. By the early 1900s Parsons' steam turbines were generating electricity, lighting towns at night and making it possible for factories to work in shifts throughout the night. In 1899 Guglielmo Marconi (or according to some accounts, Nikola Tesla) invented the radio, long referred to as the 'wireless'. The BBC started broadcasting in 1922, and before long we were listening to the King's Christmas speech, and to the rantings of Adolf Hitler.

The electric wiring systems that soon covered continents were a further giant building exercise, adopting Tesla's alternating current (AC), which was found to be more efficient than Edison's direct current (DC). Together with the improvements in the manufacture of concrete, after 1887 this permitted huge skyscrapers that reared into the sky in New York and elsewhere, transforming the shape of cities. Rather than climb up thirty or forty floors, Alexander Miles developed a safe electric lift, also in 1887. Devices using improved versions of Siemens' electric motors, running on electricity generated by steam turbines, have changed our lives forever: washing machines, vacuum cleaners, fridges, power tools and, of course, computers.

Alongside electricity came the other great energy source: oil. The oil discoveries made by Edwin L. Drake and others in 1859 did not at first seem to be of revolutionary significance. The refined product, kerosene (or paraffin), gradually began to replace palm oil and whale oil as lubricants for industrial machinery, and for lamp fuel. The new lubricants provided the profits for John D. Rockefeller to set up his Standard Oil Company in 1865.

One of oil's waste products was gasoline, which was too volatile and explosive for general use. The crucial breakthrough came when, in 1876, the German, Nikolaus Otto, developed the first engine that used gasoline, also known as petrol. Carl Benz, another German, took this engine and manufactured the world's first motor car in 1882. After that, gasoline became Rockefeller's chief source of profit as the motor car took off. One of the first vehicles made by Benz was named after his daughter Mercedes. By the 1890s motor cars were taking to the roads in larger numbers, particularly in the United States. They were mechanically still inefficient and liable to break down. And they were expensive – only for the wealthy, until 1912 when Henry Ford set up the first assembly line factories to manufacture the Model T Ford, a motor car affordable for the emergent American middle classes.

The new factories soon led to the 'scientific management' of the labour force on principles laid out by the American mechanical engineer Frederick Taylor in 1909. Workers were clocked in, their work was split into specialised tasks endlessly repeated, they were subject to constant supervision, their mealtimes synchronised with the needs of the machines. Whereas workers prior to the nineteenth century controlled what they did, by the early twentieth century they were just production units in vast enterprises managed by others.[67] Timothy Leary commented: 'In an industrial age, the virtuous person was good, prompt, reliable, dependable, efficient, directed, and, of course, replaceable. There was not much need for the individual to operate his or her own brain in a factory civilization.'[68]

The oil-electricity breakthrough brought affluence to later generations, and accelerated the global warming processes that bedevil us today. It also revolutionized food production, mainly through the process of nitrogen fixation. Atmospheric nitrogen cannot be used by living things for their growth, but when it is 'fixed' in the roots of legumes by bacteria in the soil, it forms the ammonia which plants can utilise for growth. However, nature's nitrogen fixation process was too slow for the vast increases in grain production that were needed as the population rose during the nineteenth century. Natural forms of fixed nitrogen, such as the guano deposits off the coast of Chile, were mined extensively, but by the 1870s had been used up. The 'problem' was solved in what was perhaps the most important technical breakthrough of the twentieth century. In 1908 the German university chemist Fritz Haber discovered how to split atmospheric nitrogen, using very high temperatures of 500 °C in an electrical furnace. The way was now open for scientists to produce ammonia using artificially fixed nitrogen. The industrial chemist Carl Bosch pioneered the mass production of ammonia-based fertilisers in the Haber-Bosch process. This revolutionised the production of grain. Huge increases in yields per hectare of wheat and other crops were now feasible. (Haber's next invention was the creation of poisonous gas that the German army used in the coming world war.)

The petrol engine was on hand to maximise this production potential. Cars, first on sale from the 1890s, were joined by larger vehicles: trucks, ambulances (much needed in the First World War), and buses. For agriculture the breakthrough vehicle was the petrol-driven tractor. Tractors could plough fields quicker and deeper than ploughs pulled by oxen or horses. By the 1930s, especially in the United States, farmers were able to massively increase grain yields. Stalin pushed the manufacture of tractors in the Soviet Union (though the extra grain that could potentially have been grown was cancelled out by his collectivisation of agriculture). Later, petrol-fuelled machines, especially the combine harvester, increased the speed of harvesting; and trucks got the grain to market in larger volumes more speedily.

Nikolaus Otto (petrol engine) and Haber-Bosch (nitrogen fixation) between them enabled the massive global increase of food that was the most striking human development of the twentieth century. Today there are eight billion humans on the planet compared to the 1.6 billion in 1908. It is estimated that without the technologies of the petrol engine and electricity and nitrogen fixation taking us artificially beyond nature's limits, almost half of humanity would not be here.[69]

Electricity and the petrol and diesel engine led to an increase in the speed of everything. By the early twentieth century ever increasing speeds began to dominate human behaviour and culture. Speed is exciting, but also disquieting – exemplified by Jacques-Henri Lartigue's photograph of the speeding racing vehicle at a 1913 grand prix. Ever increasing speed underlay the tensions of the twentieth century. Edward Munch's 1893 painting 'The Scream' intuitively predicts the way things were to go. As Marshall McLuhan wrote: 'Acceleration is a formula for dissolution and breakdown in any organisation. Since the entire mechanical technology of the Western world has been wedded to electricity, it has pushed towards higher speeds. All the mechanical aspects of our world seem to probe toward self-liquidation.' McLuhan argues that the 1844 take-off of the electric telegraph and the publication of Soren Kierkegaard's *The Concept of Dread* in the same year are not coincidental. 'The Age of Anxiety', McLuhan argued, 'had begun. For with the telegraph, man had initiated that outering or extension of his central nervous system that is now approaching an extension of consciousness...To put one's nerves outside, and one's physical organs inside the nervous system, or the brain, is to initiate a situation – if not a concept – of dread.'[70] By 1920 Sigmund Freud was writing *Beyond the Pleasure Principle*, his psychological treatise on the human death wish.

The petrol motor was quickly adapted to new flying machines. The Wright brothers, with the first airplane flight in 1902, opened the way to an age of new possibilities, both of speed and of fear. By 1911 the Italians were using aircraft to bomb civilians in their colony of Libya. Other countries' air forces soon followed. Picasso's painting *Guernica* illustrates the German and Italian bombing of the city of Guernica during the Spanish civil war. The look on the little Spanish girl's face in Robert Capa's photograph of an air raid over Bilbao in May 1937 is the look of the age of catastrophe (to use Eric Hobsbawm's phrase).

Excitement, volatility, and hubris drove the twentieth century. This was epitomised by the Futurist Movement in Italy in the century's first decade. F.T. Marinetti's 1910 *Manifesto of Futurism* romanticised the dangers. 1. 'We intend to sing the love of danger, the habit of energy and fearlessness.' 2. 'Courage, audacity, and revolt will be the essentials of our poetry.' 3. 'Up to now literature has exalted a pensive immobility, ecstasy and sleep. We intend to exalt aggressive action, a feverish insomnia, the racer's stride, the mortal leap, the punch and the slap.' 4. 'We affirm the world's magnificence has been enriched by a new beauty: the beauty of speed.' 7. 'Except in struggle there is no more beauty. No work without an aggressive character can be a masterpiece.' And four years before the outbreak of the first world war: 9. 'We will glorify war – the world's only hygiene – militarism, patriotism, the destructive gesture of freedom-bringers, beautiful ideas worth dying for, and scorn for women.' 10. 'We will destroy the museums, libraries, academies of every kind, will fight moralism, feminism, every opportunistic or utilitarian cowardice.' And Point 11 describes the early twentieth century in a single sentence: 'We will sing of great crowds excited by work, by pleasure, and by riot; we will sing of multicoloured, polyphonic tides of revolution of the modern capitals; we will sing of the vibrant nightly fervour of arsenals and shipyards blazing with violent electronic moons; greedy railway stations that devour smoke-plumed serpents; factories hung on clouds by the crooked lines of their smoke; bridges that stride the rivers like giant gymnasts, flashing in the sun with the glitter of knives; adventurous steamers that sniff the horizon; deep-chested locomotives whose wheels paw the tracks like the hooves of enormous steel horses bridled by tubing; and the sleek flight of planes whose propellers chatter in the wind like banners and seem to cheer like an enthusiastic crowd.'[71]

Two years later in 1912 the British liner the Titanic sailed too close to an iceberg and sank. Within another two years Europe and much of the world embarked on a war which devastated the apparent stabilities of the nineteenth century.

# 9. Capitalism

The political revolution of the sixteenth century gave rise to the competing nation states of Europe, as well as accelerating trade with and extraction from imperial territories. Factories and industrial cities sprang forth from the 1820s. The new workers (the proletariat) and middle classes (the bourgeoisie) fought for their political rights. Thus began the age of capitalism, a word first used in the early nineteenth century. By the twentieth century capitalism was challenged only by communism; but by the 1990s communism had collapsed, leaving capitalism as the world's only economic system, albeit with different versions, varying with the amount of state interference. It is the economic system that we humans benefit from, that enables us to exist, and the one that is destroying the planet's environment.

Capitalism is an extraordinarily complex system that defies one-line definitions.[72] It bases production, for the most part, on the privately owned (as opposed to state-owned) company, managed by people who make all the decisions about what is to be produced, how much to pay the workers, and what proportion of the profits (if there are any) to keep for themselves. The state may regulate their operations to some degree and take some of the profits via taxation. Capitalist owners, by the end of the nineteenth century, had strong-armed their way into the decision-making apparatus of the state, so that capitalists were essentially in charge of regulating themselves. (Today, for example, privately-owned water companies in Britain have successfully dissuaded the British government from regulating how much sewage they can discharge into the rivers and seas.)

In the historical communist state, the state bureaucracy makes decisions regarding what is to be produced and what not, how much of any particular item is to be produced, and the price to set for it. In the capitalist state, in contrast, these decisions are made by entrepreneurial managers guided by 'the market'. How much of an item to produce is determined by an assessment of the 'demand'. Since nobody can precisely predict this, companies produce things and see if they sell. If they sell at a profit, they manufacture more; if they don't, they stop producing. The price is also determined by 'the market', according to how much people will pay. It is also influenced by whether other companies can make the same item cheaper (for example by paying their workers less). Sooner or later the 'right' price is established by trial and error, taking into account the competition, the costs of production, and the profit margins of the retailers.

Smaller companies are often family firms, in which entrepreneurs are helped by relatives and succeeded by their children or other descendants. Larger companies are financed by wealthy people or institutions such as banks or pension funds that invest in the company in exchange for 'shares' (equities). The company's management gives part of the profits to the shareholders and sets aside another part for reinvestment in the company. Big decisions are made by the shareholders where a majority of 50.1% of the shares secures the decision. At first sight it seems democratic; a closer looks reveals the absolutist nature of company control, because in most companies a few shareholders, among them the managers, hold the bulk of the shares.

This managerial class usually dominates parliaments, and collectively uses part of its profits to lobby for decisions favourable to its interests, so that the nominally democratic structure of the state becomes a facade. Combinations of owners, shareholders and wealthy people in a state argue for as much freedom to do as they like, with as little regulation as possible by government. The self-interested argument was, and still is, that leaving the managerial class to its own unregulated devices will achieve an outcome for society which on balance is in the best interests of everyone. The history of the late nineteenth and twentieth century pivots around the capacity of any state to steer a line between the self-interested demands of the capitalists, and insistent demands from workers for higher wages and better working conditions. An economic slump, for example, could lead to a situation of near revolution, or to the voting in of an extremist dictatorship, as when Hitler came to power in Germany in January 1933.

Several features of the capitalist system, which are sometimes passed over in silence, need to be added to the above imperfect definition. They include:

*Ruthless competition and struggle.* Capitalism is a system of competition, with a winner-takes-all outcome. It is interesting that the phrases used to describe nineteenth-century capitalism are precisely those used by Charles Darwin in his ideas on evolution. Is that just a coincidence? The idea of the 'survival of the fittest' (a phrase not used by Darwin himself) entered politics, and was to be an important psychic component of the national competition which produced the world wars, and of Italian and German fascism in the 1920s and 1930s. The theme of competition is intrinsic in modern society: in sport, education, politics and creative endeavour. Our competitive 'superiority' over other animals is tacitly assumed to justify the massacre of wildlife that we are engaged in.

*The mechanisms of capitalist production are openly parasitic.* The argument is that the ingenuity of the capitalists in getting the production process underway justifies their taking the bulk of the profit for themselves, and paying the workers the minimum for survival. Marx called this exploitation of workers by managers and owners 'surplus extraction'. The fact is that in capitalism the quest for wealth drives the system. In 2022 Elon Musk (Tesla) and Jeff Bezos (Amazon) had become the world's first dollar trillionaires. This is not a good basis for a healthy society. It openly drives inequalities and unfairnesses, which invariably creates tensions in societies, except in the very rare cases where the state raises taxation of the rich and redistributes to the less well off (as happened briefly in Britain after the Second World War).

*Perhaps most importantly, capitalism is authoritarian.* This is camouflaged to some extent by the parallel emergence since the 1920s of the democratic state in which most people have the vote, and can collectively influence the composition of their government. However, within a company, the owners can dictate whatever they decide. The typical large company has a board of directors. The directors direct: they govern; they make the decisions. In a capitalist state no one questions that right. The board of directors appoints a chief executive officer, who is all but a dictator in his/her context. Another key director is the chief finance officer, who makes the financial decisions: how much money the company can borrow, or what proportion of profits goes towards dividends. Theoretically a board of directors can fire the chief executive officer, but this seldom happens. Given that the collective capital-owning class also effectively runs the state, it is not surprising that the state echoes the ethos of the companies and corporations, which are by definition antipathetic to democratic principles. Only on rare occasions, such as when the support of the workers is needed in wartime, are the interests of the capital-owners temporarily given a back seat – but again in their own interest.

*Capitalist theorists stress the advantages of a system where companies are constantly competing with each other.* They argue the more competition, the lower the prices, and the better off everyone is. This claim ignores the fact that a principal trend in the history of the capitalist system, especially since the 1950s, has been the one towards monopoly. The successful survive and grow, and the weak go out of business, or are bought out by the successful. Only occasionally have governments intervened to break up huge monopolies. Having no competition, monopolies can increase prices and the cost of living for customers. To the extent that companies increase their political influence, as they have done in the era of globalization since the 1970s, the trend towards monopoly has intensified. Prices increase, wages are reduced relatively, and choice reduces. Giant companies today, such as Amazon and Wal-Mart, put a lot of upward pressure on prices.

*The central requirement of capitalism is growth.* The capitalist company or corporation *has* to grow its profits, otherwise its share price will collapse and it will go out of business or be taken over. This growth imperative is insatiable, analogous to cancer: it is the distinctive feature of the capitalist system. The growth includes the constant search for new markets (witness the global proliferation of Coca-Cola). The more people there are, the more potential customers. Although not openly proclaimed, capitalism likes, indeed needs, an increasing population, and an expanding potential market. That market exploded in the twentieth century as the world's population soared from one and a half to six billion, and from six to eight billion in the twenty or so years of the twenty-first century. Should population growth by some miracle stop, or go into reverse, the entire structure of the capitalist system would collapse. Eventually everyone on the planet would have everything they needed (or could be persuaded to need). At that point the financial system would collapse. This is the heart of our species crisis.

*Connected with 'growth' is the concept of 'progress',* an idea or assumption that emerged parallel with the development of capitalism. What could possibly be wrong with progress? Besides improving things, progress means producing more things, enabling people to buy and consume more, and live better. It is about doing everything more efficiently. This inevitably means using up more of the planet's resources, and letting the waste products warm the atmosphere. Progress also means thinking up new things for people to 'need' or buy, and the formation of new companies to manufacture the new items. It is by definition incompatible with a stable maintenance of the status quo. And for national governments growth becomes a political imperative. This brings us back to the dilemma of the cancer cell: the need for expansion, but ultimately dying as a result of that expansion.

*The capitalists' constant need for innovation* is related to growth and progress. The result is constant change leading to psychic confusion and disorientation. To quote Marx on capitalism: 'Constant revolutionising of production, uninterrupted disturbance of all social conditions, everlasting uncertainty and agitation distinguish the bourgeois epoch from all earlier ones...all that is solid melts into air.'[73]

*Capitalism transforms human society's moral values, and often not in a healthy direction.* As a system it possesses no moral idea of human survival either in the short or the long term. Growth and the pursuit of wealth tend in the direction of greediness, as the system fosters consumerism. For new things to be sold, either other things have to be destroyed, or the purchaser has to be persuaded to have and want more things. In stable societies children have to be taught and disciplined against their natural impulse to have or consume too much. Capitalism reverses this idea of restraint. A 'childification' of the adult follows. This became increasingly so during the twentieth century as the advertising industry took off, and was further fostered by television which used programmes to get people in front of advertisements. 'A society that has lost its life values will tend to make a religion of death and build up a cult around its worship,' wrote Lewis Mumford in 1946, 'a religion not less grateful because it satisfies the mounting number of paranoiacs and sadists such a disrupted society necessarily produces.'[74]

*The ultra competitive, winner-take-all momentum of capitalism* not only echoes the metaphor of war, but actually unconsciously (sometimes quite openly) fosters war itself. Much profit can be made out of destruction and death. Lewis Mumford summed it up: 'The state of paleotechnic society may, ideally, be described as one of wardom. Its typical organs, from mine to factory, from blast furnace to slum, from slum to battlefield, were at the service of death. Competition: struggle for existence: domination and submission: extinction.' One is not only talking of the US companies that profited from the 2003 invasion of Iraq.

*There is no obvious alternative to capitalism.* State socialism of the Stalinist type destroys as much as capitalism does, but without the consumerist possibilities. The phrase 'the capitalist economy' becomes slightly tautological. As the twentieth century advanced it became apparent that all economies were forms of capitalism, with similar bases but different shapes. The differences depended on the amount of state regulation tolerated, or how much of the total profits should be channelled back to the less well off via taxation. The neoliberal capitalism of Thatcher and Reagan differed substantially from the social-democratic Keynesian forms in Western Europe after the Second World War. Over a century of attempts to organise capitalism's overthrow have proved to be 'tilting at the wind'. As Meghnad Desai remarked: 'Capitalism has not just survived; it has been rejuvenated, and shows no prospect of imminent collapse, or even aging...[There are] only different versions of capitalism. There is no rival mode of production on the horizon as a viable alternative. Capitalism is the only game in town. The contest is between rival versions.'[75] By the early 1970s all attempts at opposition from young people, utopian attempts to overthrow 'the system', had failed. The left-wing revolutionaries of the mid-1960s evolved into the wealthy drivers of the system of the early twenty-first century.

The capitalist system that took off in western Europe during the nineteenth century needless to say did not arrive in a perfected form overnight: it was honed and refined as the existing classes fought each other and readjusted their relationships. By the beginning of the twentieth century the factory owners and upper middle classes who owned and profited from the huge companies had acquired a great deal of political power, and were well into the process of merging with the landed aristocracies. The landowner-capitalist alliance faced a new working class which had appeared since the 1820s. To head off the threat of revolution, the parliaments, reichstags, and assemblies of the governing classes made strategic retreats where unavoidable. For example, in Germany, Bismarck, a landowning Junker, drove a programme of social reform through the Reichstag. Lloyd George in Britain did much the same during the Liberal Party administration after 1906. Typical reforms included establishing the eight-hour day, paid holidays, sickness benefits, and pensions for the workers. Social democratic parties were integrated into government, and became political features from then on.

The working classes were not only bought off with reforms, however, but subjected to a battery of what can only be called controls. These encouraged the lower classes to behave, and to support the national strategies devised by the wealthy. Base controls included the law, backed up by imprisonment for committing crimes, defined by the parliaments. The ultimate control until well into the twentieth century was the hangman's noose. The law was supported by the church, whose priests and bishops had influence over the population in the towns and rural areas. In some cases, such as with Wesley's Methodists in Britain, religious groups openly preached obedience to the state. Their basic message was that good moral behaviour in this life will, if not rewarded here, find reward in an afterlife. The message of the Bible was fused with programmes of the landowner-capitalist groups to cement loyalty to the state. The Church of England was known as the 'conservative party on its knees'. National police forces of one variation or another came into existence, in daily contact with ordinary people. The police were supported, in the upholding of the law, by magistrates and judges, with serious crimes tried in the cities. Imprisonment for crimes was designed to act as a deterrent against poor behaviour. A general atmosphere of how to behave pervaded life.

The basic controls of the law and the church were supplemented by others. All children had to pass through the developing mass education system which became increasingly necessary as the complexity of capitalist needs multiplied. The second half of the nineteenth century saw the introduction of compulsory education for children from the age of four until their early teens. Children were subjected to strong discipline from teachers, with frequent physical punishment. The stress was on loyalty and obedience. The royal family were a central focus in most

European states, with an emphasis on nationalism and, by implication, the threat from enemies. The bell and timetables ruled; a preparation for the factory or the office. A two-tier education system reflected the class divisions in which the poorer kids went to state schools to be drilled in the basic skills for industrial know-how, and those from wealthy families to well-funded schools, often privately run, where their function as future managers of the state was inculcated. Even in the wealthier institutions there was a focus on discipline and future military service which persisted until after the Second World War.

Derrick Jensen's thoughts on education in the United States in the twentieth century could apply to schoolchildren of any decade after the 1860s: 'Through the process of schooling, each fresh child is attenuated, muted, moulded, made like aluminium – malleable yet durable, and so prepared to compete in society, and ultimately to lead this society to where it is so obviously headed. Schooling as it presently exists, like science before it and religion before that, is necessary to the continuation of our culture and to the spawning of a new species of human, ever more submissive to authority, ever more pliant, prepared by thirteen years [nine years in the later 1880s] of sitting and receiving, sitting and regurgitating, sitting and waiting for the end, prepared for the rest of their lives to toil, to propagate, to never make waves, and to live each day with never an original thought nor even a shred of hope.'[76]

After the discipline of school, children grew up into adults who were subject to the discipline of the factory, and the constraints of life in the industrial town. Workers had to clock in at a given time, the start of the day's or shift's work being signalled by the factory siren, the sound of which spread for miles. The managers planned and directed work schedules, and stripped workers of decision-making capacity. Work was frequently exhausting, and by the time the closing of the shift siren sounded there was not much energy left over for political action. Novels by British writers that dealt with these conditions included D.H. Lawrence's *Sons and Lovers* and Richard Llewellyn's *How Green Was my Valley.*

Apart from in Britain (where compulsory military service was not brought in until the First World War), the European states introduced military conscription for boys in their late teens. In Germany the army was viewed as 'the school of the nation'. There was compulsory full time military service for three years, after which males were drafted into a standing reserve which entailed further annual training. From the age of around thirty, German men were then put on standby for further service should it be required by the state. The schoolteacher with the cane was replaced by the sergeant-major with a long list of punishment options for ill-discipline.[77] The object was to ensure greater fear of one's own officers than of the enemy.

To further enforce obedience, both school and the army required dress by uniform. Uniform dress codes, even in the church, pervaded societies. Dress codes were obligatory except perhaps for eccentrics or artists. In civilian life the military uniform for men was succeeded by the office uniform – the suit – which appeared in the 1880s. The stiff, buttoned-up collar together with the tie became the norm. Dress codes in factories, offices, railways, and politics (the frock coat, the top hat, and the black umbrella) were effectively compulsory. Colour was not allowed, so attire was uniformly black, and not only because black did not show the dirt.

All these controls were supplemented by the national sports systems that evolved from the 1860s onwards, made feasible by the railways which covered Europe by the 1880s. Games are a fundamental activity of *Homo sapiens*, and games systems reflect the dynamics of society, with a stress on competition. In early industrial society, sport was partly designed as a diversion from politics, as indeed was the pub. Certain sports were reserved for the working class and others for the wealthy, thus further reinforcing class divisions. For the worker, it was greyhound racing, and of course football. The first English football league was established in 1888. The Bund Deutscher Fussballspieler followed in 1890, after the game was introduced into Berlin by English expatriates in the early 1880s. The first England versus Germany game was held in Berlin in November 1899. French football began at the same time, also having been introduced by English expatriates.

Although football is overwhelmingly the world's most popular game, it was then (and largely still is) a game for the workers. When I was a boy and read the Teddy Lester novels about boys at a British public (i.e. private) school, the game they played, which was rugby, did not make sense to me.[78] This alternative to football started in the 1850s at Rugby

School after a boy picked up the ball in a game of football and ran with it. It found favour amongst the elite officer class, and its physicality anticipated military training. Another game, cricket, became popular from the 1820s in England, later to be exported to most parts of the British Empire. The white dress code, and the languid pace on the field, against the backcloth of mown grass lawns, and a game that lasted a whole day (later, in test matches, five days), suggested aristocratic leisure and wealth. Even more so did the horse riding game of polo. Thus games reflected class, and helped cement the inevitability of the national system.

The final control we can touch upon would need a book in itself to give it justice: the national press. The prerequisites for a national press were again the railways, also basic literacy for all, which was not available until mass education was made compulsory (in England by the Gladstone government of 1868-74). Further technological advances were also necessary: bulk-produced paper in 1874, and the rotary press, also in the 1870s. Alfred Harmsworth's *Daily Mail* in 1896 achieved mass circulation for the first time, as compared with newspapers such as *The Times*, which circulated only amongst the wealthy. The negative influence of the *Daily Mail* can hardly be overstated. Harmsworth's editors and journalists paid slavish deference to the aristocracy, particularly the monarchy. Deification of the monarchy – which after the reign of George III (died 1820), had no political power – became a national religion.

Nationalism was even more central to the popular press. Vituperative articles on the national enemies were featured daily; in England's case these were France or Germany, or sometimes Russia. In Britain, as the country's imperial power came under increasing threat, the *Daily Mail* pushed an aggressive line on all matters of national interest. The Kaiser of Germany was made into an enemy, especially after he had in 1895 congratulated President Kruger of the Transvaal Republic for thwarting an attempted coup by Rhodes and Jameson. During the British war against the Boers that followed in 1899, mass hysteria about the lifting of the siege of Mafeking was whipped up by the popular press in London. This hyped up national enthusiasm had been termed 'jingoism', after a famous whipping up of hysteria against Russia in 1878, which went: 'We don't want to fight, but by jingo if we do, we've got the men, we've got the ships, we've got the money too.' Popular press incitement of 'the people' against national enemies was repeated in all the advanced industrial countries in the early twentieth century – incitements that were to play an important role in bringing about the war that was now approaching.

## 10. War, 1914-45

In 1914 Europe plunged into what was in effect a thirty-one year war, the first part of which (the First World War) ended in 1918, but which erupted again in 1939 (the Second World War). It ended, finally, after a hundred million deaths, in 1945. It was the last war of rival European and Japanese imperial powers before the atomic bomb made such wars unfeasible.

The first phase, from 1914 to 1918, was mostly a European civil war that was fought by the Russians, the French and the British to prevent German hegemony in central Europe. A secondary theatre involved Japanese aggressions into China. The vicious stalemate in the European sector was only broken with the intervention of the United States on the side of the British and French. The war also led to the overthrow of the Russian Tsar in 1917 and the seizure of power by Lenin's communists. The United States, however, failed to sign the punitive Treaty of Versailles imposed on the Germans in 1919 and withdrew into isolation, leaving the Europeans licking their wounds.

The second part of the war is usually considered to have begun in September 1939, after the Nazi German attack on Poland that began Germany's second attempt to dominate Europe by force. Japan, however, had invaded and annexed the northern part of China, Manchuria, in 1931, and in July 1937 began a war against central China. During 1941 the two hitherto separate wars became intertwined wars of global imperial conquest as, in June, the Germans attacked the Soviet Union, and in December the Japanese invaded Malaya, the Philippines, and Indonesia, whilst preemptively attacking the United States at Pearl Harbour.

The failure of the Germans to defeat Stalin's Soviet Union, and the American entry into the war against them made a second German failure inevitable. As defeat loomed closer during 1942-45 the Germans carried out a genocide against Jewish populations under their control, even as the German armies were being forced back into Germany by the Soviet armies in the east and the Americans and British in the west. In the Far East, the Japanese fought to the bitter end against the Americans, only surrendering after Hiroshima and Nagasaki had been hit by atomic bombs. Japan's final ejection from China in 1945 was followed by a Chinese civil war that ended with the victory of Mao Zedong's Communists in 1949.

Those, very briefly, are the facts. The war, on and off over thirty-one years, caused millions of deaths (in the first phase mostly soldiers, in the second phase mostly civilians), and ended the era of Europe's political and military domination of the world. Eric Hobsbawm names it 'the age of catastrophe'.[79]

Let us take a closer look at what caused Europe's act of mutual self-destruction. Some historians argue that the war in 1914 began as a result of chance irrational decisions taken at the moment. If politician X had done or said *this* instead of *that*, there would have been no war, and the nineteenth-century era of industrial growth and prosperity would have continued. But there were underlying problems that made a big war likely sooner or later. These problems were not confined to Germany, which at the 1919 Treaty of Versailles, was blamed for beginning the war.

Conflict over land and resources by rival European nations had been going on for some time. Europe's population had been growing fast and the British were increasingly dependent on their colonies for food. The resources needed for growing industries for the first time included oil, which was joining coal as an energy source that drove industrial economies. In most countries there was a growing right-wing trend in national politics, with extremist groups pushing ideas of social Darwinism and racism. Unlike Britain and France, which had acquired substantial empires in the previous centuries, Germany, only united since 1871, was looking for her 'place in the sun'. Germany had developed a navy, and her army had become the strongest in Europe. France and Russia allied with each other in 1894 to warn Germany off from further expansion in Europe. This encirclement by hostile powers fuelled German extremist groups and made her army generals nervous. The French wanted to get back Alsace-Lorraine which they had lost to Germany in the Franco-Prussian war of 1870-71. The Russians wanted to expand towards the Balkans and the eastern Mediterranean, threatening Germany's ally Austria. The British wanted to hang on to their empire and continue to exploit it; but, feeling threatened by growing German naval power, they threw in their lot with the French and the Russians.[80]

Diplomatically Europe had become a tinder box.

Inside each of these nations rapid industrialisation and the emergence of large working classes was producing increasing political tensions. The demands for better working conditions and higher wages from worker unions grew more violent in the first years of the twentieth century. Extremist worker leaders, influenced by Karl Marx, talked of revolution to get rid of monarchies and capitalists. One strategy (syndicalism), particularly strong in France, was to organise violent strikes to bring the country's economy to a stop.

Governments replied by using troops to break up strikes, as happened in Britain in 1912. The Russian left-wing groups, despite the small working class in Russia's less advanced economy, were the first to push for the revolutionary overthrow of their monarchy and aristocracy. In Germany the Kaiser and the land-owning class, the Junkers, were desperately trying to hold on to their control of the state, now threatened by both a dynamic capitalist class and a worker movement. Although superficially a democracy with a popularly elected Reichstag, Germany was still controlled by the Prussian land-owning wealthy. The German upper classes had not made the political concessions to the capitalists that the British upper classes had done. Britain was facing 'troubles' in Ireland, as well as striking workers and demands for expanding the vote to women. In all these nation states the ruling classes were tempted to redirect their internal tensions against the foreign enemy. As the war began in 1914 Kaiser Wilhelm II said: 'today I know only Germans' as the trains departed to attack France. In short, the war was largely an externalisation of unresolved internal revolutionary tensions faced by monarchical regimes that had become tired and redundant.

A further catalyst was the anomie of life in the growing industrial towns and cities. The conditions of work in many factories were appalling. The diets of workers were poor, their working hours long, and their holidays short or non-existent. These conditions combined with conscription to produce a contradiction in the worker psyche: dislike of the state and demand for reform, but simultaneously an obedience to capitalist bosses and the upper classes. This contradiction was exploited in the schools and by ultra-nationalist newspapers, and redirected towards war. For many young men, going to war was a time of escape from the 'controls' of their lives that had little hope of improvement. The view of some historians is that for men, war was a chance to escape their women, and the confines of the family. How else can we explain the enthusiasm, even jubilation, of the men in uniform going off to war in August 1914, as many photographs show? As the military historian, Martin van Creveld, writes: 'One very important way in which men can attain joy, freedom, happiness, even delirium and ecstasy, is by *not* staying at home with the wife and children, even to the point where, often enough, they are only too happy to give up their nearest and dearest in favour of war.'[81] How else can one explain the Englishman Julian Grenfell writing: 'I *adore* war. It's like a big picnic without the objectlessness of a picnic. I've never been so well or so happy.'[82] Grenfell wrote these words in August 1914 a few months before he was killed in the fighting in France.

Then there were the military developments common to all European states, with the partial exception of Britain. The last big fight between France and Prussia/Germany had been in 1870-71, which led to the Prussians in Paris, and a united Germany.[83] Prussia under Bismarck introduced universal male conscription in the early 1860s, which was in part an attempt to undermine the call for liberal reform of the state and redirect it towards a foreign enemy and national unification. France's humiliation in 1871 led the other European states to follow Germany's lead and introduce conscription. In Germany in particular the army chiefs (the General Staff) became influential in formulating state policy. They were kept firmly under control by Bismarck, but once he had left the scene in 1889, the military influence on political strategy increased. As far as the General Staff were concerned, Russia was the main enemy, and from the 1880s they were calling for an expansionist war into Russia. This remained one of Germany's aims all the way until 1945.

But having provoked a Franco-Russian alliance against them in 1894, the German Chiefs of Staff had to prepare for a two-front war. Although they had the most formidable army, faced with France and Russia simultaneously, they knew they were outnumbered and things might go badly. So the General Staff drew up war plans, which depended on getting millions of men speedily to the war front by railway. This meant having to choose whether to attack west against France and remain on the defensive against Russia, or vice versa. In the early 1890s the

German focus was on going east, but by the early twentieth century the military plan developed by General von Schlieffen was for using their railways to go west and invade France first. War by railway timetable led to an inflexibility in both German and Russian war plans: multiple rail timetables would take weeks to alter. When the crunch came, the politicians were unable to have any influence on the military and had no room for manoeuvre.

On a broader level we can see that war was a fundamental boost to early twentieth-century industrial capitalism. Industries were producing the guns, the artillery, the naval ships, the uniforms, and the barbed wire. A great advantage of war to capitalism was (and is) that it causes a lot of destruction, and destroyed things have to be replaced. 'Creative destruction' as Joseph Schumpeter termed it.[84] Capitalists could live quite happily with either war or peace. Some of the old guard from the land-owning classes on the other hand were horrified at the new industrialisation and moves towards democracy. For them, war had always been a primary duty. The German officer class saw war as their destiny. The victor in the Franco-Prussian war, General Helmut von Moltke, wrote: 'Perpetual peace is a dream, and not a pleasant one at that; and war is part of God's ordering of the world...Without war, the world would wallow in materialism.'[85]

It is pointless to argue which nation was responsible for starting the war in August 1914. No major participant was 'innocent'. The build up to the war began when Germany's only genuine ally, Austria, entered a dispute with Russia. Russian ministers supported Serb nationalists who wished to rip apart the Austrian empire. A group of Serbs assassinated the Austrian heir-apparent at Sarajevo on 28 June 1914. Sarajevo was in Bosnia – then ruled by Austria – which the Serbs wanted for themselves. Backed by Germany, the Austrians decided to sort out their 'Serb problem' once and for all. But when, on 25 July, the Austrians declared a local war on Serbia, the Russians gave the critical order to mobilise their armies against Austria *and* Germany, and the nightmare of war by timetable began.

The German Schlieffen Plan was inflexible. The German army's railway timetables were geared to an attack on France, no matter what. The French affirmed their alliance with Russia. There was an escalation of mobilizations, and on 1 August 1914 Germany invaded Belgium and France because that is what their military plan required. (Bismarck was no doubt turning in his grave.) Bethmann-Hollweg, the German Chancellor, could not overrule the military, and neither could a rather bewildered Kaiser. The Russians, who had started the whole thing, also refused to stop mobilising, and invaded German territory in East Prussia. This action of military and political madness signed the death warrant of the Tsarist monarchy. The war was to see the demise of most of Europe's last remaining monarchies – France's had already fallen in 1871, and in Britain the monarchy was already a mere figurehead.

The four years of war that followed were to see the death of at least ten million men, and were the most terrible and revolutionary in European history. Soldiers on all sides were slaughtered by artillery, machine guns, and breach-loading rifles. As yet there were no tanks or aircraft to break the stalemate. Most of the killer battles of attrition took place in northern France, as the Germans tried, and failed, to get through to Paris. By late 1914 two lines of trenches faced each other from the English Channel to the Swiss border, defended by barbed wire and machine guns, and under continuous artillery bombardment. Every now and again the generals on both sides would order their troops to attack the machine-gun defended enemy trenches in suicidal bids to break through and encircle enemy armies. There were a series of terrible battles in some places, such as Ypres. The German offensive against the French city of Verdun in February 1916 lasted nine months, and led to over a million dead and wounded.[86] The British-French reply at the River Somme in July 1916 led to 21,000 British troops killed on the first day of the offensive, the worst day in British military history. French army mutinies in 1917 were hushed up. Only with the arrival of United States troops in the spring of 1918, and the British development of the tank, did the balance finally swing against the Germans.

The psychological horror of the war is well put by David Roberts: 'The First World War was a war of delusions, euphemisms and bitter ironies. Heads of state and politicians, posturing and bluffing, found that it was easy to talk themselves into a war, and almost impossible to talk themselves out of it. Rhetoric and double talk blossomed from politicians, newspapers, posters, pulpits and poets. It was so pervasive that clear thought and common sense was overwhelmed. The loftiest ideals were used to justify behaviour that was evil in the extreme. Soldiers were shot for refusing to fight for freedom. Self-preservation justified self-destruction. The love of one's fellow man justified destroying him. The words "Human Civilization" seemed to have lost their meaning.'[87]

The British naval blockade of the European continent led to drastic food shortages in Germany and throughout central Europe. The worst war conditions were in Russia, and in 1917 the Tsarist monarchy collapsed (see next chapter). Towards the end of the following year the German and Austrian monarchies also collapsed. In Berlin, during the final days of the war in October and November 1918, men of the German navy mutinied, and communist groups surged in popularity. After the final armistice, returning German troops were angry and the idea soon spread that they had been 'stabbed in the back' by 'socialists and Jews'. German politics was in dangerous flux in 1918-19 as the extreme left-wing Spartacists' socialist supporters were destroyed by groups of ex-soldiers called Freikorps. These civil disturbances were made worse by the flu epidemic that swept Europe from mid-1918 onward, leading to millions more deaths. In Germany conditions were worsened with the hyper-inflation of 1922-23, which wiped out the savings of most of the population.

The shortage of young men in combatant countries meant that women were recruited to work in factories that manufactured shells and guns; they were also mobilized into basic urban jobs, such as bus and tram driving, factory work, and, of course, hospital nursing. Society throughout Europe was caught between grief and anger. Women in all countries grieved for the men who did not return. Vera Brittain's *Testament of Youth* was just one example: the thoughts of a young woman, whose fiancé had been killed in France, as she wandered around London's Whitehall on the day of the armistice on 11 November 1918.[88]

The harshly punitive Treaty of Versailles forced on Germany in 1919 was never accepted by the Germans. In Italy there was resentment for the opposite reason: not receiving enough for being on the winning side. Everywhere politics was in flux, and everywhere parliamentary liberalism and democracy were threatened. The Russian revolutions of 1917 and 1918 brought the communists of Lenin and Stalin to power, and socialist and communist groups sprang into existence in all countries in the early 1920s, including China. This, in response, provoked the rise of right-wing groups who sought to control the working classes. In Italy Mussolini led his fascists to seize power in Rome in October 1922 (the word 'fascism' derives from the bundle of axe and sticks used by the high-ups in the original Roman Empire, which Mussolini used as a romantic reference). Right-wing groups, heavily militarised, were not only virulently anti-communist but anti-liberal and anti-democracy as well. Liberal groups of the old ruling class and the newer social-democratic parties found themselves threatened by right-wing and left-wing revolutionaries who wanted to abolish democracy.

In Germany Adolf Hitler led the National Socialist German Workers Party (*Nationalsozialistische Deutsche Arbeiterpartei*) whose name was abbreviated to Nazis. In the 1920s, Nazi support was tiny, and democracy in the Weimar Republic was still hanging on, despite the election of the war-time chief of staff, Hindenburg, as president in 1925. This changed as the economic depression tightened its hold in Germany during 1930-32. Huge gains for the Nazis in the elections to the Reichstag in September 1930 and March 1932 were followed, in January 1933, with Hitler's fully legal appointment as German chancellor. After Hindenburg's death in August 1934, Hitler combined the offices of chancellor and president, designating himself the fuehrer (leader). The moderates and monarchists thought they could control Hitler, and use him to head off social revolution. They miscalculated.

Hitler had been a soldier in the 1914-18 war and refused to accept the peace treaty of Versailles: his basic aim was to start all over again to assert German expansion and hegemony in Europe. The Nazi movement was militaristic from the start. The Sturmabteilung (SA) squads wore brown uniforms and the Schutzstaffel (SS) under Heinrich Himmler wore black uniforms. The Nazis were able to manoeuvre Hitler into power as an effective dictator after 1933. All other political parties were banned. Opponents were put into concentration camps (an invention of the British in the South African Boer War in 1899-1902). German workers, who normally voted social-democrat or communist, found themselves controlled by the party apparatus; many joined the Nazi party as an escape from unemployment. Unions were banned, except the pseudo-unions run by the state. Everybody in Germany was 'coordinated', and made subject to the all-powerful state.

A rearmament programme was begun, despite the paper restrictions of the Versailles treaty. Effective use was made of the radio, and Hitler made broadcasts to millions. Aircraft and Mercedes Benz vehicles took him round the country to cheering crowds.[89] Germans were sent back to work building the autobahns and manufacturing weaponry for the next war. Women were to stay at home and bear children for the Reich.

To these basic themes of German fascism was added a potent racism and antisemitism, based on a belief that only 'pure' Germans could be citizens. Antisemitism was virulent and, as we shall see, led to tragedy in the second part of the war. More than this, though, was the belief in the perfectibility of humans, with the Germans at the pinnacle as a blond master race. Academics researched eugenics. The ill and deformed were to be prevented from having children, and from late 1939 were to be killed by the state. A bastardised form of Darwinism set the tone: the right of the stronger to dominate. Some of these ideas had been central to German military thinking prior to 1914, including the inferiority of the 'Slavs' and Russians. War against Russia and seizure of their territory for German 'Lebensraum' (living space) was the Nazi aim throughout, with the pact signed with Stalin in August 1939 a short-term tactical manoeuvre.

German fascism was a toxic mix of racism, German nationalism, a militaristic expansionism that loathed democracy, and fantasies of past 'Nordic' heroes. Unlike communism, the basic tenets of which were (theoretically at least) common to communist parties everywhere, German fascism was unique. Although some of its features were evident in Franco's Spain and fascist groups in central Europe, the only 'pure' fascists were those in Germany.

The Second World War was to be the last European war of the old style, in which heavily armed nation states fought each other over territory and direct control of people and resources. Japan's defeat and the failure of its attempt to control China was similarly the last attempt to do things that way. After Hiroshima that type of war was ruled out.

After 1939, the second part of what was effectively a 31-year war differed from the first part (the First World War) in that it was directed as much against civilians as against armies. Huge displacements of population took place. The Germans and Japanese carried out well planned strategies of extermination, such as the Japanese massacres at Nanking in December 1937,[90] and the German massacres throughout the western Soviet Union and Poland (quite aside from the death camps). Massacre was a policy adopted by all nations engaged in the war, even the 'decent' ones. From 1942 Churchill in Britain gave the green light to the head of the RAF bomber command, Arthur 'Bomber' Harris, to have the RAF carpet-bomb Germany. For the next three years German cities were bombed to smithereens. There was no particular strategic advantage in this. Similarly the United States' air force, under Curtis LeMay, once its navy had occupied islands within reach of Japan, embarked on massacre bombing raids. Japan's capital city Tokyo was almost completely obliterated by US bombers in March 1945, and hundreds of thousands of civilians killed. The will to win any war between powerful, fully mobilised nations inevitably leads to genocidal atrocities.

This second phase of the prolonged period of war, even more than the first part after 1914, was characterised by more or less complete control of industries and the economy by the warring states. The industrial effort required by war put an end to the slump of the 1930s, with unemployment being soaked up by the production needs for aircraft, tanks and other weapons. For the first time the United States mobilised its full industrial potential, so that by the end of the war the US emerged as the strongest nation on the planet. The US military industries continued to churn out weapons and bombs after the war, leading to the germination of what President Eisenhower in 1960 called 'the military-industrial complex'. The 'golden age' which followed after 1945 was partly based on this (see chapter 14).

In 1945, unlike in 1918, Germany was completely occupied by the victorious Russian, American and British armies. This time Germany was partitioned. The Marshall Plan poured money into Europe, especially into Germany, to finance the reconstruction of what had been destroyed. Those who feared that the war would be followed by economic dislocation and depression, as in the 1920s and 1930s, were proved wrong – to their pleasant surprise. The economic take-off after the war was further encouraged by the new policies of welfarism for the returning troops and their families. Clement Attlee's welfare state in Britain was a good example. New homes were built for troops, and there was heavy investment in the building of roads. Some of the Nazi infrastructure policies of the 1930s were successfully copied by the victor powers.

We can see in retrospect that the 31-year war was centred on the position of Germany in Europe. Prior to 1914 German power had been increasing and threatened the established imperial powers France, Britain and Russia. It was still an age when imperial rivalries were habitually settled by war: this was no different, except that the numbers and the weaponry meant that these nations vied with each other for self-annihilation, helped by failures in political capacity and imagination. Embarking in 1914 on a strategy that made defeat likely, the Germans were left licking their wounds in the 1920s. Hitler's Nazis after 1939 had another go at dominating Europe and Russia by military force. Again: failure. After 1945 Germany was for a second time left to sift through the ruins. This time, however, under Chancellor Adenauer and his successors, German policy was genuinely peaceful. German and French politicians cooperated in setting up the beginnings of a peaceful European union.

The French and the British, at first with some reluctance, began to give up their imperial possessions, and discovered to their surprise that they had lost nothing. Much of Africa, Asia and South America had raw materials that they could sell only to the rich world. Their need to import industrial goods that they could not make for themselves meant big profits for the rich nations. Direct imperial control was found to have been a costly waste of money. This 'soft imperialism' approach was only politically feasible after Western Europe was fully democratised in the 1950s.

In addition the atom bomb made the old national and imperial wars of Europeans and Japanese obsolete. The further development of the hydrogen bomb in 1952 meant that a war in which states used nuclear weapons would be an act of national and species suicide.

Three aspects of these war decades that are difficult to separate from the pure military events need further examination: Stalin's regime in the Soviet Union in which countless millions were killed in what is termed 'the terror'; the Nazi genocidal massacre of Jewish people from 1941 to 1945; and the development of the atomic bomb by the United States and its use against Japanese cities in 1945. These were actions of civilized governments in a time of great stress. Any assumption that they are unrepeatable in the future would be foolhardy. We look at each of these terrible episodes of human cruelty in the three chapters that follow.

## 11. Stalin and the Terror

At the beginning of the twentieth century Russia was overwhelmingly rural, a vast country dominated by rural landowners with large estates. Russian serfdom had only been gradually abolished after the early 1860s, and in 1914 much of the rural population was still effectively tied to the land. Industrialisation was in process, but Russian capitalism, and the capitalist liberal class that went with it, was retarded in comparison with Germany, France and Britain. Illiteracy was widespread, and the urban proletariat was still tiny, since industry was so backward. This did not prevent a strong urban-based social-democratic movement being formed in the 1890s. It was heavily influenced by the ideas of Karl Marx, although, without a large, aggrieved proletariat, an urban revolution centred on workers in Russia seemed implausible.

Social democratic groups differed over whether to focus on the urban proletariat or the rural peasantry. According to a strict reading of Marx, European societies progressed from a feudal era, dominated by land owners, into an industrial-capitalist era dominated by the liberal (or, to use Marx's term, bourgeois) capital-owning class. The eventual aim was, once capitalism was developed, to achieve a state run by the workers, who would control industry in their own interests. At that point the state would 'wither away', and the class struggle would end. The transition to a worker controlled state, most Marxist factions stressed, could only happen through revolution, which would of necessity be violent.

In Russia the problem for Marxists who thought this way was that there was not, as yet, an industrial proletariat: the transition from feudalism to capitalism still had some way to go. This problem was much debated amongst the Marxist social-democratic factions, many of whom were in exile. At a conference in London in 1902 their debates led to a split. One group, the larger one, accepted that there could not be a worker revolution in Russia until capitalism was much more highly developed and there would be enough workers for a revolution. This might mean tactically siding with the liberal capitalists for a while. A smaller group, led by Lenin, advocated that in Russia's 'special situation', they should seize power straight away and then assess how to proceed.

Lenin's group called themselves Bolsheviks (majority), even though they were a minority. The other group, who were actually the majority, were labelled Mensheviks (minority). The Mensheviks adhered to the Marxist textbook; the Bolsheviks were more flexible and opportunistic.

A combination of an aggrieved peasant-serf population in the rural areas, striking workers in the towns, and tsarist Russia's defeats in a war with Japan led, in late 1904, to violent revolutionary actions throughout Russia. One such action is shown in the brilliant Sergei Eisenstein film, *Battleship Potemkin* (1925), which recreates a mutiny amongst the Black Sea battle fleet, and, in the famous Odessa Steps sequence, the shooting down of civilians. Both Bolshevik and Menshevik groups, including the young Trotsky, were among the fomenters of the upheavals. In a bid to head off the need for reform, tsarist ministers in 1906 established a national elected assembly, the Duma. There were social-democrats among the delegates, but, as in Germany, the electoral system was weighted in favour of the wealthy. Revolutionary tensions worsened and strike disturbances increased. The need to defuse the tensions induced the tsarists to push an aggressive war policy against Germany and Austria. Extremist Bolsheviks, like Joseph Dzhugashvili (Stalin), were imprisoned or, like Vladimir Ulyanov (Lenin), driven into exile.

The war against Germany, initiated by the Russians, sealed the fate of the Tsarist monarchy. By 1916 the morale of the troops was shattered, and conditions of hunger and deprivation in the cities were terrible. By early 1917 the Tsar was finding it difficult to keep his defeated troops loyal. In February, when women in Saint Petersburg came out on to the streets, the Tsar's police and troops refused to shoot at them as they had done in previous riots, and the Tsar had to abdicate. A provisional government, headed by Kerensky, prepared for proper elections for an assembly that would write a new constitution. But Kerensky made the mistake of continuing the war against Germany, and, in the summer of 1917, this led to a mass mutiny of the Russian army. It was in Germany's interest to stir up trouble in Saint Petersburg, and to this end Germany ferried Lenin from Switzerland to the Russian capital by train through German territory. The Bolsheviks, unleashed by Lenin's uncompromising leadership, took the gamble at the end of October 1917 and staged a coup. Sailors from the Kronstadt fleet took control of the Winter Palace, and

Kerensky went into hiding. Russia's first (and last) properly democratic elections were held for a constituent assembly, with the largest party being the non-Marxist socialist revolutionaries; but in January 1918, before the constituent assembly could write a new constitution, the Bolsheviks dissolved the assembly and prepared to rule by force in the name of the peasantry and proletariat. A new dictatorship had seized power in Russia. It was not to collapse until 1991.

The two years that followed saw hunger and famine throughout Russia, while monarchists and liberal groups ('the whites') fought the Bolsheviks ('the reds') in an appalling civil war. Hundreds of thousands starved to death in the famine or were killed in the civil war. The Bolsheviks took ruthless measures against opponents. In April 1918 Lenin and Trotsky in desperation signed the Treaty of Brest-Litovsk with the Germans, giving up territory including Ukraine, so they could concentrate on the fight against the whites. The Bolsheviks were successful in mobilising a new Red army, whose ranks were filled both by revolutionaries and tsarist generals who had thrown in their lot with the new regime. Led by Lenin they shot the Tsar and his family, rounded up and killed Mensheviks and Socialist Revolutionaries, eliminated the whites, and were even able briefly to invade Poland. The new revolutionary Soviet state, formally established in 1922, survived all efforts by the victor powers in the First World War to bring it down.

From the early 1920s Soviet Russia was a pariah state in Europe. Only the defeated Germans were prepared to have political relations with the new Red army. The entire Russian economy had collapsed over the previous three years. What industry there was had come to a halt. Peasants throughout the country had seized landlord estates for themselves. Tearing up the Bolshevik theory that the focus should be on the proletariat (the industrial workers) Lenin, who was an economic realist, proposed a combination of a pro-peasant policy, and a 'new economic policy' which was a way to encourage private production and a move in the direction of capitalism. But in 1922 Lenin was incapacitated by a stroke, and died in early 1924. His most likely heir-apparent was Trotsky, the most powerful man in the Politburo, and effectively the minister for the Red army. But Trotsky did not move with enough energy, and the dominant figure who emerged was Stalin.

His real name was Joseph Dzhugashvili: Stalin (steel) was his undercover code name. He was born in Gori in Georgia. He was short, good-looking and ruthless. He had played a pivotal role in the civil war in Ukraine, and rose in the ranks of the Bolshevik party to the relatively minor post of general secretary. His uncouthness and ambition led Lenin, shortly before his death, to warn the other top leaders to marginalise him. But Stalin was able to use his position as general secretary to control the key party appointments, and his influence grew rapidly after Lenin's death. Within the Politburo he cunningly played off the opposing factions.

Apart from the struggle for power for its own sake, the basic disputes within the Politburo were over how to modernise Russia and carry the revolution further. Should one go easy on the peasants? How to industrialise? Should private enterprise be tolerated? Changing his position tactically from month to month, Stalin first got rid of Trotsky, who was forced into exile in 1927, and in the following two years expelled both a 'leftist' group centring on Kamenev and Zinoviev, and a 'rightist' one under Bukharin. By 1928, Stalin had achieved complete control within the Politburo; at the Party Conference that year he was hailed enthusiastically as leader. From then on he was effectively a dictator.[91]

Stalin also controlled what was called the Ministry of Home Affairs, which had developed into a secret police apparatus. After a sequence of acronym titles, it was known as the NKVD (People's Commissariat for Internal Affairs). In 1928 the first Soviet concentration camps were established, to which political offenders and criminals were sent for forced labour to begin the serious work of extracting resources, the base materials for industrialisation. The entire system of camps was termed by its inmates the Gulag. The forced labour camps were administered by the NKVD, under Genrikh Yagoda from 1932 to 1936.

For Stalin the realistic fear was that as Germany revived, a future German-Russian war was likely, if not inevitable. Russia's backwardness in the late 1920s meant that in such a war, defeat was likely. As Stalin insisted in 1931: 'We are fifty or a hundred years behind the advanced countries. We must make good this distance in ten years. Either we do it or we go under.'[92] In this short breathing space, a twin policy was enforced: all out industrialisation, and the collectivisation of land and farms over the entire Soviet Union. Private land ownership was abolished, wealthy land owners killed, and peasants forced onto collective farms (called kolkhozes) run by the state. Surplus people were to migrate to the urban areas and the new industrial complexes. The richer peasants with large land holdings, designated 'kulaks', were rounded up by the army and the NKVD and banished to Siberia or sent to the concentration camps. Peasants and farmers, receiving notice from the state that they were to be moved to a collective farm, or banished from their land that their families had been tending for generations, resisted with determination. Police squads were brought into the rural areas to enforce the moves. Anyone who showed any sign of opposition was termed a kulak and shot or deported. In retaliation, many of the peasants killed their cattle and burnt their crops. The result was the famine of 1932-33 in which around three million people starved to death, particularly in Ukraine.

For Stalin, this was a deliberate act of terror, which showed his regime meant business.[93] By 1933 factories were going up all over Russia, their workers a combination of urban people and those forced off the land. Trainloads of peasants came into the cities looking for work. Iron and steel factories went up everywhere. The concentration camps were located near ore deposits. Convicts dug the mines, cut down the timber in the forests, and built the canals, railways and roads. Conditions in the camps were brutal, with very high death rates.

To tighten the screws further the regime attacked religion and took over or destroyed the churches. In July 1931, for example, the party communicated to the people the regime's decision to demolish the famous Basilica of Christ the Saviour in Moscow. As Ryszard Kapuscinski writes: 'Let us for the moment give free range to our imagination. It is 1931. Let us imagine that Mussolini, who at that time rules Italy, orders the Basilica of St. Peter in Rome to be razed.'[94] The Basilica of Christ the Saviour was to be turned into a palace for the soviets, but remained a building site until it was rebuilt in the 1990s.

By the early 1930s the whole of Russia had been turned into what amounted to a prison camp.[95] The country was guarded by military patrols, and barbed wire surrounded the entire border (the length of the equator). All residents had to have 'papers' which could be demanded for inspection by NKVD militias. Citizens could be 'banished' from their homes, and not allowed within a 100-kilometre limit of any city. The charges were invariably fictitious. Informers were everywhere, and one could be called in by the local police to answer the most ridiculous charges on the basis of the testimony of a neighbour who might be rewarded with a 'package'. As production collapsed during the switchover to rural cooperatives and forced industrialisation, there were shortages of food and material goods; so a system of rationing was introduced. For the party elite there were 'packages' and special stores; for everyone else shortages and queues. All trade unions were made illegal, except special pseudo-unions run by the party.

Literature, always revered in Russian culture, was effectively silenced. Writers had to submit what they wrote to be censored. The only literature permitted was that which sang the praises of the regime. All writers had to show a positive view of communist Russia and praise the way things were going in the rural areas. The literary style that followed was known as 'socialist realism'. Regime appointees who ran the Writers' Union vetted everything and had a stranglehold on what could be said and what not. Police informants being everywhere, it was safer to keep quiet, a process called 'internal migration': one kept one's thoughts to oneself. The press was controlled by the regime. The news was dominated by the Party newspaper *Pravda* (Truth). Language was permeated by euphemism and often meant the opposite of what it seemed to say.

The system of terror that evolved in the 1930s extended to the highest levels of the Communist Party. Despite his control of the Politburo and the party secretariat, Stalin was nervous. Some unease at his policies had been shown by some members of the Politburo, and he feared counter-revolution. Kirov, the upwardly mobile chief of Leningrad (as Saint Petersburg had been renamed), though loyal, was charismatic and a potential future successor to Stalin. Events in Germany during 1933-34 may have given Stalin ideas – especially Hitler's use of the Reichstag fire in February 1933 to declare his dictatorship, and his murder of opponents within the Nazi party in June 1934 ('night of the long knives'). In early December 1934 Kirov was murdered in Leningrad. Stalin rushed by train to the city, and inaugurated a bloodbath of his opponents. There has been persistent though inconclusive speculation that Stalin himself ordered Kirov's killing.

There followed a series of 'show trials' during 1935-1938, in which critics of the regime were put on trial and charged with the most improbable crimes. Most of them confessed after being tortured and their families threatened. Bukharin, Zinoviev and Kamenev were among those shot, as was the head of the NKVD, Yagoda. The state's senior prosecutor, Vyshinsky, headed the show trials, sometimes with Stalin secretly watching. The state went on a witch hunt of all real and fictional opponents of the regime. For Russians the terrible year 1937 had begun. If found guilty under Article 58 of counter-revolutionary activity the only sentence allowed was death.

The witch hunts were led by Nikolai Yezhov, who had taken over from Yagoda as head of the NKVD. The great terror, or the Yezhovshchina ('Yezhov's operation'), as the Russians termed it, involved the killing of hundreds of thousands of men and women, most of them faced with fictional charges. Among those killed were prominent Bolsheviks and their families, most of the top generals in the Red army, including the commander-in-chief Mikhail Tukhachevsky, and writers, musicians and artists. Moscow sent out instructions that certain quotas of victims were necessary. Robert Conquest in his book *The Great Terror* gives some examples: 'Yezhov telegraphed the NKVD chief in Frunze, capital of Kirgizia: "You are charged with the task of exterminating 10,000 enemies of the people. Report results by signal." The form of reply was, "In reply to yours of...the following enemies of the people have been shot," followed by a numbered list. An order to Sverdlovsk NKVD called for 15,000 executions. Another to a small town near Novosibirsk, ordered 500, far above the normal capacity, so that the NKVD had to shoot priests and their relatives, all those who had spoken critically of the regime, amnestied former members of White Armies, and so on, who would ordinarily have got five years or less. In February 1938, a recent Soviet account tells us, Yezhov himself went to Kiev to call a special NKVD conference to order 30,000 more executions in Ukraine.'[96]

Those identified for arrest were usually woken by the police in the early hours of the morning, and taken away in black vans. Their families never saw them again. It was usual for victims to be interrogated in the local prisons – in Moscow the three most notorious were the Butyrka, Lubyanka and Lefortovo. They would be subjected to 'the conveyor belt', continuous interrogation by successive teams of NKVD. They were deprived of sleep, subjected to humiliations, such as not being allowed to relieve themselves, and, if they did not confess to some ludicrous charge, beaten and tortured, and their families and children threatened. Faced with a panel of regime judges, without any legal representation, they would quickly be found guilty on the basis of absurd 'confessions', and more often than not taken to some cellar and shot through the head. Alexander Solzhenitsyn wrote later: 'If the intellectuals in the plays of Chekhov who spent all their time guessing what would happen in twenty, thirty, or forty years had been told that in forty years interrogation by torture would be practised in Russia; that prisoners would have their skulls squeezed with iron rings; that a human being would be lowered into an acid bath; that they would be trussed up naked to be bitten by ants and bedbugs; that a ramrod heated over a primus stove would be thrust up their anal canal (the "secret brand"); that a man's genitals would be slowly crushed beneath the toe of a jackboot; and that, in the luckiest possible circumstances, prisoners would be tortured by being kept from sleeping for a week, by thirst, and by being beaten to a bloody pulp, not one of Chekhov's plays would have gotten to its end because all the heroes would have gone off to insane asylums.'[97]

Observers outside Russia tended to believe the justifications put out by the Stalin regime. As Hitler once remarked, the bigger the lie, the more people are likely to believe it, as they lack the imagination to think otherwise. Only in 1956, with Khrushchev's secret speech to the Party's Twentieth Conference, did the truth about the Yezhovshchina come out. Virtually all the charges had been baseless, and most of the victims were later exonerated. After Stalin's death in 1953, Russians were able to write about their experiences. One was the poet Anna Akhmatova, whose husband and son had been taken to the gulag. Another was Alexander Solzhenitsyn, who described the continuing arrests and deportations to the gulag in the late 1940s. Two accounts I will dwell on briefly: that by Nadezhda Mandelstam, whose husband, the poet Osip Mandelstam, was a victim, who described their experiences in two extraordinary books: *Hope against Hope* and *Hope Abandoned*;[98] and that by Yevgenia Ginzburg, who described her arrest and imprisonment in her accounts: *Into the Whirlwind* and *Within the Whirlwind*.[99]

Osip Mandelstam was a Jewish poet from Saint Petersburg. He was one of a group of four Russian poets whose reputations were to survive the Stalin years, the others being Anna Akhmatova, Boris Pasternak and Marina Tsvetaeva. Mandelstam was prominent in what the Russians termed 'the intelligentsia', not particularly political, and neutrally favourable to the communists. Friendly with Bukharin, Mandelstam found it increasingly difficult to publish his poetry after the latter was sidelined in the Stalin capture of power in the late 1920s. Travelling in Ukraine during the famine and 'kulak' deportations of 1931-32 he was shocked at what he witnessed. Rather unwisely he wrote an angry poem about Stalin in this context, which he read out to a private group amongst which was a police informer. It read:

We live deaf to the land beneath us,
Ten steps away no one hears our speeches,
All we hear is the Kremlin mountaineer,
The murderer and peasant-slayer.
His fingers are fat as grubs
And the words, final as dead weights, fall from his lips,
His cockroach whiskers leer
And his boot tops gleam.
Around him a rabble of thin-necked leaders –
fawning half-men for him to play with.
They whinny, purr or whine
As he prates and points a finger,
One by one forging his laws, to be flung
Like horseshoes at the head, the eye or groin.
And every killing is a treat
For the broad-chested Ossete*.[100]

(*Ossetia was north of Georgia where Stalin was born, its people of Iranian stock. There were rumours that Stalin had Ossetian blood.)

Mandelstam was arrested in May 1934, and interrogated by the NKVD. This was before Kirov's assassination and the unleashing of the full terror; Mandelstam and his wife were merely banished, after an intervention by Boris Pasternak. Stalin phoned Pasternak to say that he had reviewed Mandelstam's case and 'everything would be all right'. He mocked Pasternak for not having done enough for Mandelstam. 'But he's a genius, isn't he? If I were a poet and a friend of mine were in trouble, I would do everything to help him.'[101] Sent by train with a militia escort, Mandelstam and his wife Nadezhda spent the next months in Cherdyn, before being moved to Voronezh. Back in Moscow during 1937, and misreading the atmosphere of that year, the couple accepted an offer, apparently from the Soviet Writers' Union, for a vacation at a Party rest home near Moscow. There Mandelstam was arrested and Nadezhda never saw him again. Later she was able to establish that her husband had been sent in a prisoner train across Russia to Vladivostok, where he was to serve a five-year sentence for 'counter-revolutionary activities'. The fate of such prisoners was to be onward shipped to Magadan in the Arctic Circle, but Mandelstam died – probably in December 1938 – before he could be transferred. He was forty-eight.

Nadezhda Mandelstam's *Hope against Hope* is a sobering account of the fear that the Yagoda and Yezhov years instilled in the entire Russian population during the mid and late 1930s. People in their homes would be alarmed if a car stopped outside their house, or they heard a lift stop on their floor. 'The principles and aims of mass terror,' she wrote, 'have nothing in common with ordinary police work or security. The only purpose of terror is intimidation. To plunge the whole country into a state of chronic fear, the number of victims must be raised to astronomical levels, and on every floor of every building there must always be several apartments from which the tenants have suddenly been taken away.' But, she added, the NKVD could not kill everyone, and 'there are always witnesses who survive to tell the tale.'[102]

One who did survive was Yevgenia Ginzburg, who taught history at Kazan University.[103] In February 1937 she was taken by the NKVD and accused of being a member of a 'Trotskyist' group, and underwent the usual interrogation, fake trial and sentence. She expected the death sentence, but after a firm denial of the fictional charges, she was surprised 'only' to receive a sentence of ten years in the gulag. For two years she was held in solitary confinement in a prison near Ekaterinburg, in a tiny cell without any ventilation. Then, along with thousands of other convicts, she was put on the train to Vladivostok, then sent by ship through the Sea of Okhotsk to Magadan.

In this town, within the Arctic Circle, prisoners were selected for work in mines or cutting lumber. Rations were sub-minimal for survival. Prisoners were tracked out to the work sites under armed guard. The work quotas were impossible to achieve, and yet rations were reduced if they were not realised. Convicts were shot for any infringements. Hunger led to slow starvation, and incidents of cannibalism were common. For lesser misdemeanours a prisoner was put into a punishment cell, without heat, and sparsely clothed. Camp officials had to meet quotas for punishments. Ordinary criminals were favoured over 'politicals', and there was anarchy amongst the convicts. Sentences were increased without any reason, as Ginzburg's was in 1949. She was saved when a camp doctor gave her the relatively bearable job as a nurse in a camp hospital. To survive in the camps one needed such a stroke of luck. After Stalin's death in 1953 Ginzburg was finally rehabilitated, but she never saw her husband again.

Kapuscinski wrote of the Bay of Nagayev, the sea entrance to Magadan: 'This is a place-symbol, a place-document, with a symbolic weight similar to that of the gate of Auschwitz, or the railway ramp at Treblinka. This bay, the gate, and the ramp are three different designs of the same scene: the descent into hell.'[104] Similar camps existed over the entire Soviet Union. (For a riveting account of work conditions of convicts along the Kolyma River see Varlam Shalamov's *Kolyma Tales*.)

At least 700,000 people lost their lives in the Yezhovshchina of 1937-38, and millions of others in the fifteen years that remained of the Stalin years (that excludes casualties in the 1941-45 war). It has been argued that this forced labour system speeded up the industrial production without which Russia would have lost the war against Hitler's Germany. Russians I spoke to during the Gorbachev thaw of 1988-89 denied this, arguing that it was precisely the gulag system that had brought defeat so close. Most history books imply that Stalin took rational political decisions out of fear that the objectives of the revolution were endangered, stressing the electrification of the Soviet Union and the manufacture of lots of tractors. The Russians who survived and wrote of their experiences say something different: that the Bolsheviks were thugs from day one. Unlike Hitler's Nazis who came to power legally, Lenin's group staged a coup in early 1918 with the overthrow of the Constituent Assembly. From then on they were a minority group who were to rule by terror. Stalin was a ruthless killer for whom democracy and the norms of political life were anachronisms (as we shall see Hitler also used terror and loathed democracy).

Tzvetan Todorov wrote in 1991: 'Totalitarianism is the extreme of our political life...the opposite of democracy. It is in an altogether different sense of the word that the camps represent the extreme of the totalitarian regime: they are its quintessence, its most intense and concentrated manifestation; the camps are the centre, so to speak, rather than the peripheral extreme. If one considers totalitarianism from a political or a philosophical point of view, one is hard pressed to decide which of its attributes most accurately defines it. Is it the single-party system? The conflation of state and ideology? The revolutionary project? From the standpoint of the individual's experience, however, the pertinent trait is incontestably terror, and this terror the camps both distil and amplify. Hannah Arendt is correct in seeing terror as the essence of totalitarian government, even if to characterize it in such a way ignores other important attributes of the totalitarian system.'[105]

Were fascism and communism/Stalinism ideological opposites, an extremist 'right-wing' ideology confronting its 'left-wing' antithesis? Or is it better to see them as two versions of totalitarianism, as Hannah Arendt argued in her *Origins of Totalitarianism*?[106] Her book, written in the early 1950s, traces the roots of what she termed totalitarianism back to the later nineteenth century. The forced labour camps of South Africa's gold mines in the 1890s and the British system of concentration camps during the Boer war of 1899-1902 were among its roots. The First World War provided the conditions for totalitarian regimes to emerge, and inventions – such as barbed wire (first manufactured by J.F. Glidden in 1874 [107]), the radio, motor vehicles and railways – provided the tools that made totalitarian rule possible. The psychological brutality of the fighting in the 1914-18 war smashed the unwritten nineteenth-century rules of relatively decent behaviour.

Both communism and fascism, whether Mussolini's or Hitler's version, were rooted in the First World War. Hitlerism and Stalinism emerged in nations that had suffered shattering defeat, and both were brutalised by the war. Both were nationalistic, seeking to gain, or regain, what their monarchical predecessors had failed to attain. Both were anti-worker, with free worker unions being replaced by state-run pseudo-unions. Each was centred on the Party, with all rival parties banned. Each emphasised the 'leader': in Germany the fuehrer, in Russia 'the boss'. The will of a single man dominated; he was surrounded by cronies, Mandelstam's 'fawning half-men'. In each the individual was subordinated to the nation. There was total 'coordination' – *Gleichschaltung* to use the German word – of individuals. We had the emergence of the 'fascist personality' and what in the Soviet Union Nadezhda Mandelstam called 'the wolf tribe' – individuals who would carry out whatever orders they were given either out of fear or for self-advancement.

Everything in both types of regime was controlled: culture, art, film, the universities, scientific ideas, the popular press, literature. Both systems were anti-Christian, the communists destroying the churches, the Nazis forcing the Catholic and Protestant churches to serve their political ends. They were both utopian, the communists looking forward to the classless society and 'the withering away of the state', the Nazis to a fantasy of a pure race future which interblended with romantic ideas about the legendary past. That is to say both rejected the reality of the present. Both in effect rejected capitalism, the communists openly abolishing it, the Nazis using it, but as a tool that had to be kept under control. There was a moral relativity in each of the thought systems, with much abuse of language, what George Orwell called 'double-speak'.

The basic idea was that the end was all important, and if there were innocent victims, so be it. Each was focussed on the (fictional) internal enemy, the Stalinists on kulaks, Trotskyites and spies for Japan; the Nazis on Jews, communists and freemasons. The enemy was only fit for the concentration camp, the Russians starting with camps in 1928, the Nazis imitating them after mid-1933. On the one hand the Gulag; on the other Auschwitz, Treblinka, Sobibor. There was systematic use of terror by both regimes, the Soviet version run by the NKVD secret police, the Nazi one by the SS and the Gestapo. Both became militarised, with SS divisions fighting alongside the German army and NKVD high-ups supervising the Russian generals in the 1941-45 war. In the Soviet Union: Dzerzhinsky, Yagoda, Yezhov, Beria; in the Hitler state: Himmler, Heydrich and Müller. In both states the art of sadism was perfected. Both

Stalin and Hitler were preoccupied with preparations for war. In both, the focus was tanks, aircraft, armaments. The Nazis, admittedly, tried to give the population butter as well as guns, whereas in Russia social deprivation ruled. There are differences in detail, but there is a strong case for saying they were versions of the same thing.

# 12. Auschwitz

Hitler's National Socialists were to kill millions of Jewish people during the Second World War. Other groups were also killed en masse, such as gypsies and homosexuals, but it is the focus on one race group which differentiates the German killings from the Stalinist killings, where the victims were marked out by their alleged political 'crimes'. A large proportion of the Jewish victims were murdered in death camps which were in effect factories for the mass murder of humans. The most notorious camp, Auschwitz, was in fact the name given to a group of camps in south-western Poland, where work-to-death camps, such as those in the Soviet Union, and a death factory were combined into a dual operation. In Auschwitz between one and a half and two million Jews lost their lives. Other single purpose death camps in Poland included Chelmno, Sobibor, Treblinka, and Belzec. After the war ended in 1945 the neologism 'genocide' began to be used for the mass killing of Jews. Another term increasingly used since the 1940s is 'the Holocaust', sometimes referred to as 'the Shoah'.

How can one account for this disaster? Anti-Jewish attitudes were prevalent in Europe well before the twentieth century, though such antisemitism was not especially strong in Germany, where less than one percent of the population was Jewish. Racial dislike of Jews was much stronger in Eastern Europe, especially in Poland and Russia, which had higher concentrations of Jews. For centuries Jews had been used as scapegoats by monarchical regimes, often to divert attention from unpopular political actions. In tsarist Russia murderous attacks on Jews called 'pogroms' were occasionally organised by the regime. The last decades of the nineteenth century saw an intensified prejudice against Jews throughout much of Europe, for example amongst the political right in France, boosted by bastardised versions of Darwin's evolutionary theories. By the twentieth century a new pseudo-science called eugenics was focusing on the ideal perfect human bodily appearance and mental make-up: uncoincidentally, the ideal human race type was the European. European eugenicists studied the 'black natives' of Africa (which Britain, France and Germany were busy invading), and identified them, along with the Jews, as inferior racial 'types' or *Untermenschen.*

Antisemitism was prevalent in the Austrian empire where, at Braunau am Inn, Hitler was born in 1889. He imbibed his antisemitism in Vienna prior to 1914 during his late teens and early twenties. The shock of Germany's defeat in 1918 and the humiliating terms of the Treaty of Versailles intensified German and Austrian antisemitism amongst the political right. The returning soldiers blamed their defeat on the collapse of the home front, which, they alleged, was orchestrated by Jews, socialists, communists and Bolsheviks – who were all blurred together as objects of hate. From then on, right-wing groups in Germany, whose fervent aim was to overthrow the Treaty of Versailles and avenge the *Dolchstoss* (stab in the back), merged this with antisemitism. The communist seizure of power in Russia was seen as being engineered by Jews. The United States, whose declaration of war on Germany in April 1917 effectively decided the outcome of the First World War, was seen as being run by capitalists among whom Jews had the upper hand. Jews were portrayed as bacilli threatening Germany.

All this was nonsense, but it did not prevent Hitler parading his antisemitism in *Mein Kampf*, published in 1926. Most of those who became his lieutenants, such as Joseph Goebbels, were strong antisemites. Even when pursuing rational political strategies, antisemitism always remained a major part of Hitler's thought and psychological make-up. Whenever things were going badly for Germany, it was the Jew who was to blame. The 'problem of the Jew' for Hitler was there even when he was focussing on other things. (There were many things the Nazis did not like: for example, in 1928 their party newspaper, the *Völkischer Beobachter*, described Berlin as: 'A melting pot of everything that is evil – prostitution, drinking houses, cinemas, Marxism, Jews, strippers, negroes, dancing, and all the vile offshoots of so-called "modern art".'[108])

The escalation in the Nazi vote after 1929 was thus bad news for Germany's half a million Jewish people (around 0.7% of Germany's population), many of whom began plans for emigration when Hitler became chancellor in January 1933. Others hoped that the Nazi antisemitic rhetoric would tone down now that they were in power, or that Hitler's position as chancellor would be brief. But that was not to be. The first concentration camps were set up in Germany during the course of 1933 and Jews and socialists were among the first to be imprisoned in them. By 1935 the danger to German Jews was unambiguous. In September that year came the Nürnberg Laws, a series of anti-Jewish measures, which were to be added to over the next six years. The new Reich's Citizenship Act specifically excluded Jews as citizens, allowing only 'Aryans'. Jews were soon to be refused permission to marry Aryans.

In March 1938 German troops marched into Austria and fused it into a greater Germany (*Grossdeutschland*). Most of Austria's Jews were now targeted for humiliation. At this stage Jews were effectively being encouraged to emigrate out of Germany. Others took the train to Trieste in Italy then went by ship to Haifa in Palestine. The problems for Jews facing the dilemma of whether to leave or risk things by staying were various, among them: people's reluctance to leave their homes; the hindrance many states such as the US put in place making it difficult for them to get in; and some Jewish people's refusal to join the colonisation of the Arab territory of Palestine. Most of them saw themselves as loyal Germans; indeed many Jewish men were decorated soldiers who had fought in the Kaiser's armies in the First World War.[109]

Conditions worsened during the rest of 1938 and 1939, especially after the *Kristallnacht* of 8 November 1938, when Jewish synagogues and shops throughout Germany were set on fire or had their windows smashed (hence 'crystal night') in retaliation for the assassination of a German official in Paris. Jews were banned from becoming medical doctors, dentists, vets, or lawyers. All Jews had to carry identity cards. In December 1938 their pensions were reduced. Successive laws compelled them to give up all gold and silver, and firearms; and to join a Reich's Union of Jews. Their food coupons were withdrawn, their houses seized and sold to Aryans, and they were removed to special 'Jewish residences'. They were no longer permitted to drive a car, own a radio, a telephone, or a typewriter. Most of the pleasures of life were taken from them. They were refused permission to walk in parks, use public libraries, go to the cinema, use a swimming pool, or go for a boat ride on the Elbe River. From 19 September 1941 they were compelled to wear a yellow star prominently on their coats.

In January 1939 Hitler made a speech to the Reichstag announcing that should Germany face another war, it would be bad news for the Jews, who, he said, would not survive it. But as yet there was no formulated policy of extermination, even when, in September 1939, the European war began. As the war began, the fear of German Jews at the possible outcome was captured by the Jewish academic, Victor Klemperer, in his diary entry for 3 September 1939: '...popular opinion absolutely certain of victory, ten thousand times more arrogant than in 1914. The consequences will either be an overwhelming, almost unchallenged victory, and England and France are castrated minor states, or a catastrophe ten thousand times worse than 1918. And the two of us [Klemperer and his wife] right in the middle, helpless and probably lost in any case...And yet we force ourselves, and sometimes it even succeeds for a couple of hours, to go on with our everyday life: reading aloud, eating (as best we can), writing, garden. But as I lie down to sleep I think: Will they come for me tonight? Will I be shot, will I be put in a concentration camp?'[110]

The Nazi version of totalitarianism was preoccupied with racial purity, and the breeding of blond, blue-eyed German Aryans. There was a mania for bodily health and fitness. The job of the women was to produce beautiful Aryan children free from hereditary defects. A social Darwinist mentality stalked the universities and the party. By 1937-38 Himmler's Schutzstaffel (protection squads, better known as the SS) were exploring ways of creating a pool of superior and athletic super-soldiers, with 'pure' blood. The insanity of this notwithstanding, a series of measures to this end was put in place. Immediately, in July 1933, an Act for the Prevention of Offspring with Hereditary Diseases was passed.

As in any society, Germany in the 1930s had its percentage of children and adults suffering from physical or psychic problems.[111] Many were accommodated in special hospitals or asylums if their families could not care for them. As the war began in September 1939 and German armies were invading Poland, things took a sinister turn. Hospital chiefs were ordered to kill some of their inmates who had 'become a burden' on state finances. The killings began in December 1939. The victims were asylum inmates, the mentally ill, and the incurably ill. But amongst them were perfectly healthy, normal individuals whose families had decided, for one reason or another, to get rid of: for example a 'hysterical housewife'. Various ways of killing were experimented with: gassing in sealed vans was one; another was injections with phenol or other poisons.

By 1940, gas chambers at certain institutions were in operation inside Germany. The most notorious were Hadamar, north of Frankfurt; Hartheim, near Linz; Sonnenstein, near Dresden; Grafeneck, near Münsingen; and Brandenburg on the Havel River. Victor Klemperer, who lived near Dresden, wrote in his diary for 21 May 1941: 'Sonnenstein has long ceased to be the regional mental asylum. The SS is in charge. They have built a special crematorium. Those who are not wanted are taken up by a kind of police van. People here call it "the whispering coach". Afterwards the relatives receive the urn. Recently one family here received two urns at once.'[112]

The doctors and nurses were in some cases uneasy at their task, but most carried out instructions. Letters were sent to the family saying that the victim had died of heart failure. The killings, and the instructions, were devised in Berlin at a centre at Tiergartenstrasse 4 (codenamed T4) under the charge of senior Nazis, among whom were Philipp Bouhler and Karl Brandt. Once killed, the bodies of victims were burnt. The smoke of the cremation fires aroused the curiosity of residents in the vicinity of the hospitals, and rumours spread about what was happening. In August 1941 Bishop Galen of Münster gave a sermon in the cathedral denouncing the killings as unchristian, to Hitler's fury. The killing of adults slowed, but those of children were to continue right to the end of the war in 1945.

When the German armies overran northern France in May and June 1940 and the French capitulated, Hitler's 'Jewish problem' was put temporarily on the back burner. By that time there were only a small number of Jews left in Germany: around 160,000. On the other hand, the successful invasion and occupation of Poland in the latter months of 1939 had led to Germany incorporating a huge additional Jewish population, and the 'problem' became worse.

Poland was divided into three regions: the western part, which Germany had lost in 1919, was re-annexed; the eastern part, which was taken over by the Soviet Union – following the agreement between Stalin and Hitler of August 1939; and the central region, named the Generalgouvernement, which was under German control. In Poland antisemitism had been more vicious than in Germany, and the policy to round up Poland's Jews and send them into the Generalgouvernement began with help from Polish collaborators.

The task of working out a strategy for solving 'the Jewish question' was given over to the central SS administration in Berlin, known as the Reichssicherheitshauptamt (Imperial Security Head Office) or RSHA for short. This was headed by Himmler's deputy Reinhard Heydrich. During 1940 and early 1941 Jewish ghettos were established in key Polish cities, such as Warsaw and Lodz: Jews were ordered from their homes and relocated to the ghettos, which were sealed off from the rest of the city or town. Special Jewish councils did the self-administration. These measures preoccupied the German authorities, while they thought up a longer term solution. One idea discussed after the 1940 victory over France was to send Europe's Jews to the then French colony of Madagascar, off the coast of south-east Africa. The failure to defeat the British, however, and the continuing control of the high seas by the British navy, rendered this idea impracticable. Many Jews were killed during the invasion of Poland and the setting up of the ghettos, but as yet there was no idea of a mass killing.

That changed during 1941. Rather than focus on defeating the British, for example in north Africa, where Egypt and the Suez Canal might have been secured, an overconfident Hitler decided to tear up the August 1939 Non-Aggression Treaty with Stalin and attack the Soviet Union. This meant a two-front war, which could become dangerous for Germany if Britain was joined by its ally the United States. Roosevelt, re-elected US president in November 1940, favoured entering the war, but was for the time being restrained by the US Congress.

As the Soviet Union had a very large Jewish population, a secret high-up Nazi meeting in March 1941 discussed what to do about the prospective enlarged 'problem'.[113] Following Operation Barbarossa, the attack on Russia which began on 22 June 1941, the German armies secured huge areas of new territory in Russian Poland and Russia's western regions of Belorussia and Ukraine, both areas with large Jewish populations. In July and August the focus in the rear of operations was on shooting captured Russian officers, saboteurs, and male Jews (at first Jewish women were left alone). By September, however, Jews everywhere in the Soviet Union under Nazi control were being shot in batches: men, women and children. The 'work' was given over to four killer squads called *Einsatzgruppen* (quick response units). One notorious mass execution took place at the turn of September-October 1941 at Babi Yar in Kiev, where over 30,000 Jews were shot to death in a ravine. (In 1938, as mentioned, Yezhov had personally ordered the killing of 30,000 people in Kiev.) As the German armies drove eastwards into Lithuania (then under Soviet rule), some of Poland's Jewish population were deported by train to Minsk, Riga and other Lithuanian cities with the story that they were being relocated. There they were shot in forests.

Although the German armies had won spectacular victories, by August 1941 the German high command and the top Nazis were beginning to be uneasy. Soviet military resistance was continuing strongly. There were disputes between the high command and Hitler over the strategy. Russia was huge and the German armies finite. Should they go for Moscow, or focus on southern Russia and aim for the oil in the Caucasus? Autumn and winter were not far off. By October confidence had revived after more victories, but only momentarily. Hitler had nightmares about a repeat of the First World War: stalemate followed by defeat. Paranoia increased his hatred of the Jews (and communists) whom he blamed for everything. It was this phase – September-October 1941 – that saw the decision for a 'final solution' of the Jewish problem: all Jews in every part of Europe under German control were to be killed.

When exactly did the decision become irrevocable? Historians are still debating the question.[114] Some believe that the 'final solution' decision was taken in July and certainly no later than August 1941, as Germany's victories increased optimism for a new order in Europe in which no Jews would remain. The fate of the Jews, according to this view, was a consequence of German victories. In recent years other historians have disputed this. They say the decision for the final solution was taken as late as 12 December 1941 after the war began between Germany and the United States. There is evidence for this view in minutes of meetings Himmler and Goebbels had with Hitler in mid-December. Goebbels wrote in his diary for 13 December 1941: 'With respect to the Jewish Question, the Führer has decided to make a clean sweep. He prophesied to the Jews that if they again brought about a world war they would be set for annihilation in it. This wasn't just a catch word. The world war is here and the annihilation of the Jews must be the necessary consequence.'

Hitler, it appears, while on the verge of making up his mind in October, had held back from giving the final order as there was still hope that the United States would stay out of the war, and that the Soviet army would collapse. The Jews were, at that stage, hostages. But the Soviet counter-offensive at Moscow in November 1941, and the war between the United States and Japan that began on 7 December, made a US-Germany war unavoidable.

Referring to President Roosevelt, Hitler fumed in a radio speech: 'It was the Jew in all his Satanic vileness, which gathered around this man, but also to whom this man reached out.' A German victory was now unlikely, and, as a direct consequence of this fact, the green light to kill all the Jews was given. The final solution was, in other words, the outcome of Germany's inevitable defeat. David Cesarani puts it thus: 'With the German declaration of war on the United States on 11 December 1941, the war became global. Jews ceased to be hostages whose lives were held as a guarantee of American non-intervention; instead they became culprits who deserved sanguinary retribution. Ultimately, the course of the war rather than decisions within the framework of anti-Jewish policy, triggered the descent into European-wide genocide.'[115]

The next three years, from January 1942 to April 1945, when Hitler committed suicide, saw one German defeat after another. The German retreats in the Soviet Union, North Africa, Italy and France were accompanied by the murder of as many of Europe's Jews as the Nazis could get their hands on. Huge resources and manpower were transferred from military operations to the organisation of the mass killing of Jewish civilians. This was done via a number of methods: continued mass shootings, as at Babi Yar; Jews being worked to death in concentration camps and factories; and mass gassings in special death camps, drawing on the T4 techniques used in the German home front killing of the mentally ill. The entire railway system in German-controlled Europe was diverted to the transporting of Jews to killing places, to the detriment of military operations.

In Nazi-occupied Soviet Union and Poland the *Einsatzgruppen* and other squads continued their work. Christopher Browning in his book *Ordinary Men* recounts how older men from German cities were drafted into the killing squads such as Reserve Police Battalion 101 from

Hamburg. Many were workers and socialist in their political views, decent men in civilian life. Browning provides harrowing accounts of the killing operations, with the majority of victims being women and children. German soldiers were, however, given the option of not participating in the killings; but only a few preferred not to. The killers were plied with alcohol. Browning puts his finger on a key problem of our times. He writes: 'Most of all one comes away from the story of Reserve Police Battalion 101 with great unease...In every modern society, the complexity of life and the resulting bureaucratization and specialization attenuate the sense of responsibility of those implementing official policy. Within virtually every social collective, the peer group exerts tremendous pressures on behaviour and sets moral norms. If the men of Reserve Police Battalion 101 could become killers under such circumstances, what group of men cannot?'[116]

The psychological hesitations of the men doing the shootings, and the sheer number of Jews to be killed, meant that more efficient means were necessary. In November 1941 experiments were begun with killing people in gas chambers along the line of the T4 operation. The first site was at Chelmno in western Poland. Among the first victims were Russian prisoners of war. But Jews were gassed as well. Further death camps were set up in the eastern part of the Generalgouvernement Poland, at Belzec, Treblinka and Sobibor.

A conference of SS and RSHA high-ups took place at Wannsee in Berlin in January 1942 for the more detailed devising of a continental strategy. Why not combine pure gas chambers with work camps? Thus was born the idea of Auschwitz. Auschwitz, which began operations in May 1942, was to become the camp with the largest number of Jewish victims. Jews arriving by rail from all over Europe, including Italy, Greece and Marshal Pétain's France, were subjected to a 'selection' right on the railway platform. The elderly, children, and frailer people were sent straight to the gas chambers, their minds set at ease with the promise that they were only going to the showers. Instead they were locked into an enclosed chamber, into which the poison gas Zyklon B, an insecticide manufactured by IG Farben, was funnelled. The bodies were then either buried or burnt, the work being carried out by Jewish inmates, wearing striped pyjama suits. Younger and stronger arrivals had their heads shaved, and were set to work on construction sites and in local factories which were part of the prison camp complex. If you were lucky you might last a year; when adjudged as being too weak to continue to work the prisoner would be set aside for the gas chamber in a further 'selection'.

By mid-1942 the death camps were in full operation. Jews sent to Treblinka, Sobibor and Belzec, in contrast to Auschwitz, were gassed at once. Himmler visited the camps to see how things were going from time to time. The commandants and operators of the camps were a German version of Nadezhda Mandelstam's wolf-tribe.

Heinrich Himmler, head of the SS in charge of the whole 'final solution', gave a speech to senior SS officers at Poznan on 4 October 1943. He is quoted as saying: 'I also want to speak to you here, in complete frankness, of a really grave chapter...I am referring to the evacuation of the Jews, the extermination of the Jewish people...Most of you men know what it is like to see a hundred corpses side by side, or five hundred or a thousand. To have stood fast through this and – except for cases of human weakness – to have stayed decent: that has made us hard. This is an unwritten and never-to-be-written page of glory in our history, for we know how difficult it would be for us today – under bombing raids and the hardships and deprivations of war – if we were still to have the Jews in every city as secret saboteurs, agitators, and inciters. If the Jews were still lodged in the body of the German nation, we would by now have reached the stage of 1916-17...We do not want, in the end, because we destroyed a bacillus, to be infected by this bacillus and to die...All in all, however, we can say that we have carried out the most difficult of tasks in a spirit of love of our people. And we have suffered no harm to our inner being, our soul, our character.'[117]

But Germany *had* already reached the stage of 1916-17. Defeat was inevitable, and that is why the final solution was happening.

The ten-part film series *Shoah* made by Claude Lanzmann provides a chilling picture of the rail transport of Jews to the east Poland death camps. For Auschwitz, an account by a survivor is to be found in Primo Levi's *If This Is a Man.*[118] Levi was an Italian Jewish chemist who, after the fall of Mussolini in 1943, took part in guerrilla operations in northern Italy. He was captured by fascists, handed over to the Germans, and put on the train to Auschwitz, where he arrived in March 1944. His book is an account of his nearly being worked to death. He was only saved (like Yevgenia Ginzburg in Kolyma) by luck. His chemist's expertise proved useful in the local rubber factory, and he maintained enough energy to survive a period in mid-1944 in Auschwitz that saw the killing of 400,000 Hungarian Jews. The Auschwitz killings came to a halt in October 1944, but the forced labour continued. In January 1945, as the Russians approached, Levi was fortunately in the sick bay, and was not part of the remaining prisoner groups taken off by the SS which set out on foot to walk to Germany in thick winter snow, a journey in which many died or were shot. When the Russians entered Auschwitz, even these war-hardened soldiers blanched.

Primo Levi was able to return to Italy only via a railway journey that lasted several months. He was later to write about his experiences in his partly fictionalised memoirs. He observed: 'We who survived the Camps are not the true witnesses. This is an uncomfortable notion which I have gradually come to accept by reading what the survivors have written, including myself, when I re-read my writings after a lapse of years. We, the survivors, are not only a tiny but also an anomalous minority. We are those who, through prevarication, skill or luck, never touched bottom. Those who have, and who have seen the face of the Gorgon, did not return, or returned wordless.'[119] His warning for future generations was: 'The Nazi camps were the apex, the culmination of Fascism in Europe, its most monstrous manifestation...In every part of the world, whenever you begin by denying the fundamental liberties of mankind, and equality among people, you move towards the concentration camp system, and it is a road on which it is difficult to stop.'

Levi's warning can be read alongside another warning by British historian Gerald Reitlinger written after the war and after the atomic bomb was dropped on Hiroshima: 'For remote control killers, working from their office desks, are the shadow under which the present age lives. It was not for nothing that [Otto] Ohlendorf [commander of *Einsatzgruppe D*] justified his ninety thousand murders at Nuremburg [the allied trial of Nazi leaders in 1946] by allusions to the "press-button killers of the atomic bomb". The vaster the massacre, the more awful the weapons, the easier it becomes to arrange them. The little armies of office chiefs and stenographers are not nauseated by their work, because they do not see it...The men who stayed glued to their desks...lacked the imagination to see what happened at the end of the telegraph line.'[120]

# 13. Hiroshima

On 16 July 1945 a team of scientists reacted with astonishment, but also jubilation, to their successful detonation of the first atomic bomb in the US desert of New Mexico. The bomb was of special design and needed to be tested; the explosive substance was plutonium, element 94. Three and a half weeks later on 9 August 1945 a similar bomb was dropped on the city of Nagasaki in Japan: it killed around 40,000 people – men, women and children. Three days before the Nagasaki bombing, an alternative design bomb, based on uranium 235, had been dropped, untested (so confident were the scientists that it would work) on Hiroshima: it killed over 100,000 people. The two bombings finally persuaded the Japanese government to accept defeat in the Second World War. The months July and August 1945 have ever since divided human history into two eras: before and after the atomic bomb.

Less than eight years later, in 1952, an even more powerful bomb was tested in the Pacific Ocean: the hydrogen bomb, with an explosive impact several hundred times that of the Hiroshima and Nagasaki bombs. There are today twenty or thirty thousand of these devices, under the political direction of the US, Russia, Britain, France, China, India, Pakistan, and possibly North Korea. If they were ever to be used they would wipe out human civilization. Since 1952 threats that these weapons would be used have occurred at regular intervals. The missiles are ready to be fired at a few minutes' notice, once the political orders have been given. Thus began an age of universal fear unlike what had gone before.

The scientists involved in the development of these weapons faced criticisms. Why did they go ahead with the experiments into bombs that they knew would kill huge numbers of civilians? The man who led the team that built the 1945 bombs, Robert Oppenheimer, replied: 'It is my judgement in these things that when you see something that is technically sweet you go ahead and do it and you argue about what to do about it only after you have had your technical success.' His colleague, Edward Teller, who led the hydrogen bomb team, put it more explicitly: 'To abstain from progress is a medieval idea. I am in favour of any advance in knowledge or any development of the greater power of man.'[121]

The Polish poet, Wisława Szymborska, begs to differ. In her poem 'Discovery', she writes:

> I believe in the great discovery.
> I believe in the man who made the discovery.
> I believe in the fear of the man who will make the discovery.
> I believe in his face going white,
> his queasiness, his upper lip drenched in cold sweat.
> I believe in the burning of his notes,
> burning them into ashes,
> burning them to the last scrap...
> I believe in the refusal to take part.
> I believe in the ruined career.
> I believe in the wasted years of work.
> I believe in the secret taken to the grave.[122]

Teller or Szymborska? This conflict is the invisible backcloth to the facts of how the atomic bomb was developed.

One of the primary questions of later nineteenth-century science was: what is the nature of matter?[123] What is the smallest particle? If you go on chopping up, say, a grain of sand, at what point can you chop no further, because you have the smallest possible particle of sand? The physicist James Clerk Maxwell believed in the existence of very small particles that were already being called 'atoms', and which, he imagined, had existed in unchangeable form since the beginning of the universe. But as late as the 1890s, despite big advances in physics and chemistry, the question still had no answer.

The initial breakthrough in understanding the structure of matter came in 1896 at the Cavendish Institute, the University of Cambridge, England. Its head of physics, J.J. Thompson, discovered the electron. This was a negatively charged fundamental particle, but was it an atom? In 1911 at the University of Manchester its head of physics, the New Zealander, Ernest Rutherford, came up with the idea of an atom having a nucleus, a central core that was paired with one or more electrons, which were either in the core or went round it: he did not yet know. A pupil of Rutherford, the Dane, Niels Bohr, took this further with his theory that electrons went round the atomic nucleus in certain pathways.

But how was the nucleus itself structured? Rutherford, now at the Cavendish Institute, took the next step in the 1920s by demonstrating the existence of protons, and suggesting that a number of these made up the nucleus of an atom. The positive electrical charges of the protons were counterbalanced by negatively charged electrons – one electron for each proton in the nucleus. The experiments were ingenious and fiddly, and often done on small budgets. Things were not made any easier when the German physicist, Werner Heisenberg, in the mid-1920s established mathematically that any research into electrons would have to take into account that it was not possible to know their velocity and position simultaneously. Experiments were made more difficult still by the fact that the protons' positive electrical charges make it complicated to bombard them with positive alpha particles of helium, one of the ideas physicists were working on.

The field opened up when in 1932 another British physicist, James Chadwick, then at Cambridge, discovered the other key component of the atomic nucleus, the neutron, a particle about as large as a proton, but with no electrical charge.[124] With the neutron's discovery the structure of atoms could finally be visualised. In 1936 Niels Bohr at Copenhagen showed that the nucleus of an atom is made up of protons and neutrons, with each positively charged proton 'balanced' by a negatively charged electron, which circles the nucleus in a flight path. Physicists established that the number of protons in an element's nucleus coincides with its 'atomic number', whilst the combination of its protons and neutrons produces its 'atomic weight'. Further research demonstrated that some elements occur in forms with varying numbers of neutrons, each of these known as 'isotopes' of the element. For example, there is an isotope of uranium with 143 neutrons instead of the normal 146, giving it – with its 92 protons – an atomic weight of 235 rather than 238.

Chadwick's 1932 discovery of the neutron began the science of nuclear physics. At physics departments throughout Europe – in Rome, Copenhagen, Berlin, Paris, Cambridge and Göttingen – experiments were devised to get a more complete idea of how the nucleus of an atom was structured. Because it has no electrical charge the neutron proved to be more suitable than the proton to bombard with alpha particles, as neutrons would not be repelled by a positive charge. In Rome, the Italian physicist, Enrico Fermi, and his team fired alpha particles on all elements in the periodic table up to uranium. The uranium experiment produced a surprise: new atoms were observed which Fermi assumed were isotopes of uranium higher up in the periodic table. A German chemist, Ida Noddack, thought this was a premature assumption. Perhaps what had happened, she wrote critically of Fermi's work, was that the neutrons fired at the uranium nucleus had induced it to split into 'several large fragments, which would of course be isotopes of known elements but would not be neighbours [in the periodic table].' Noddack's suggestion, which turned out to be correct, was in 1934 rejected as being impossible.[125] The idea that an atom could break apart was not then regarded as plausible.

The Nazis began their anti-Jewish measures in the spring of 1933. The 'Law for the Restoration of the Professional Civil Service', promulgated on 7 April, stipulated that only racially pure Germans could hold posts in the civil service, which included the universities. At a stroke all Jewish academics throughout Germany lost their jobs. Other official and unofficial measures against Jews, and the prospects of more to come, persuaded many Jewish academics to emigrate. Many of the physicists and chemists involved in nuclear research were Jews living in Germany, who now fled to the United States or to other European countries – especially Britain, and Denmark. Amongst them were physicists who were to play a vital role in developing the atom bomb in the United States: Edward Teller, Albert Einstein, George Gamow, Hans Bethe, Otto Frisch, Lise Meitner, Eugene Wigner and Rudolf Peierls. Although the Italian, Fermi, was not Jewish, his wife Laura was, and fearing anti-Jewish measures from Mussolini's fascists, they duly departed for the United States at the turn of 1938-39.

The Jewish physicist Leo Szilard was in England in the summer of 1933, having fled Nazi Germany. He was a Hungarian, from Budapest originally. Richard Rhodes in his book *The Making of the Atomic Bomb* relates how, as Szilard was crossing Southampton Row in central London one day, he had a sudden thought: what if you could split an atom, and have its parts split others in a chain reaction? – you might be able to release infinite energies that could be used to make very powerful bombs.

He attempted to get patents on the idea, but during the next four years came to the realisation that any such development was impossible.[126] He was wrong.

Back in Germany Lise Meitner was at the Kaiser Wilhelm Institute (KWI) in Berlin. Although she was Jewish, she had been born in Austria, and hence was not a citizen of Germany. She was working at the KWI under Otto Hahn on the chemical analysis of elements being fired at by neutrons, when her citizenship status changed. It was March 1938 and Hitler had seized Austria in the *Anschluss*. Later that year, in November, Meitner fled Germany for a new job in Stockholm. Letters she received from Hahn just before Christmas contained news of some peculiar experimental results. Hahn had identified the elements in the 'fragments' broken off when uranium was bombarded with neutrons. The fragments were barium, a much lighter element with 54 protons, compared with uranium's 92. It seemed that the uranium atom had split, but that surely had to be a mistake? Hahn's letter was asking Meitner for her opinion.

Meitner was that Christmas on holiday at the Swedish village of Kungälv with her nephew Otto Frisch, also a physicist. On a walk in the snow they intuited what had happened. The uranium nucleus, being huge and unstable (it is the heaviest nucleus with 92 protons and 146 neutrons), had split into smaller elements such as barium. But that was not all. The combined mass of the fragments was a tiny bit less than the mass of the original uranium atom. Following Einstein's law $E=mc^2$, the loss of mass must have been converted into energy: 200 million electron volts they calculated – a huge amount for a single atom.[127] Ida Noddack had been right after all. And so had Leo Szilard.

The word got out and spread like wildfire among the nuclear physicists. Frisch informed Niels Bohr who was just about to leave by ocean liner for New York. There was a rush to get the hypotheses into the science journals. Within a month, during which time Enrico Fermi had arrived in the US in flight from Mussolini, US scientists confirmed the result. That summer of 1939, when Hitler had annexed what remained of Czechoslovakia, the implications of the splitting of uranium were being exhaustively discussed. It was realised that if the splitting single atom of uranium gave off two or more neutrons there was a possibility of a chain reaction in which all the atoms in the uranium mass would split; and each would give off 200 million electron volts, which, in a chain reaction, would be released in a trillionth of a second. If this could be used as a weapon it would be a bomb of fearful power.

Presciently Niels Bohr guessed that what was splitting in the reaction was the U235 isotope of uranium, rather than the fundamental U238. But U235 was only 0.7% of the uranium mass, and if it was only U235 that fissioned (the biological term that was now being used), it would need a factory size facility to collect enough of it to make a bomb. And the physicists were faced with the further problem: what would be the minimum mass of uranium (the 'critical mass') needed for a chain reaction? Initial calculations suggested a bomb would weigh many tons and be undeliverable.

By now it was September 1939 and Hitler had begun the European war. Scientists in both the US and Britain found that politicians had too much on their minds to focus on wild ideas of a super bomb coming from the university physics departments. Committees were set up to liaise between nuclear scientists and government, but nothing further was done. Einstein was persuaded to write a letter to Roosevelt outlining the possibilities and dangers, but it was ignored.[128] The main danger was that if the British and Americans did not get going, the Germans might well build a bomb first. The politicians thought this far-fetched. Research went ahead sporadically, with money in constant shortage.

In early 1940 Otto Frisch, having found a niche for himself at Birmingham University in England, was joined by Rudolph Peierls. While Nazi armies were overrunning France in the early summer of that year, Frisch and Peierls did some fresh calculations. They worked out that if one bombarded the isotope U235 with fast neutrons, a chain reaction might be possible from just a few pounds of U235. In short, a bomb was theoretically feasible. They approached the head of the department, Mark Oliphant, to give him the news.

Things moved faster from then on. The British government set up a committee in which the politics and science were considered together – the MAUD committee. (Maud was the name of Niels Bohr's childhood governess; although everyone thought it was the code for something.) The drive to build a bomb had seriously begun. Frisch wrote later: 'I have often been asked why I didn't abandon the project there and then, saying nothing to anybody. Why start on a project which, if it was successful, would end with the production of a weapon of unparalleled violence, a weapon of mass destruction such as the world had never seen. The answer was very simple. We were at war, and the idea was reasonably obvious; very probably some German scientists had had the same idea and were working on it.'[129] Indeed German scientists were, but Heisenberg, Hahn and others in Germany were not getting sufficient practical support from the Nazi high-ups, though uranium deposits in German-occupied Bohemia were put under guard.

Research in the United States produced the next discovery. Among the isotopes given off by U238 when it fissioned was an element with an atomic weight of 239. This 'decayed' into several variations, one of which was a new metal which had not been seen before. In December 1940 a team at the University of Chicago led by Glenn Seaborg identified and named the new element 'plutonium': Pu239.[130] Like U235 it was shown to be highly fissile. But unlike U235, plutonium could be relatively easily manufactured – at least in theory – from natural uranium. That winter research in the United States showed that the Frisch-Peierls calculations of the critical mass of U235 were right – all that would be needed for a bomb was 7 kilograms of U235. It was now April 1941 and Hitler was gearing up for the invasion of the Soviet Union, while Japan was continuing its conquests in China.

There were two feasible routes to the manufacture of a new type of bomb: one using uranium 235, the other plutonium 239. Calculations showed that the explosion of 7 kilograms of U235 would be about 20,000 times more devastating than any existing explosive, and could destroy the whole of a city the size of New York. James Chadwick checked the calculations and wrote in 1969, reflecting back: 'I remember the spring of 1941 to this day. I realized then that a nuclear bomb was not only feasible – it was inevitable. Sooner or later these ideas could not be peculiar to us. Everybody would think about them before long, and some country would put them into action. And I had nobody to talk to. You see, the chief people in the laboratory were Frisch and [Joseph Rotblat]. However high my opinion of them was, they were not citizens of this country [Britain], and the others were quite young boys. And there was nobody to talk to about it. I had many sleepless nights. But I did realise how serious it could be. And I had then to start taking sleeping tablets. It was the only remedy. I've never stopped since then. It's 28 years, and I don't think I've missed a single night in all those 28 years.'[131]

The committees set up to discuss matters by the governments of both Britain and the United States continued their work. Britain, where the technical feasibility of a bomb had been established, tried to put pressure on the United States. To isolate enough U235 to make a bomb would require a massive expenditure. To produce plutonium was less difficult technically, but would also require huge financial investment. The United States dragged its feet. Roosevelt's administration in Washington, however, was faced with the growing threat of a war with Japan. In October 1941 Roosevelt set up what was in effect a bomb committee with himself in charge.

The Japanese attack on Pearl Harbour in early December 1941 brought the United States into war with Japan, Germany and Italy, and from then on the making of the bomb was fast-tracked. The assumption at that time was that a device could be produced in about two years. The danger was that if Germany got there first, it could win the war. Should such a device not be feasible, well, the Germans would also fail. The US planners felt that nothing would be lost by going ahead.

During 1942, as the United States navy fought back against the Japanese in the Pacific Ocean, the Soviet armies fought the Wehrmacht in the eastern Ukraine, and Jews were being gassed in the (by now) fully operational death camps, Roosevelt made the decision to finance the manufacture of a bomb. The operation was known as the Manhattan Project. Robert Oppenheimer was appointed head of the science team, and General Leslie Groves was put in overall charge of organisation. In September 1942 they looked for operational venues, and settled on a range of hills in the New Mexico desert where they took over some school buildings at a place called Los Alamos. The recruitment of the science team began.

The first functioning nuclear 'pile', later to be termed a 'reactor', was built at the University of Chicago by a team headed by Enrico Fermi; it had gone critical on 2 December 1942, an important date in history. Fissions in a uranium chain reaction create both U235 and Pu239 but in very small amounts. The difficulties facing Groves and Oppenheimer were twofold: how to manufacture sufficient fissile material, both of U235 and Pu239, in reactors; and how to figure out a workable bomb design from scratch. During 1943 two reactors were built at Oak Ridge, Tennessee, the one producing plutonium and the other uranium 235. At the same time a second group of reactors to produce plutonium was set up at Hanford in Washington State. The Hanford B Reactor, built by the Du Pont Corporation, was the first reactor that produced plutonium. The establishment of these industrial facilities in so short a time was an astonishing feat. Groves demanded that the facilities be built and production got under way under 'impossible' schedules. The first plutonium and U235 were delivered to Los Alamos during March-April 1944 and by early 1945 in amounts sufficient for bombs.

Oppenheimer's team of physicists matched Groves's achievement. When enough of the isotope U235 was available, the design experiments went ahead. It was conceptually simple. The critical mass of U235 was divided into two parts, the one part machined into a hollow sphere placed at one end of the bomb tube; the other formed into a bullet that could be discharged along the tube into the hollow sphere at very high speed. This would create the critical mass that would explode. The necessary calculations, experiments and machinings took several months, and the work – with U235 from Oak Ridge – was completed by the early summer of 1945. This was the design of the Hiroshima bomb. The scientists were so confident that it would work that they did not feel it necessary to test it.

A bomb made from P239, plutonium, was more complicated, since a 'gun type' design could cause the plutonium to explode prematurely and 'fizzle'. This technical problem was solved by Seth Neddermeyer and George Kistiakowsky, who advocated squeezing a ball of plutonium using a group of lenses around the core, which would explosively compress the plutonium to the necessary critical mass. This more complex 'implosion' design needed to be tested. A test site was established at Alamogordo in the New Mexican desert where the first atomic explosion took place on 16 July 1945, an event known as the Trinity Test. The bomb yielded the equivalent of 18,600 tons of normal explosive. Philip Morrison, one of the scientists watching, noted: '...we saw an unbelievably brilliant flash. That was not the most impressive thing. We knew it was going to be blinding. We wore welder's glasses. The thing that got me was not the flash but the blinding heat of a bright day on your face in the cold desert morning. It was like opening a hot oven with the sun coming out like a sunrise.'[132] And he was ten miles away. The new US president, Harry Truman, had a confident step when he met with Stalin and Churchill at Potsdam the following day.

There remained the question of dropping a bomb, especially on a civilian population. When the Second World War began in 1939, President Roosevelt had made this appeal to world leaders: 'The ruthless bombing from the air of civilians in unfortified centres of population during the course of hostilities which have raged in various quarters of the Earth during the past few years, which has resulted in the maiming and in the death of thousands of defenceless men, women and children, has sickened the hearts of civilised man and woman, and has profoundly shocked the conscience of humanity...I am therefore addressing this urgent appeal to every Government which may be engaged in hostilities publicly to affirm that its armed forces shall in no event, and under no circumstances, undertake the bombardment from the air of civilian populations or of unfortified cities, upon the understanding that these same rules of warfare will be scrupulously observed by all of their opponents. I request an immediate reply.'[133]

Roosevelt's appeal went unheeded. The Second World War was the first in which civilians rather than soldiers became primary targets. The Germans ruthlessly bombed Warsaw from day one. A British bombing raid on Berlin during the summer of 1940 led to the use of German aircraft to bomb London and other British cities, such as Coventry, in what became known as the blitz. Once the British army had been thrown back across the Channel in 1940, the only means of attacking Germany was from the air. From 1941 the British Bomber Command under Sir Arthur Harris began the systematic bombing of German targets. At the beginning only military targets were attacked. By 1943 this had evolved into 'area bombing', the deliberate and systematic bombing of heavily populated areas of key German cities in an attempt to destroy Germany's civilian morale and thus to shorten the war. This strategy was blessed by Churchill who called for 'absolutely devastating, exterminating attacks by very heavy bombers...upon the Nazi homeland.'

The most infamous of the British attacks was that on Hamburg in late July 1943, where incendiary bombs were used to set the city burning and to kill as many people as possible. This attack's secret operation plan – code-named Operation Gomorrah – was explicit: 'It is estimated that at least ten thousand tons of bombs will have to be dropped to complete the process of elimination...Intention: to destroy Hamburg.'[134]

On the night of the bomber raid the entire city of Hamburg was engulfed in a firestorm in which the street tars melted, and blazing winds reached deadly temperatures. A woman resident remembered: 'Women and children were so charred as to be unrecognizable; those who had died through lack of oxygen were half charred and recognizable. Their brains had tumbled from their burst temples and their insides from the soft parts of their ribs. How terribly these people must have died. The smallest children lay like fried eels on the pavement.' Another woman survivor recollected that as she fled: 'We got to the Löschplatz all right but I couldn't go on across the Eifestrasse because the asphalt had melted. There were people on the roadway, some still lying alive but stuck in the asphalt. They must have rushed on to the roadway without thinking. Their feet had got stuck and then they had put out their hands to try and get out again. They were on their hands and knees screaming.' In his *On the Natural History of Destruction* W.G. Sebald relates how '[People] lay doubled up in pools of their own melted fat.' Those who managed to get out of the city fled throughout Germany. Sebald quotes someone who 'describes a group of forty or fifty such refugees trying to force their way into a train at a station in upper Bavaria. As they do so a cardboard suitcase "falls on the platform, bursts open and spills its contents. Toys, a manicure case, singed underwear. And last of all, the roasted corpse of a child, shrunk like a mummy, which its half-deranged mother had been carrying around with her, the relic of a past that was still intact a few days ago".'[135]

Hamburg was only one such target. By 1945, when it was clear that Germany had been defeated, British and American bomber forces targeted the beautiful city of Dresden a week or two before the Russian armies occupied it. Once again there was indiscriminate slaughter of its inhabitants, around 20,000 of whom were killed during the night of 13 February. The writer Kurt Vonnegut was an American prisoner of war in

Dresden at the time, and recollected: 'They went over with high explosives first to loosen things up, and then scattered incendiaries...They burnt the whole damn town down...Every day we walked into the city and dug into the basements and shelters to get the corpses out, as a sanitary measure. When we went into them, a typical shelter, an ordinary basement usually, looked like a street car full of people who'd simultaneously had heart failure. Just people sitting in their chairs, all dead. A fire storm is an amazing thing...It's fed by the tornadoes that occur in the midst of it and there isn't a damn thing to breathe. We brought the dead out. They were loaded onto wagons and taken to parks...The Germans got funeral pyres going, burning the bodies to keep them from stinking and spreading disease.'[136]

The United States forces advanced westwards across the Pacific Ocean during 1942, 1943 and 1944, seizing islands occupied by the Japanese, losing thousands of troops in vicious fighting, until eventually they seized and occupied the Marianas, a group of islands within air range of Japan. Systematic bombing of Japan's cities began from the island of Tinian towards the end of 1944. A new plane, the Boeing B29, had the necessary range to hit Japan and carried a serious bomb load. Commander of operations in that theatre was Curtis Le May, who disregarded his president's 1939 appeal not to target civilians. There was a list of justifications, such as: the Japs were sub-humans, there was a need to save one's own troops' lives, to shorten the war, they started it, and bombed our ships...The attack on Pearl Harbour had led to an American loathing of everything Japanese.

By March 1945 Le May's bombers were giving Tokyo, Yokohama and other Japanese cities the same treatment the British and Americans were giving those in Germany. Tokyo, with its mainly wooden dwellings, was nearly burnt out by a strategy of systematic dropping of incendiaries. Around 100,000 people died in Tokyo on the night of 9-10 March 1945, with a further 40,000 seriously injured. According to the Strategic Bombing Survey 'probably more persons lost their lives by fire at Tokyo in a six-hour period [that night] than at any time in the history of man.' Le May offered up the excuse that it was not possible to separate people's homes from military factories in the Japanese urban theatre: 'The entire population got into the act and worked to make those airplanes or munitions of war...men, women, children. We knew we were going to kill a lot of women and kids when we burned a town. Had to be done.'[137]

The assembly of the atom bombs at Los Alamos was nearing completion by the early summer of 1945, but would be too late to use on Germany, which had surrendered on 6 May. But which city in Japan should be selected for the first use of an atomic bomb? Faced with a massive slaughter of civilians even Japan would give up the fight. Several cities had been left relatively untouched as they were top of the list of candidates for an atomic bomb test. An early favourite was Kyoto, but it had too many historic and religious buildings. Hiroshima moved to the top of the list. It was a port on a river in a flat plain surrounded by mountains. The best air crews were briefed, and one led by the top pilot Paul Tibbets was selected for the job. This time the bomb would be the untested uranium U235 device. The B29 – named the Enola Gay after Tibbets' mother – flew and arrived over Hiroshima on 6 August at 8.15 on a sunny morning as people of the city were going to work. The bomb aimer, Thomas Ferebee, got his aim good on the centre of the city. There had only been a single plane, so nobody on the ground had bothered to seek shelter.

The blast (the equivalent of about 18,000 tons of TNT) shocked the aircrew as they saw what happened. Robert Lewis, the Enola Gay co-pilot, wrote: 'I don't think anyone expected to look at a sight quite like that. Where we had seen a clear city two minutes before, we could now no longer see the city. We could see smoke and fires creeping up the sides of the mountains.' The tail gunner Robert Carron remembered: 'I saw fires springing up in different places, like flames shooting up on a bed of coal...I can still see it – that mushroom and the turbulent mass – it looked like lava or molasses covering the whole city, and it seemed to flow outward up into the foothills where the little valleys would come into the plain, with fires starting up all over.'[138]

Residents of the city near the epicentre of the blast were killed at once, their bodies evaporating. Evidence from survivors is available in books by Richard Minear, *Hiroshima: Three Witnesses,* and Michihiko Hachiya, *Hiroshima Diary.*[139] Residents fled into the river and canals where they died as the water boiled. A doctor wrote: 'Between the [heavily damaged] Red Cross Hospital and the centre of the city I saw nothing that was not burned to a crisp. Streetcars were standing at Kawagoe-cho and Kamiya-cho and inside were dozens of dead bodies, blackened beyond recognition. I saw fire reservoirs filled to the brim with dead people who looked as if they had been boiled alive.' And a husband helping his wife escape the city: 'While taking my severely wounded wife out to the riverbank by the side of the hill at Nakahiro-machi, I was horrified, indeed, at the sight of a stark naked man standing in the rain with his eyeball in his palm. He looked in great pain but there was nothing I could do for him.'[140] Hearing about this, Dr Michihiko Hachiya had a nightmare. 'The night had been close with many mosquitoes. Consequently I slept poorly and had a frightful dream. It seems I was in Tokyo after the great earthquake and around me were the decomposed bodies heaped in piles, all of whom were looking at me. I saw an eye sitting on the palm of a girl's hand. Suddenly it turned and leaped into the sky and then came flying back towards me, so that, looking up, I could see a great bare eyeball, bigger than life, hovering over my head, staring point blank at me. I was powerless to move. I awakened short of breath and with my heart pounding.'[141]

Bombs destroy not only people, Richard Rhodes notes, but everything: 'Destroyed...were not only men, women and thousands of children but also restaurants and inns, laundries, theater groups, sports clubs, sewing clubs, boys' clubs, girls' clubs, love affairs, trees and gardens, grass, gates, gravestones, temples and shrines, family heirlooms, radios, classmates, books, courts of law, clothes, pets, groceries and markets, telephones, personal letters, automobiles, bicycles, horses – 120 war horses – musical instruments, medicines and medical equipment, life savings, eye glasses, city records, sidewalks, family scrapbooks, monuments, engagements, marriages, employees, clocks and watches, public transportation, street signs, parents, works of art.'[142]

The bomb destroyed an entire society.

At Los Alamos there was jubilation. Otto Frisch, who had played a part in the development of the bomb, wrote: 'Then one day, some three weeks after [Trinity], there was a sudden noise in the laboratory, of running footsteps and yelling voices. Somebody opened my door and shouted, "Hiroshima has been destroyed!"; about a hundred thousand people were thought to have been killed. I still remember the feeling of unease, indeed nausea, when I saw that many of my friends were rushing to the telephone to book tables at the La Fonda Hotel in Santa Fe, in order to celebrate. Of course they were exalted by the success of their work, but it seemed rather ghoulish to celebrate the sudden death of a hundred thousand people, even if they were "enemies".'[143]

Three days later on 9 August 1945, after the Japanese government had dithered over the decision to surrender, a further bomb, this time plutonium, was dropped on the city of Nagasaki. Another 40,000 to 50,000 people were killed; not so large a death list as in Hiroshima because of a slight mis-aim, and the absorption of the blast by surrounding hills. So ended the Second World War, leaving President Truman justifying the bombings alternatively as saving his own troops' lives or warning off the Russians who had just invaded Manchuria.

More powerful bombs had already been envisaged. Since 1942 nuclear scientists, notably Edward Teller, had been doing calculations for a *fusion* bomb, which would dwarf the power of the fission device. Just as the fission of an atom of a heavy element leads to the release of formidable energy, so does the fusion of lighter elements. Physicists already knew that the fusing of two atoms of the hydrogen isotope, deuterium, would produce an atom of helium with a combined mass less than the two atoms of deuterium. The 'missing' mass is converted into energy, which in turn produces a chain reaction in the deuterium. Unlike a fission bomb, whose size and yield are finite, the chain reaction in a deuterium device can be as large as required. But the initiation of the fusion process requires temperatures of around 400 million °C. That was unobtainable until 1945, when such temperatures were produced inside the exploding fission device. Plans for the fusion bomb (now called the hydrogen bomb) which could destroy hundreds of square miles of territory were shelved. They were to reappear in the early 1950s.[144]

# 14. The Golden Age and its Breakdown

The years from 1914 to 1945 had been brutal. A hundred million people died in the two phases of the prolonged period of world war, during which there occurred the Soviet Yezhovshchina purges, the Nazi extermination camps, and the mass killing of civilians from the air in Europe and Asia. The war participants licked their wounds in 1945 fearing that the post-war years would be as grim as they had been after 1918. However what followed were thirty years of decent political behaviour and rising prosperity for nearly all people on the planet. In Britain these years are referred to as the 'golden age', in France as 'les trentes glorieuses'. This 'golden age' lasted until the late 1960s: it was based on rising incomes, an industrial boom, very cheap oil, a global revolution in food production, and a new social phenomenon known as teenagers.[145]

The foundations of the new era of prosperity were the redistribution policies of Roosevelt's New Deal in the United States, and the economic stimulus of the Second World War. The New Deal was a complex set of policies designed to get people working again after the onset of severe economic depression in the early 1930s. John Maynard Keynes's *General Theory of Employment, Interest and Money* (1935) had an important influence on policy. There was a big increase in government intervention in industry, and money was moved from the rich to the poor to stimulate spending. The wealthy accepted these policies grudgingly because of the threat of a communist revolution and the danger of a serious attack on the capitalist system, as had occurred in Stalin's Russia.

To get the economy out of depression a lot of spending was needed. In Germany Hitler had 'solved' problems of economic depression with massive spending on rearmament and the building of roads. Similarly, military spending on war in the United States between 1940 and 1945 provided the critical stimulus for the economy, which ended the depression. During those six years the GDP of the United States increased twenty-five times as factories churned out the tanks, aircraft and guns to defeat the Japanese and Germans. Harold Evans wrote: 'At no period before or since has there been anything to equal the 15% rise a year in general industrial expansion created by the war and the vitality of a free people given a chance to show what they could do.'[146] Unemployment – which had seen 9.4 million Americans still out of work in 1939 – was soaked up by the explosion in industrial production and was further reduced by the paid conscription of men for the military. The combination of war and the redistribution of income ended depression and deflation. By 1944 in fact the US had entered a period of moderate inflation.

A new post-war economic system, the Bretton Woods system, was set up in 1944 to ensure financial stability. It was agreed that all the major currencies of the free world were to be tied to the US dollar, which in turn was tied to gold at the rate of US$ 35 to 1 ounce of gold. Currencies were further underpinned by capital controls on large money movements across borders. If a country got into financial problems, for example through overspending or a slump in exports, the new International Monetary Fund (IMF), set up in 1946, was there to provide loans, which were conditional on economic reforms in the borrowing country. The idea was to keep all countries financially solvent and cooperating on expanding trade. Along with the IMF, the Bretton Woods negotiations established a World Bank to provide loans to poorer countries, as well as a General Agreement on Tariffs and Trade (GATT) that saw a general reduction on trade tariffs between the major industrial nations. The demon of the protectionist competition of the 1930s was contained. In addition, the United States' Marshall Plan of 1948 funnelled billions of dollars into Europe to help finance its rebuilding after the war, on condition that everything needed came from the United States. These investments were the complete opposite of how the US had withdrawn from Europe after the First World War ended in 1918.

Paralleling these measures to smooth the flow of trade were equally vital policies to enable people to buy manufactured goods and keep unemployment low, thus slaying another demon of the 1930s. These policies included the limited distribution of wealth from rich to poor. Taxes on high incomes were increased – up to 90% for the very wealthy, as also were taxes on capital gains. Part of the extra income for governments was devoted to welfare for the less well off, both for social fairness and to maintain 'purchasing power'. Financially distressed people, such as women with children, who had fallen on hard times, were to be given financial assistance. As important was the introduction of national health systems where medical treatment was heavily subsidised by the state. The classic example of these policies was that of the Labour administration of Clement Attlee in Britain between 1945 and 1951. The effort to provide these benefits was in part a reward for the soldiers, sailors and airmen who had won the war against the Nazis.

A similar path was pursued in the US in the thirty years after 1945. When industry was booming, state spending was reduced, and when people's purchasing power fell and there was recession, state spending was increased so as to keep people in work. These practices extended the Rooseveltian policies of the New Deal years. During the 1950s the Eisenhower administration, for example, embarked on the biggest surge of road building in US history. Besides reducing unemployment, this facilitated the rapid movement of manufactured goods. In Britain, the state itself took over the owning and running of a few key industries, such as chemicals and railways, which had hitherto been privately owned. Certain industries were felt to be too vital for the public interest to allow them to be run by private interests for profit. The idea was also to protect capitalists as their own worst enemies, and prevent them from angering the working and middle classes who might rise up and imitate the Stalinists in the Soviet Union. The capitalists were compensated, but were not always happy.

This overall strategy has been given various names. One of them is 'the Keynesian consensus', as it was Keynes who had originally proposed these measures in the 1930s in order to counter the economic slump that had facilitated the rise of fascism and communism. Another name is 'social democracy': a capitalist democratic system whose central strategies are fairness, the maintenance of purchasing power, and prosperity. Other names have been the 'welfare state' or the 'mixed economy' (the mixture being capitalism and socialism). Such a state is not 'socialist' as it is far from a state-controlled economy. It is self-interestedly capitalist, but a variant of capitalism that in the post-war era produced the golden age.[147]

Social-democratic economic strategies provide only part of the explanation for the golden age. Just as important, and underlying everything, was cheap energy, especially oil.[148] Oil was coming on tap at an abundant rate during the 1940s and 1950s. Petrol was so cheap it was almost given away.[149] Cheap fuel along with efficient roads and railways meant cheap food. Along with cheap fuel went a revolutionary explosion of technology. Jet passenger airliners, such as the Comet and Boeing 707, were made in production lines like cars. By the early 1960s the middle classes in Europe and the United States were beginning to fly to holiday destinations overseas for the first time. Motor vehicle production took off, running on cheap fuel and boosting the iron and steel industries. More middle class households could think of buying a car on hire purchase. New electrical appliances were produced and improved: radios, televisions, vacuum cleaners, washing machines, fridges, electric ovens. Huge investments were made in the rebuilding of Europe – the bomb sites were cleared and new homes and factories built in their place. The construction boom further absorbed unemployment. One is reminded of Schumpeter's remark that 'creative destruction' in wars is good for capitalism.

The de-colonisation following the war, although vigorously opposed by the old guard such as Winston Churchill, was profitable for the ex-imperial countries, particularly Britain and France. They cut administrative and military expenses, and, to their surprise, discovered that they had lost nothing. Newly independent countries, such as India (independent in 1947), found themselves initially tied to the US and Europe for exports and imports. In the late 1950s and 1960s, most European countries gave their colonies independence. It was better and cheaper to decolonise and go over to free trade access; and in any case that is what the United States demanded. Let the newly independent ex-colonies overspend after the 1950s and run up high debts, which in turn tied them to conditions imposed by the IMF and World Bank that were favourable to the wealthy countries and their corporations. Many liberation leaders in Africa became increasingly kleptocratic and bribable; available to do deals with rich-world corporations for their resources.

The 1950s also saw the beginning of the cold war, as the communist Soviet Union and the United States competed with each other in nuclear arms and mutual threats. The Soviet Union exploded its first atomic bomb in August 1949. This led to an arms race involving competing production of hydrogen bombs, and mutual threats of nuclear annihilation. This was followed by another race – to be the first into space, which was won by the

Soviet Union's Sputnik in 1957. All this competition gave a large boost to military spending in the United States, with factories and their suppliers producing an infinite range of new military hardware. The economy of the United States was heavily militarised, as private firms built the weapons demanded by the politicians and the armed forces. When he left office in 1961, President Eisenhower (who had commanded the US forces in the Second World War) felt it necessary to warn the world about the growing power of 'the military-industrial complex' – 'the increasingly vast agglomeration of men and resources which lived by the preparation of war', as Hobsbawm described it.[150] The economies of the rich world were now partly dependent on the profits of the armaments industries. Millions of small arms were exported to the third world – the poor world – whose wars were very profitable to the manufacturers.

The combination of government spending, income redistribution, cheap oil, and an explosion of new technology led to an unprecedented affluence. When wartime rationing and spending restrictions ended in the early 1950s, stock markets in the US and Europe began an unparalleled rise in share prices that was to continue into the early 1970s. Shops were bursting with all the technological comforts of the affluent lifestyle, from vacuum cleaners to motor cars. Italy, for example, having produced 18,500 fridges in 1951 produced 5,247,000 in 1971. Getting people to buy things with wages that were increasing in real value boosted the entire advertising industry. As one Nokia phone advert exhorted: 'you just want it because you want it.'

The consumer society, as it was soon labelled, was accompanied by the fear of being wiped out by the hydrogen bomb. The television entered people's homes with advertisements to buy this or that, alternating with sombre broadcasts of the latest Soviet threat. I remember visiting the British motor show at the Olympia Exhibition Centre in London in late October 1962, drooling over the new E-type Jaguar, whilst nervously expecting London to be wiped out by nuclear bombs – it was the time of the Cuban missile crisis (see chapter 21).

Transistor radios, a must-have product, fuelled the rock 'n' roll revolution in popular music. Bill Haley and the Comets in 1954 were followed by Elvis Presley and his twisting hips (which the BBC tried in vain to block), Chuck Berry, Buddy Holly, the Beatles and the Rolling

Stones. Money was poured into education to meet the needs of the new technological world. The previous generation had tended to leave school at 13 or 14; from the 1950s it was necessary to stay in school until 16 at least, and an increasing percentage of pupils stayed on until 18 to complete A levels or the equivalent, such as the Gymnasien in Germany. For the first time young western people from the lower middle and working classes were able to go to university, financed by the state. Affluent teenagers, with their trendy clothes, clashed with their parents' generation which had been deprived of such things. In Britain young people were even paid to go to university. As Britain's prime minister, Harold Macmillan, said in 1957, 'you've never had it so good'. The Leica photographer, Henri Cartier-Bresson, was not so optimistic, remarking: 'In the Fifties the world had been totally changed by scientific studies made during the war. These technological changes became part of our lives, creating deeper and deeper tensions so that we are in a world that seems headed for suicide.'[151]

The late 1950s and 1960s also saw a transformation of family and social relationships. By the early 1960s the contraceptive pill was becoming available, enabling women to have sex without the fear of becoming pregnant. Betty Friedan's 1963 book *The Feminine Mystique* blasted the idea that women should stay at home and rear children. She called the imprisonment of the woman at home in the family 'the problem that has no name', and led a revolt against the three Ks: *Kinder, Küche, Kirche* (children, kitchen, church).[152] Women increasingly went to university alongside men, and often performed better. Careers opened up for women, though women's wages tended to remain lower than those for men. 1965 was the first year that the French fashion industry manufactured more trousers for women than skirts.

In addition there was a relaxation in morality, with declining church attendance, and a tearing up of taboos related to writing about sex. Henry Miller's *Tropic of Cancer*, originally published in 1934 and promptly banned, was republished in 1961. With the unbanning of D.H. Lawrence's *Lady Chatterley's Lover* that same year, young people rushed to buy the Penguin copy in the bookshops. The mini-skirt was in. Homosexuality was unbanned in many countries, and by the early 1970s 'gay' clubs, like those in San Francisco, were nurturing the HIV virus (which was not identified as such until 1983). The more affluent the society, the more the family weakened. Divorce rates soared as women obtained equal legal rights to end unsatisfactory marriages. In Britain in 1938 one in fifty-eight marriages ended in divorce – by the early 1980s it was one in two-point-two.

As a man's wage or salary increasingly could not meet the costs of all the new necessities, the gap had to be met by the woman of the family working too. Fertility rates declined and the single-child family became common. A reorganisation was taking place in the way people lived and related to one another. And the owners of capital were beginning to get ideas of how to profit from this. As novelist Michel Houellebecq noticed: 'the sexual revolution was to destroy the last unit [the family] separating the individual from the market.'[153] Herbert Marcuse noted that previous taboos on behaviour, which had been 'sublimated' in other activities, were now abandoned, but that the new freedom was used as a form of control. He called this 'repressive desublimation'. Marcuse wrote: 'radio and television set the pattern of conformity and rebellion...The experts of the media transmit the required values; they offer the perfect training in efficiency, toughness, personality, dream, and romance. With this education the family can no longer compete. In the struggle between the generations, the sides have shifted. The son knows better...[the father's] authority as transmitter of wealth, skills, and experience is greatly reduced; he has less to offer and therefore less to prohibit.'[154]

Thus consumerism was born. The growth of the consumer society was accompanied by what, at first glance, appears to have been a youth rebellion against the injustices of the political world. It was partly the outcome of the vast knowledge imbibed by young people at school and university, which made them feel superior to their parents' generation; and partly an opposition to the war against Vietnam in which the US administrations of Kennedy and Johnson had unwisely become involved. From 1965 the rebellion against the Vietnam War tore society apart in much of the Western world. There was mounting anger which grew during 1967 into almost revolutionary tensions. A chant sung at anti-war rallies was: 'Hey, hey, LBJ, how many kids did you kill today?' One of the student leaders in the United States, Mario Savio, wrote angrily: 'There is a time when the operation of the machine becomes so odious, makes you so sick at heart, that you can't take part; you can't even passively take part, and you've got to put your bodies on the gears and upon the wheels, upon the levers, upon all the apparatus and you've got to make it stop. And you've got to indicate to the people who run it, to the people who own it, that unless you're free, the machine will be prevented from working at all.'[155]

The 1960s saw what appeared – on the surface – to be a rebellion against practically everything. There was an 'anti-university' in London, with students lying in corridors smoking marijuana. Varieties of what was termed 'concrete poetry' ridiculed conventional forms of art. One I remember was a music performance in which the violinist sawed his violin in half. Allen Ginsberg's poem *Howl* illustrated the mood.[156] The opposition to 'capitalism' was, though, accompanied by an increasingly affluent lifestyle, with much drinking of alcohol and listening to the latest hits on the new long-playing records. Arthur Miller put his finger on the problem: 'The sixties radical opened his eyes to a system pouring its junk over everybody, or nearly everybody, and the problem was to stop just that, to escape being overwhelmed by a mindless, goalless flood which marooned each individual on his little island of commodities.'[157] Or, to quote the Rolling Stones, 'In sleepy London Town there's just no room for street fighting man.'[158]

The political world struck back with De Gaulle's use of riot police against Paris students in May 1968, the election of Nixon as US president later that year, and the shooting of students protesting at Kent State University in the United States in 1970. It would not be long before the radical rebels of the mid-1960s transformed themselves into the corporate elites of the 1980s and 1990s. Timothy Leary, the rebel professor and drug evangeliser, described the transition: 'Back in the 1960s when I flew in for a lecture, the student committee showed up at the airport wearing long hair, sandals, blue jeans, and cheerful, impudent grins. The radio would be blasting out Mick Jagger and Jimi Hendrix as we drove to campus. The students eagerly asked me about "high" technologies – methods of consciousness expansion, new brands of wonder drugs, new forms of dissident protest, up-to-date developments in the ever-changing metaphysical philosophies of rock stars: Yoko Ono's theory of astrology; Peter Townsend's devotion to Baba Ram Dass. I kept abreast of these subjects and tried to give responsive answers. Today [1994] it's different. The lecture committee arrives at the airport wearing three-piece suits, briefcases, clipboards with schedules. No music. No questions about Michael Jackson's theory of reincarnation or Sheena Easton's concept of sugar walls. The impudent grins are gone. The young people are cool, realistic, corporate-minded. They question me about computer stocks, electronic books, and prospects for careers in software.'[159]

The 'turn on, tune in, drop out' generation of the 1960s was brought back to Earth as the golden age gave way in the 1970s to an era of inflation and economic recession, the worst since the early 1930s. The combination of inflation and recession, which economists call stagflation, was unusual. There were several mutually reinforcing causes. Governments had been spending too much, while union demands had pushed wages too high: both were inflationary. More critically, the United States was the world's pivotal economy, with the currency against which others were pegged. As the US became heavily in debt largely because of the Vietnam war, central banks sold dollars in favour of gold. From 1968 the US Federal Reserve Bank found it increasingly difficult to maintain the dollar at $35 to an ounce of gold. In August 1971 Nixon was compelled formally to break the dollar's link to gold: that is to say the dollar now floated; its value depending on financial markets. In subsequent years, as the dollar floated, its value fell against other currencies, and against gold, so that by 1980 gold stood at US$ 800 per ounce, not $35.[160] The result was runaway inflation. In turn the price of oil, on which economies depended and which was quoted in dollars, soared, pushing up the cost of transport, and everything that had any oil input. The price of oil was pushed up further after the Arab-Israeli war of October 1973, as the Organisation of Petroleum Exporting Countries (OPEC) ramped up prices.

As prices of everything rose, real value of wages fell, leading to a reduction in spending. After the long bull market since the early 1950s, the year 1974 saw the worst stock market crash since 1929. Share prices fell and dividends were cut. The other investment made by those with money was in US government bonds which also lost value. Although interest rates were pushed up, they were not pushed up as much as inflation. If bonds returned say 8%, but inflation was 12%, you made less than nothing on government debt. In response, government bonds crashed in price, leading to large capital losses for wealthy owners of the bonds (though the low real interest rates led to fixed investment in equipment and structures hitting high levels). With both share (equity) and bond prices falling, and dividends being cut, rich people's income and net worth were both heavily reduced.

The more people were out of work, and the less people who had work were able to purchase with their static wages, the more unions went on strike. This led to showdowns between governments and unions, particularly in England during 1973. Governments were forced to cut back on welfare expenditure. This led to more trouble with workers. There were echoes of the year 1930, which had led to the collapse of Germany's social democracy.

The rich were getting angry, and blamed the years of the Keynesian consensus, social-democracy and strong unions. Matters were made yet worse after the 1979 revolution in Iran when oil prices went yet higher. Something had to be done. In 1980 the new US Federal Reserve Bank chairman, Paul Volcker, increased interest rates to 20%, an action unprecedented in modern economies. This was good news as far as the rich were concerned, though in the short term it made matters worse, leading to a new stock market slump in 1979-81.

Structural change became the central political issue at the end of the 1970s.[161] There was a backlash against social democracy of the Roosevelt-Attlee sort. In Britain there was a swing to the political right, as shown by the election in 1979 of Margaret Thatcher's Conservative government. The following year, 1980, Ronald Reagan, a flag bearer for the far right, became president of the United States. Thatcher and Reagan's advisers pushed the policies now referred to as 'neoliberalism' – an attempt to get back to the liberalism of the nineteenth century, before governments had begun to intervene in economic policies so as to deflect revolutionary threats. Neoliberalism embraced the unorthodox policies advocated by the Austrian economists Ludwig von Mises and Friedrich von Hayek and their American followers Milton Friedman and Leo Strauss.[162] Hayek and Strauss had both migrated to the United States; at the University of Chicago during the 1950s they had established what was termed the Chicago School of Economics, which set the guiding principles of the economic policies which dominate our lives today.

A major first change was agreeing to the demands of the wealthy for the removal of government restrictions on the movement of capital around the world. Currencies – since August 1971 no longer tied to gold or the dollar – could be bought and sold for financial speculation. The big banks could now put huge pressure on the economic policy of any country by controlling the value of its currency. Bands of investors at banks such as Goldman Sachs bought and sold currencies and watched carefully the responses coming from government finance ministers. A government not pursuing 'appropriate' (from the point of view of the rich) economic policies was punished by the crashing of its national currency. At a stroke the political power of governments was weakened and handed over to banks, corporations and speculators. Their power was boosted by the arrival of the computer which made such a switch in financial controls possible.

The goal was the reversal of the Rooseveltian New Deal type policies so that corporations would no longer be regulated.[163] Strategies of 'deregulation' were developed and pursued by 'think tanks': groups of intellectuals paid for by the wealthy to advocate policies favourable to them. The central aim was that trade between nations and corporations was to be as free from duties and regulation as possible. Corporate influence simultaneously increased over the affairs of the General Agreement on Tariffs and Trade (after 1994 renamed the World Trade Organisation).

Another request by corporate neoliberals was that government-owned industries should be 'privatised', that is sold to groups of investors, preferably at give-away prices. Once a state-owned industry had been privatised, prices could be pushed up and state assets sold off, and profits channelled to the new private owners and shareholders. This led to large job losses, as well as a decline in the real value of wages of those still in employment. Trade unions that expressed outrage were met with all-out attacks by governments, the prime example being the Thatcher battle with coal miners in Britain in 1982-83 from which the corporations emerged victorious. What followed was a gradual transition from decent, reasonably well paid jobs to poorly paid 'McJobs' – named after the McDonald's fast food corporation, famous for the exploitation of its workers and the planet's resources.

The euphemisms 'privatization' and 'deregulation' sound bland, but their consequences were disastrous. As Sharon Beder noted: 'If privatization and deregulation are taken to their logical end, which is the aim of advocates, the public will be unable to influence the development of essential services, the terms of their provision, the reliability of their supply, their accessibility or their price. These will be decisions made by cartels of transnational corporations whose primary motivation is profit and power. Current trends suggest these service transnationals will become not merely "power centres" but "global centres", owning systems extending across entire continents, including electricity, natural gas, water, waste management and telecommunications. Given what is at stake, it is little wonder that the push for privatization and deregulation have been strong and relentless, bulldozing citizen opposition out of the way.'[164]

A feature of Rooseveltian social democracy had been high taxes on high incomes, known as 'progressive taxation' because the higher the income the higher the taxes, reaching 90% or so for the very rich. During the 1970s, however, the rich began to agitate for a reduction in their own taxes and a heavier relative burden on the less well off. Their argument was that by reducing their taxes they could be more enterprising, to the benefit of everyone. More money for them, they alleged, would lead to a 'trickle down effect' that would provide more money for the middle and lower classes, and state revenues and employment levels would be maintained.

That is of course not what happened. The losses of finances by the state as they cut taxes for the wealthy – regressive taxation – led to big cutbacks in state spending, and much reduced welfare and health provisions for most citizens. Taxes for the middle classes were not cut; in fact they were increased by the introduction of indirect taxes, such as sales tax on necessities. Between 1977 and 1990 the tax levels of the wealthiest 1% in the United States were cut by 36% whilst 90% of US families paid more taxes, and the state received $70 billion less in income. In other words, the poor were beginning to subsidise the rich. Margaret Thatcher in Britain attempted to pass a poll tax law in which everyone, rich or poor, would pay the same annual tax to the state. Even her right-wing Tory party rebelled at that: and this time the crowds did come out on to the streets. Of course state spending on the military was not cut.

If the weight of taxation is placed on the non-rich, state spending will be cut to balance the drop in income; jobs and amenities for most of the population will be cut; total spending will suffer; and, in the long run, capital owners will be disadvantaged. But only in the long term.

After Reagan's election in late 1980 ensured a government committed to favouring the rich, the stock market soared. The turning date was August 1982, after which, with one or two setbacks, it was to go on rising until 2008. It was the longest bull market in history, yet the trickle-down effect did not happen; instead there was a wealth boom amongst a tiny rich minority, and increased inequalities. By the mid-1980s, city beggars, who had disappeared from the streets during the decades of social democracy, were again sleeping in church porches, under bridges, and outside banks. With barely rising real wages, many people maintained their lifestyles by borrowing money, laying the foundations of a debt crisis that was to explode in 2007-08. Thus governments and the wealthy classes tacitly abandoned the commitment to provide jobs for all, which had been a feature of the era 1935-75.

As machines and electronic technology enabled corporations to increase profits by cutting jobs, the quest by ordinary people for a job that would sustain a family became more difficult. In 1979, for example, the Ford company was able to manufacture 960 Ford Escorts and Granadas a day with 4270 workers; by 1990 they could make 1200 such vehicles with 1880 workers. Hobsbawm notes: 'The historic tragedy of the Crisis Decades was that production now visibly shed human beings faster than the market economy generated new jobs for them.'[165] As Wassily Leontief noted in 1983: 'The role of humans as the most important factor of production is bound to diminish in the same way that the role of horses in agricultural production was first diminished and then eliminated by the introduction of tractors.'[166] To make matters worse, low income jobs were shifting to China or the poor world.

To conclude: by the early 2000s the state had come to be dominated by the power of corporations, whose interests were not specifically national, rather than by national electorates. Computers and jumbo jets transformed both trade and politics, permitting instant global transfer of money, instructions and goods. Corporations could now switch production to whichever part of the world costs and taxes were lowest. Nuclear bombs made the old type of war obsolete, removing a central function of the national state. Nixon's breaking of the link between the US dollar and gold in August 1971 enabled the wealthy investor class to play off national currencies against each other and secure the backing of national governments for their financial interests. What they wanted, and got, was low taxation, fewer restrictions on currency movements, deregulation, privatization, and the curbing of union powers.

By the early 1990s the corporations, the wealthy and the powerful had combined to achieve large advantages for themselves. During the G.W. Bush administrations of 2001-09, there were a further US$ 1.7 trillion worth of tax cuts, half of which went to those with incomes of over $200 million a year. Yet further tax cuts for the rich were passed in the Trump administration after 2016.

With the collapse of the Soviet Union and communism in 1991, well might Francis Fukuyama boast about the 'end of history': the favourable realignment of power for the rich that they referred to as 'the Washington Consensus'.[167] The network of corporate alliances that now spanned the world called itself the 'International Community' – despite the fact that the majority of people on the planet did not belong to it.

## 15. The Corporate (Neoliberal) World Order

The democratic powers of rich nations' citizens, based on one adult one vote, have, since the late 1970s, been eroded in favour of what could be called one dollar one vote. Corporations began partially to escape the control of their nation states. They globalised their production, switching operations to countries where they could achieve the highest output for the lowest cost. Governments could be negotiated with to reduce taxes in return for the building of factories or the provision of financial offices that would provide local jobs. Popular options were Ireland, Malaysia, Indonesia, the Philippines and Mexico. Should local unions push for higher wages, corporate managers could (and did) shift to another country. This constant threat lowered local wages: jobs were offered without pensions, health benefits, or annual increases. Wages became a reducible expense; or workers might be replaced with computerised machines.

A proportion of the extra profit was channelled into donations to politicians, many of whom could in effect be bribed into voting for laws that favoured the corporate agenda. Politicians served on corporate boards once they had retired from politics, whilst corporate executives were recruited into government, often to ministerial posts. Inside government, bankers might push their own agendas; oil men could argue for war in Iraq for example.

'Think tanks' were set up, financed by corporate profits, to push for policy changes favouring corporate interests or to resist changes that might threaten those interests. Examples include the American Enterprise Institute, the Institute of Economic Affairs, and the Centre for Policy Studies. A super think tank, the World Economic Forum, has since 1983 met at Davos in Switzerland every late January to push the interests of global capital. The world's presidents and top politicians attend (including those from China), often accompanied by celebrities of the moment to add glamour to the event. The venue is surrounded by barbed wire, and armed soldiers keep protesters out. Davos is the symbol of an increasingly undemocratic world.

Today's corporations make large payments to public relations firms to manipulate the public and government. Lobbyists are paid to hang around the corridors of power and speak into the ears of politicians. Corporate financial means are much larger than the funds available to the citizen groups advocating fairness and social justice. Should a corporation be polluting the environment, for example, the PR firms will downplay this by paying for TV programmes or magazine/newspaper articles that seek to persuade the public that 'toxic sludge is good for you'.[168] Burson-Marsteller, one of the largest PR firms, is clear about its function: 'the role of communications is to manage perceptions which motivate behaviours that create business results.'[169]

The broad strategy of corporate lobbyists and PR firms is first to detect and then to head off changes that could harm profits. In particularly critical areas, such as damage to forests or climate change, a tactic is to set up 'front groups' that sound as if they are part of public opinion but in reality are pushing the corporate line. The same with discussion groups on TV. Perhaps only half a percent out of 900 expert scientists in their field deny that global heating is happening; however, on TV panels and discussion groups one may find 50% arguing that it is not. The object is to pretend that the matter is being 'debated', thus sowing doubt in the minds of readers and viewers. Such manipulation destroys the consensus that is often necessary to bring about beneficial change.

As governments face declining revenue from taxes, it is not only health and welfare budgets that are hit. Money for education, the schools and universities, is reduced as well. The corporate strategy is to step in as heroes to the rescue, but with conditions. Coca-Cola for example might fund education so long as Coke machines are available in school foyers. Lowered education budgets enable corporations to get access to children and begin to bend their minds at an early age, a trend against which teachers are often helpless. In universities, corporations fund fellowships or professorial posts (bearing the corporate name) for studies that they regard as important, thus undermining the autonomy of academics. Unsurprisingly, critiques of their activity are voluntarily muted. That is the purpose: to censor what academics may research or what they may say.

Via such means, the idea that government is there to serve its citizens is weakened. National governments partially abandon their regulatory functions, so as not to antagonise the businesses that support them. To the extent that corporations are authoritarian structures, in which the managers and major shareholders rule, democracy is hollowed out.[170] Corporate anti-values and ways of thinking spread into every facet of life, accompanied by a bullying, hubristic arrogance, and a diminution of honesty and integrity. David Korten summed it up in 1995: 'The past two decades have seen the most rapid and sweeping institutional transformation in human history. It is a conscious and intentional transformation in search of a new world economic order in which business has no nationality and knows no borders. It is driven by global dreams of vast corporate empires, compliant governments, a globalised consumer monoculture, and a universal ideological commitment to corporate libertarianism.'[171]

By the 1990s the worldwide collective of corporations had become in effect the invisible global government. Its components include the Organization of Economic Cooperation and Development (OECD) based in Paris; the G8, where heads of state get together and argue about economic agendas; and the IMF and the World Bank (International Bank for Reconstruction and Development), which have mutated since the 1970s into guardians of the neoliberal system. They will provide loans to countries that get into difficulties, but on condition that economic structural adjustment is pursued, including the privatisation of state assets, deregulation, and the cutting back of social services. Collectives of investment banks now sell the currencies of countries that do not comply with required neoliberal policy. Similarly, privately owned 'rating agencies' – Standard & Poor, Fitch, and Moody's – 'rate' national economies: good policies attract higher ratings for their currencies, making borrowing cheaper and debt levels more sustainable.

A further component of this unofficial global administration is the Geneva-based World Trade Organization, established in 1994 out of the previous General Agreement on Tariffs and Trade (GATT). Although its stated objective is to facilitate free trade between nations, the administering committees of the World Trade Organization are dominated by the wealthy countries, especially the United States, whose representatives are frequently from the large corporations. Countries with weak negotiating punch are taken advantage of. Imports by rich countries from poor ones may be subjected to quotas that act as unofficial duties; whilst rich countries' exports to poorer countries may be subsidised to enable them to outcompete local industry. The WTO may give favoured-nation treatment to countries that pursue appropriate policies; those who misbehave are not favoured. In other words, to quote Amory Starr: 'free trade is really forced trade, in which local control over economies is superseded by the most powerful global interests and subjected to their law.'[172]

A subdivision of the WTO that also benefits the big corporations is its General Agreement on Trade in Services, or GATS, which opens up key services and industries in less influential nations to the corporate activities of the wealthy nations.[173] GATS allows local water services, hospital systems, telecommunications, or electricity systems to be opened up to foreign corporate competition, so undermining the regulatory capacity of national governments. Take, for example, postal services. Most national governments want the postal system to reach everyone at the same price, no matter how far they may be from the cities. Thus, in most countries' postal services, the people in the urban areas subsidise those in rural areas. However, if a profit-seeking foreign corporation takes over a postal system, they can insist either that rural people pay more, or that the delivery of post to these areas is reduced. In such a scenario the national government loses its ability to regulate prices or maintain universal access. Similarly a national government can find its ability to control corporate activities on grounds of safety or health is being limited, and that this ability is dependent on the permission of the WTO. An example would be an international oil company circumventing a national ban on fracking. Likewise, a national government may lose its ability to favour a start-up local company over a branch of a global corporation, because the corporation can apply to the WTO to declare a 'level playing field' – in effect eliminating local competition.

The other WTO subdivision with huge capacity for control is the Trade Related Intellectual Property Rights committee (TRIPS). This permits corporations to buy up monopoly rights to long-established traditional knowledge, and patent that right of use as an exclusive global monopoly. For example, the name 'basmati rice', a type of rice widely used in India, has been 'purchased' by the Texas company Rice Tec, and the company is legally entitled to ensure no one else can use the term, even in India. It is not only names: a local medicine or plant (including its seeds), which may have been in use for centuries, can be bought up by a foreign corporation for its own exclusive use – a practice that has been referred to as 'biopiracy'. TRIPS may also grant patents to corporations for the monopoly right to produce drugs and medicines, with the result that prices are drastically raised, while 'generic' versions of the same drug are made illegal. For example, the drug firm Pfizer has gained the patent on the drug fluconazole and sells it at US$ 6.20, two hundred times more than the cost of the generic version of the same drug which sells at US$ 0.03.

Sharon Beder sums up: '"free" trade is not about doing away with rules altogether, but rather replacing rules for companies with rules for government, and replacing rules that protect citizens, consumers and the environment with rules that protect and facilitate traders and investors.'[174] 'The World Trade Organization and its rules,' she continues, 'represent the culmination of years of corporate political mobilization, much of it carried out before civil society became aware of what was being accomplished. The WTO is today an instrument of business interests. It represents the triumph of corporate coalitions over democratic regulations that are intended to protect the human rights of workers, consumers and communities, as well as the environments in which they live and work or which they value.'[175]

Corporations cooperate with each other at a 'strategic' level to bend political systems to their will, even while at the 'tactical' level they still compete with each other. Although most nations may still be nominally democratic, the democratic process has been undermined by corporate financial penetration of governments. This has come about as a result of a slow-motion takeover which has been for the most part invisible. Neither has there been a revolutionary agenda or political manifesto. Rather, corporations have seized technological opportunities, drilling wider holes in the fabric of democracy to pursue their goal of growth, both of production and profits. The new global corporation has become, in the words of Robert Monk, 'so powerful that it has outstripped the limitations of accountability, becoming something of an externalising machine, in much the same way that a shark is a killing machine – no malevolence, no intentional harm, just something designed with sublime efficiency for self-preservation.'[176]

Three features of today's corporate-dominated world are worth stressing. The first is a widening of inequalities among the planet's human inhabitants, whether between classes, nations, or individuals globally.[177] At the time of the industrial revolution around 1830, the GDP of the richest countries was about five times those of the poorest. By 1960 that had become 38 times. Today it is 100 times. Within nations, the 'Gini coefficient' is used to make a comparative gauge of wealth levels between the different population sectors. A Gini coefficient of zero would mean everyone has equal wealth, whereas at a Gini coefficient of one, a single person would own everything. The countries with the best (closest to zero) Gini coefficients are usually (it varies from year to year) Japan or the Scandinavian countries at around 0.25. The country today with the worst Gini coefficient is South Africa at 0.72, a country whose inequalities have worsened dramatically since the end of apartheid. To take an example from South Africa: in 2005 the CEO of the grocery corporation Shoprite took home an annual salary of ZAR 59 million, 5,000 times the wage of his lowest paid worker.[178]

Another example is noted by Bradshaw and Wallace in their 1996 book *Global Inequalities*. They compare the 1995 take-home pay of the then Nike CEO, Philip Knight, who earned US$ 1.3 million, and a woman named Sadisah who worked in Nike's Jakarta factory in Indonesia. Sadisah earned US$ 1.50 a day (= US$ 480 a year) or one three thousandth of the CEO's pay. She made 3,000 pairs of shoes per year, and with her US$ 480 annual pay could buy six pairs, or 0.02%, of her annual 3,000 pair output. The promoter of Nike shoes, the basketball legend Michael Jordan, earned US$ 21 million in that year.[179]

In the early twenty-first century the world's richest 358 people had a net worth equal to that of 45% of the world's population. In 2016 the top 20% (quintile) of the global population held 85% of the wealth, and the bottom quintile a mere 1.4%. In the US in the same year the top 20% of households had received 50% of the national income, and the bottom quintile 3.6%. These discrepancies are aggressively defended by the corporate rich and the media (much of which they control). After the global financial collapse of 2008, largely caused by the mismanagement and corruption of the rich, cutbacks in government spending were designed to hit the poor the hardest, the same poor who they depicted as sponging, lazy chancers.

Alongside these national inequalities is the 'situational' inequality of some people being born into affluent nations while others are born in countries afflicted with civil war, economic collapse, climate change and overpopulation or a combination of all four. Children born in Syria are not as fortunate as those born in Denmark. Refugees struggling across deserts or hostile borders to reach countries where a living might be possible are a feature of the daily news: from Central America across the Mexican deserts into the United States; from central Africa across the Sahara and Mediterranean to Italy; from Iraq across Turkey into Greece; or across France and the English Channel into southern England. Such refugees are likely to come in larger numbers as global population mounts, and climate change critically affects their homes and livelihoods. The politics of their reception will be increasingly hostile,[180] though exceptions will be made in accordance with the needs of corporations for cheap labour.

A second characteristic feature of a world fine-tuned by the corporate collective is the mental deceit and distraction designed to camouflage the purpose, even the existence, of corporate encouragement for consumerism: an array of media and 'techniques' that create a false reality in our minds. One strategy is open deception; another is distraction of the public away from the serious issues. As John McMurtry describes it: 'The big lie [in today's world] is disseminated by round-the-clock, centrally controlled multi-media which are watched, read or heard by people across the globe day and night without break in *the occupation of public consciousness instead of national territories.* Group think, not soil, is the breeding ground of the new totalitarianism.'[181] Noam Chomsky, comparing today's corporations with Bolshevik and fascist totalitarianism, writes: 'This is an oversimplification, but for the eighty percent [of the public]...the main thing is to divert them. To get them to watch the National Football League. And to worry about "Mother with Child with Six Heads", or whatever you pick up on the supermarket stands...Or look at astrology. Or get them involved in fundamentalist stuff or something or other. Just get them away. Get them away from things that matter. And for that it's important to reduce their capacity to think.'[182]

These strategies were pursued unswervingly by giant media companies such as Time Warner, Viacom, Bertelsmann, News Corporation (with its Fox News) and General Electric. Apart from distracting people into trivia, the aim was (and still is) to get people in front of advertisements. The 'news' is invariably slanted politically in the direction favoured by corporations. Nothing is dealt with in depth. Brief sound bites follow each other at a bewildering pace. A policy of lies of omission ensures that issues of crucial importance are not touched upon at all. Well paid 'experts' are brought in to justify whatever line the corporate interest wishes to pursue. Another object is depoliticisation, and the creation of a culture of envy and a wish for emulation. 'Celebrities' have, since the 1980s, been paraded in the media to entice young (and not so young) people into accepting the system and its values, a key part of which is the 'winner takes all' culture. The way sport is presented in the media also has these aims. An angry McMurtry writes: '"Sport" as it is ironically called, is the corporate gang's daily morality play of trained group-think, fanatic factionalism and ever more money for those with most. Defeating others by overpowering monopoly is the heroic display most highly revered. Pistols, bombs, collisions, space thrusts, take-overs, wars, round-the-clock terror, get rich schemes, endless machines and fast-lane consumption are "our way of life" before adoring crowds and female bodies.'[183]

A third major feature of the corporate global economy, and the most dangerous one, is that, in the Gaian context, the goals of the corporate collective are effectively opposed to our survival as a species. Unlike groups of citizens in a democracy that are, in the last resort, committed to what is best for society and their own survival, corporate bodies are concerned solely with profits. The condition that investors place on corporate executives is that these profits grow from year to year. Growth – of production, sales, profits – is the only goal: to sell more things or services each year than the one before. This goal can be achieved in four ways: 1. to devise new things to sell that people can be persuaded to need; 2. to persuade people to buy more of the same thing than they did before; 3. to reach people (such as those in the deepest Amazon forests) who hitherto had done without consumer goods; and 4. implicitly to encourage population growth so that there are more people on the planet to buy things. When this combination of strategies fails, corporations reshuffle themselves to new management that endeavours to 'turn things round'.

Such a system is only viable in the short term because it ignores the Earth's resource base. Everything produced, or everything that facilitates more consumption, takes something out of the environment. Over the longer term, at some time in the future, it has to lead to environmental collapse. Corporate managers, as intelligent private citizens, do understand this, but in their roles as managers, this awareness is irrelevant. They know full well that they can be replaced by up and coming challengers at a moment's notice. Neither individually nor collectively is it possible for them to apply the brakes, let alone shift into reverse.

Because of its deception and opacity, opposition to our new corporate world order is difficult, more difficult even than opposition to a dictatorship inside a single nation state. Where does one begin? How to oppose the depoliticisation of people and what Chomsky calls 'the philosophy of futility'?[184] Should the opposition be in the media, or out there on the streets? Which streets? Demonstrations at IMF or WTO meetings are met with increased police and military repression. Lobbing pink teddy bears over the razor wire at Davos is a filmable media event, but not all that effective. In the early 2000s opposition groups did get together a global organization called the World Social Forum, which held annual meetings at Porto Alegre in Brazil, but its early promise faded. At this point no revolutionary idea on a global scale has been formulated to combat the political power of the corporate neoliberal world order. The corporations have money and political influence; and they are globally united, as compared to the national and ideological divisions of people.[185] They have a single agenda versus the diverse agendas of those who would oppose them. Their misrepresentations, however outrageous or untrue, are believed by a large percentage of people. As politics became more fraught during the 2010s, workers and lower middle classes, bafflingly, tended to vote for parties pursuing policies inimical to their interests, as in the pro-Brexit vote in the British general election of December 2019.

Even light opposition to corporate interests is met with legal action. So-called Strategic Lawsuits Against Public Participation, or SLAPPS, are frivolous lawsuits used from time to time by corporations which are designed to harass, distract, and intimidate opponents. One example was when Fox News (part of Rupert Murdoch's media empire) attempted to prevent the publication of Al Franken's book *Lies and the Lying Liars Who Tell Them*. The SLAPP was thrown out by the courts, but the legal process held up the publication of the book for months. A local South African example was when South African Breweries took offence at Justin Nurse's Laugh It Off T-shirt company in Cape Town. Nurse had produced a red T-shirt bearing the slogan *White Guilt – Black Labour* to imitate South African Breweries' Black Label beer. SAB took him to court; they lost, but left Nurse licking his wounds, including financial ones.[186]

Another case was that involving McDonald's fast food chain suing Helen Steel and David Morris for libel in the early 1990s. Steel and Morris were activists from London Greenpeace, who had picketed McDonald's at some of its London branches, accusing McDonald's of, amongst other things, promoting unhealthy food, exploiting workers, damaging the environment, and murdering animals. Faced with a routine SLAPP from McDonald's, most of the Greenpeace members apologised and undertook not to criticise them again. Steel and Morris, alone, refused to apologise. They were soon faced with a libel trial in London in which they had to prove to the court their allegations against the firm. McDonald's employed the best libel barrister in the UK, whereas Steel and Morris were denied a jury, and had to undertake their own defence. Eventually, after a libel trial, lasting 314 days, they won on some key points, although they lost on others.[187]

McDonald's did not bother to collect the money awarded them. The company's routine SLAPP had misfired and the company received a very bad press. But their global activities were not in the slightest bit jeopardised. All that was unusual was that the recipients of the SLAPP had fought back. The publicity, even though negative, was very good for McDonald's.[188] The McDonald's CEO, Ray Kroc, epitomises the intolerant corporate executive. His stated philosophy was: 'We have found out that we cannot trust some people who are nonconformists... We will make conformists out of them in a hurry. The organization cannot trust the individual; the individual must trust the organization.'[189] Any fascist or communist leader of the 1930s might have said this.

Where, to repeat, is the enemy? How can one fight against McDonald's with its thousands of restaurants in hundreds of countries, a corporation that is able to pay for the best lawyers, whether in the US, Russia or China? A single corporation does not have a fixed abode geographically. It is a legal concept, led by people who can move around, disappear, reappear or fade. It is difficult to envisage the targeting of the corporate world's facilitating structures such as the OECD, IMF, World Bank and WTO, let alone the corporate-dominated network of political power centres in which they are intermeshed.

'This system,' concludes David Korten, 'is inherently unstable and is spiralling out of control – spreading economic, social, and environmental devastation and endangering the well-being of every person on the planet.'[190] William Greider compares it to an out-of-control machine: 'Imagine a wondrous new machine, strong and supple, a machine that reaps as it destroys. It is huge and mobile, something like the machines of modern agriculture but vastly more complicated and powerful. Think of this awesome machine running over open terrain and ignoring familiar boundaries. It plows across fields and hedgerows with a fierce momentum that is exhilarating to behold and also frightening. As it goes, the machine throws off wreckage. Now imagine that there are skilled hands on board, but no one is at the wheel. In fact, this machine has no wheel nor any internal governor to control the speed and direction. It is sustained by its own forward motion, guided mainly by its own appetites. And it is accelerating.'[191]

John Berger writes despairingly: 'It is not easy to grasp the nature of the tyranny for its power structures (ranging from the 200 largest multinational corporations to the Pentagon) are interlocking yet diffuse, dictatorial yet anonymous, ubiquitous yet placeless. It tyrannises from offshore – not only in terms of fiscal law, but in terms of any political control beyond its own. Its aim is to delocalise the entire world. Its ideological strategy, besides which Osama bin Laden's is a fairy tale, is to undermine the existent so that everything collapses into its special version of the virtual, from the realm of which (and this is tyranny's creed) there will be a never-ending source of profit. It sounds stupid. Tyrannies are stupid. This one is destroying at every level the life of the planet on which it operates.'[192]

# 16. The Post-Gutenberg Age

If we look back at the printed book as it spread in Europe after the later fifteenth century, its broad 'message' (in Marshall McLuhan's sense) was bold, definitive, clear-cut thought.[193] The rapid spread of information that print made possible led to revolutionary advances in newly developing sciences – the 'scientific revolution'. The resulting explosions in knowledge and technology and the needs of industries and bureaucracies revolutionised schooling systems. Because of print, the length of time that a child needed to become fully literate produced a sharp distinction between adults and children, with adults able to ration the knowledge that children had access to. Print, finally, encouraged a psychic blend of individualism, boldness, obedience and conformism that lay behind Western Europe's imperialising of much of the planet. Such was the 'message' of the printed book. By the latter part of the twentieth century it seemed as if it had always been that way.

The message of the screen is different. The emergence of television, computers and smartphones is producing a transformation in the way we think and in the structures of society. In the early days it was widely believed that the internet would give everyone greater freedom to communicate and express their personal views and that this would subvert central authority. This confidence, it is now clear, was illusory. As Jerry Mander noted: 'computer technology may be the single most important instrument ever invented for the acceleration of centralised power.'[194] The computer boosts total managerialism and authoritarian bureaucracy on a global scale. The growth of corporate power globally, the subversions of effective democracy, and the explosion in computer use since the 1980s are not coincidental. The screen is a formidable force for Taylorism (the 'scientific' management of the workplace so as to increase worker productivity). It permits an invisible totalitarianism which is nearly impossible to evade: what Brett Scott calls 'automated surveillance capitalism'.[195]

Computers and their manipulations by corporate management reinforce uniformity of thinking. Indeed, there is a *requirement* for the uniform. The medium makes imitation necessary. Original thinking is unnecessary, and increasingly suspect. As every university teacher knows, today it is easy to download a pre-written essay on any subject required. Plagiarism detection programs have been essential in any university department. These programs are now obsolete as students now have access to AI programs which can write an 'original' essay in 'your own voice'. The universities are fighting a losing battle.

With the information overload imposed on us by the computer-google system our minds are increasingly becoming mechanisms that merely transfer electronic information from one place to another. Nixon's secretary of state, Henry Kissinger, put his finger on the change: '[My generation] knew we would not be able to read every book ever written and that we would not be able to remember every book that we had read, so we had to develop concepts that enabled us to recognise comparable phenomena and to project them into the future. The generation brought up on computers has no such need. They don't have to remember them. They don't have to understand them because they can always summon them again.'[196] The floods of information produced on the smartphone make impossible what McLuhan called 'the introspective life of long, long thoughts and distant goals, to be pursued in lines of Siberian railroad kind'.[197] Or, put less elegantly, there is a general dumbing down: complex ideas get reduced to bullet points, abbreviations and oversimplifications.

Out of this emerges the 21st century personality: always threatened with burn-out; impatient but passive; hyperactive but resigned. Concentrating becomes difficult; one flits from one thing to another. Electronic media replace the real by the virtual or fictional; the distinction between fantasy and reality is blurred. That is in turn linked to the rise of superstition, the growing attacks, especially in the United States, on science,[198] and our alienation from the environment. We become more susceptible to the manipulative lies of politicians and corporate managers.

Contemporary dictators were and are only too ready to make use of forgetfulness of the past or its falsifying. Lewis Mumford warned in the late 1960s of 'technology's ultimate gift...a more absolute mode of control: one that will achieve total illiteracy, with no permanent record except that officially committed to the computer, and open only to those permitted access to this facility. This repudiation of an independent written and printed record means nothing less than the erasure of man's diffused, multi-brained collective memory: it reduces all human experience into that of the present generation and the passing moment.'[199] More recently Timothy Snyder writes: 'I often think about historians who, decades or centuries hence, will make sense of the moment we experience now. What will we leave behind that they will be able to read?' He adds: '"Information" in the digital age is infinite, knowledge even scarcer, and wisdom fleeting.'[200]

The screen cuts us off both from the past and any idea of the future. Eric Hobsbawm writes in his *Age of Extremes*: 'The destruction of the past, or rather of the social mechanisms that link one's contemporary experience to that of earlier generations, is one of the most characteristic and eerie phenomena of the late twentieth century. Most young men and women at the century's end grow up in a sort of permanent present lacking any organic relation to the public past of the times they live in.'[201] Martin Amis writes: 'The modern situation is one of *suspense*: no one, no one at all, has any idea of how things will turn out.'[202]

In this memoryless context, more urban than ever before, and cut off from the natural world, a contemporary type of human being is evolving who is not all that well equipped to deal with the dangers mounting around us. He/she tends to be narcissistic, self-absorbed and incapable of love or 'seeing' the other. As Asoka Bandarage noted: 'To succeed in the competitive, professional world, people have to develop the qualities of mobility, impatience, firmness, efficiency and total commitment to self. But these are often antithetical to qualities such as stability, patience, gentleness, a tolerance for chaos and commitment to others needed to succeed as parents. As both men and women are forced to value professional rationality and paid work outside the home before the work of childrearing, the emotional foundation of the entire society weakens.'[203]

This weakening of the family and family bonds is accompanied by what Neil Postman calls 'the disappearance of childhood'. Postman stresses how television reorganises the adult-child relationship. He writes: '[Television] makes it unnecessary to distinguish between child and adult. For it is in its nature to homogenise mentalities. The often missed irony in the remark that television programs are designed for a twelve-year old mentality is that there can be no other mentality for which they may be designed.'[204] Robert Bly calls it 'the sibling society', which 'prizes a state of half adulthood, in which repression, discipline, and the...impulse control system are jettisoned. The parents regress to become more like children, and the children, through abandonment, are forced to become adults too soon, and never quite make it.'[205]

The emphasis on consumerism worsens these psychological dangers. Zygmunt Bauman observes that 'consumerism is not about *accumulating* goods...but about *using* them and *disposing* of them after use to make room for other goods and their uses. Consumer life favours lightness and speed; also the novelty and variety that lightness and speed are hoped to foster.'[206] Thus, in Alan Durning's words, 'commercial television promotes the restless craving for more by portraying the high consumption lifestyle as a model to be emulated.'[207] We create for ourselves a 'cash and keys society', as Richard Wilkinson calls it: 'Cash equips us to take part in the transactions mediated by the market, while keys protect our private gains from each other's envy and greed.' He adds: 'Instead of being people with whom we have social bonds and share common interests, others become rivals, competitors for jobs, for houses, space, seats on the bus, parking places.'[208]

Robert Bly argues that 'capitalism has siphoned off male energy so as to allow deep exploitation of children' and 'to allow direct control of children by consumerism'.[209] The novelist Michel Houellebecq's remark that 'the sexual revolution was to destroy the last unit separating the individual from the market' has already been mentioned.[210] Relationships become increasingly 'liquid' to use Bauman's term.

These trends produce a demoralisation that Vaclav Havel, the president of the Czech Republic in the early 1990s, defined as: 'A person who has been seduced by the consumer value system, whose identity is dissolved in an amalgam of the accoutrements of mass civilisation, and who has no roots in the order of being, no sense of responsibility for anything higher than his or her own personal survival, is a *demoralised* person. The system depends on this demoralisation, is in fact a projection of it into society.'[211] There is a weakening or perversion of moral life, where to distinguish 'good' from 'bad' or 'evil' is in practice discouraged. Discussions of topics such as truth, honesty, love and compassion, are often viewed as eccentric, if they are not actually forbidden.

This discouragement is already visible in the junior schools in the United States and elsewhere. William Kilpatrick in his book *Why Johnny Can't Tell Right From Wrong* describes the undermining of teachers' rights of moral assertion in schools.[212] The same in universities, where teachers have tended to lose their moral nerve in the face of corporatisation, and the use of lawyers to challenge disciplining, for example, over plagiarism. The academic Luciana Bohne describes it as a general crisis in education: 'Let me put it succinctly: I don't think serious education is possible in the United States. Anything you touch in the annals of knowledge is a foe to the system of commerce and profit run amok. The only education that can be permitted is that which acculturates one to the status quo, as happens in expensive schools, or that which produces people to police and enforce the status quo.'[213]

The growing political influence of corporations has been accompanied by a growing manipulation of academic thought. The pursuit of truth has tended to be ridiculed since the early 1980s, when Marxism began to be replaced by postmodernism as the intellectual fashion. With postmodernism, to argue for the truth of something has become suspect. An atmosphere of moral relativity has insinuated itself into the realms of higher education. Judgements are discouraged if not prohibited. In effect everything is true, yet nothing is true.

This parallels the attack on 'truth' that, during the 2010s, was conducted by kleptocratic figures in various countries including Putin in Russia.[214] An example is the rise of attacks on ideas of evolution in the United States, and the demand that biblical superstitions be taught as if they were scientifically valid. The disapproval of strong viewpoints is taking place in a world in which the practical details of existence are becoming increasingly complex, and are understood only by small minorities of scientists and specialists – a world in which science itself is under attack. An example was the difficulty the virologists had in getting US president, Donald Trump, to take the Covid-19 epidemic seriously in the United States. As the cosmologist Carl Sagan argues in his book *Demon Haunted World*: 'We've arranged a global civilisation in which most of the crucial elements – transportation, communications, and all other industries, agriculture, medicine, education, entertainment, protecting the environment, and even the democratic institutions of voting, profoundly depend on science and technology. We have also arranged things so that almost no one understands science and technology. This is a prescription for disaster. We might get away with it for a while, but sooner or later this combustible mixture of ignorance and power is going to blow up in our faces.'[215]

The pursuit of truth has tended to be replaced by the pursuit of the corporate value of 'excellence'. A reflection of this is the remoulding of the university administration along the lines of corporative executive structure. Just about every university has 'passion for excellence' central to its advertising. Examples here where I am in South Africa include the University of KwaZulu-Natal's 'the quest for excellence is a lifelong process', the *Business Day*'s reference to the fact that 'car dealers strive for excellence', and my own university's 'excellence through the ages'. The problem is that 'excellence' is a concept that has zero moral content. Anything can be excellent, including the gas used in gas chambers. After Hiroshima, the devisers of the atomic bomb at Los Alamos were gratified to receive 'the Army-Navy E for excellence' award for their work.[216]

'Excellence' has been accompanied by what amounts to a 'cult of acclaim' reminiscent of the norms of Stalinist socialist realism of the 1930s and 1940s. The cult is nurtured in the media and educational institutions, which combine with televised political platitudes to create a mental world in which certain things are true and other things wrong and unacceptable. Any career advancement gambit requires the sniffing out of what is permitted to be said and what is best left unspoken. Goals and values that corporations do not support are under-stressed or not mentioned. It becomes possible to mislead sufficient percentages of the public with open media lies, as was illustrated with the US and British governments' lies in the run up to the Iraq war in 2003. The manipulation of public opinion has become a well funded science.

With the weakening of accepted public values, the idea of 'evil' has itself become dangerously blurred. Jean Baudrillard writes: 'Terrorism in all its forms is the transpolitical mirror of evil. For the real problem, the only problem, is: where did Evil go? And the answer is everywhere...In a society which seeks – by prophylactic measures, by annihilating its own natural referents, by whitewashing violence...by performing cosmetic surgery on the negative – to concern itself with quantified management and with the discourse of the Good, in a society where it is no longer possible to speak Evil, Evil has metamorphosed into all the viral and terroristic forms that obsess us.'[217]

Robert Bly in his *The Sibling Society* has a passage which provides a good postscript to this discussion: 'We are all human beings now, standing in the rubble of a destroyed literate society looking at the ruins of education, family and child protection. Technology has destroyed interrelationships in the human community that have taken centuries to develop. The breaking of human beings' connection to land has harmed everyone. We are drowning in uncontrollable floods of information. We are living among dispirited and agonized teenagers who can't find hope. Genuine work is disappearing, and we are becoming aware of a persistent infantilizing of men and women, a process already far advanced.'[218]

# 17. Population Growth and Environmental Destruction

At the time when humans first took up agriculture around 14,000 years BP, our global population was an estimated 5 million. By the time of Jesus Christ, 2,000 years BP, that had risen to between 100 and 200 million. Over the following 1,500 years, until around the time of Christopher Columbus, that number had more than doubled to around 500 million, despite the temporary declines in population after the Black Death pandemic of the mid and later 1300s. By the time of the first railways, say 1830, the 500 million had within 330 years doubled to 1000 million (a billion). That in turn doubled to 2 billion by the early 1930s – the time of the Great Depression and Hitler's rise to power in Germany. Despite the Second World War and a global loss of life of between 60 and a 100 million people, by 1945 we were at 2.5 billion. By Kennedy's inauguration in 1961 that had risen to 3 billion. Within less than twenty years, around 1980, the 3 billion had grown to 4 billion, at which point we were consuming 100% of the planetary photosynthate (defined later in this chapter). Within a further ten years, by 1990, that 4 billion had grown to 5 billion, and the next ten years saw a similar increase, making our numbers 6 billion by the year 2000. We reached 7 billion by 2012. In November 2022 we reached 8 billion. That means that in the previous ten years we added (after subtracting deaths) an extra 274,000 people every day, or 11,400 every hour. And numbers will continue to rise. If the last decade's compounded rate of population growth (1.34% per annum) were to continue, there would be 11.6 billion people in 2050. Demographic experts, presuming that the rate must reduce, predict that the 2050 figure will be closer to 9 or 10 billion. They also debate what date and at what figure human population will cease to rise. The current popular guess is 2070 at 12 billion. For reasons that we will examine, that appears to be the maximum possible.[219]

Whole libraries of books have been written to explain this extraordinary and accelerating increase. Earlier phases of growth were based on the invention of agriculture, and given impetus by the smelting of iron, and the use of cattle and horses to pull ploughs. Iron tools enabled the more efficient destruction of forests in much of Europe and its conversion to fields and pasture for animals. In the Middle Ages the improvement in seed varieties and the careful nursing of land via crop rotation maximised grain production. A further critical boost was provided, at least for Europe, with the development of firearms. This permitted imperialistic seizure of other parts of the world by Europeans, and the forcing of slave labour onto plantations to grow cotton, sugar and other crops. Slaving allowed an increase in Europe's energy imports. This, along with the accompanying political and capitalistic reorganisation, led to earlier marriages, higher birth rates, and lower death rates. In the nineteenth century the plundering of the rest of the world by Europeans raised imports of food; and this, combined with various life enhancing developments such as cotton clothing and better sanitation, led to dramatic population rises.

The twentieth century witnessed even more dramatic boosts to population increase because of electricity and oil. Electricity enabled the Germans Fritz Haber and Carl Bosch to fix nitrogen for the first time, and so created the capacity for the mass production of the ammonium nitrate fertilizers, which allowed much higher grain production and further population take-off. Petrol and diesel engines allowed tractors, combined harvesters and other agricultural machines to push agricultural production to undreamed-of levels. Colin Mason notes: 'modern agriculture uses land to convert petroleum into food.'[220] It has been estimated that about 40% of the global population today is alive because of factory-manufactured nitrogen fertilizers.[221] The green revolution after the 1940s drove up population growth in India, China and elsewhere. Grain production by food corporations such as Cargill or Archer Daniels Midland continues to be maximised for profit – these corporations, like all corporations, are dependent on growth. Grain exports from primary producers (the US, Canada, Australia and Russia) to poor world nations facing shortages are a means to keep them politically dependent – an added incentive to grow surpluses of grain.

Trends in the global statistics are alarming because grain output is falling relative to the increases in population. By the late 1970s total annual global grain output had reached 1.4 billion tons. The world's population was then 4 billion, so that meant 340 kilograms of grain per person a year on average. By 2009 the per person total was 305 kilograms of grain per year. Today, with 8 billion people, this has been reduced to under 290 kilograms per person.

Population growth has in addition meant a huge reduction in the area of cultivable land, as well as a reduction in the amount of land available per person on which to grow food.[222] In 1950, for each of the 2.6 billion humans on the planet, there was 0.23 hectares of cultivable land available; by the year 2000 this had been reduced to 0.11 hectares per person. As population pushes in the direction of nine or ten billion the average amount of land per person will decrease further. Seed producers cannot keep up – their capacity to create grains with higher yields is already at its outer limit. The problem is magnified by the increasing amount of land given over to cattle grazing for both milk and meat. As people become wealthier, as has happened in China over the past forty years, they go for higher consumption of meat, so an increasing proportion of land is directly or indirectly given over to meat. The land given over to the production of ethanol for fuel makes things worse.

An equally big issue is water – unsalted or fresh water, without which crops cannot be grown or life exist. The Earth contains a large amount of water – around 1.4 billion cubic kilometres. Of that, however, only 2.5% is fresh water, and of that, 75% is locked up in ice caps. That leaves around 8,000 cubic kilometres accessible by us. As of now around 4,000 cubic kilometres (50%) of that is available, and is used by us annually, and returned to the planet polluted. The demand will double by 2080, which puts an absolute limit on human population.

The minimum annual requirement of water for a healthy human being is 40 cubic metres.[223] Many countries won't be able to supply this as we advance further into the 2020s and 2030s. Water tables are falling everywhere, even in the massive aquifers, such as the Ogallala in the United States, the Guarani Aquifer in southern South America and the Great Artesian Basin in Australia. River flows are reducing – some of the world's major rivers, such as the Yellow and the Yangtze in China, no longer flow the entire year. As fresh water becomes scarcer, it proves to be an irresistible private profit attraction to the large water corporations, e.g. Bechtel, RWE-Thames Water, Vivendi, Suez-Lyonnaise, and SAUR-Bouygues. Their aim is to buy up the entire planetary available supply, and charge us for it.[224] Should a kleptocracy get its country into unserviceable debt, the WTO and IMF invariably make their loans conditional on water privatization. This is already leading to citizen movements, some of them violent, to bring water back into public ownership, such as the Cochabamba rioting in Bolivia in 2000-2001.

It must be stressed that all the figures I have quoted are averages. Annual food consumption is skewed between the rich and poor parts of the world. In North America the average food intake per person per annum is 700 kilograms of grain, while in Africa it is 200 kilograms. South Africa, where I live, is in between, with an average of 325 kilograms per person per annum, but within that average are vast gaps in consumption between the wealthy and the poor. These contrasts in food consumption are echoed by consumption of water. The average person in the United States consumes about 1,200 cubic metres of water per annum, compared to the 290 cubic metres of the average South African.

There was a theory, which started in the 1950s, that as people became wealthier, the number of children per couple would decline. The assumption was that if one could increase the wealth and hence the food intake of poorer people, their high fertility rates would reduce in turn, and the global population would stabilize. This 'demographic transition' has not come about, at least not to any significant extent. Births, or 'fertility rates', are still much higher in Africa than in other parts of the world. In richer parts of the world, such as Germany or Japan, the average number of children per woman is less than two (in France it is less than 1.4) whereas in Kenya it is between six and seven.

At first glance this seems illogical. Wouldn't wealthier people have more children than poor people? The explanation lies in what is called the 'intergenerational flow of wealth'. In the rich world the costs of rearing a child are heavy, and the prospective parents can do other things with their money. They prefer directing their libido into other directions, most involving increased consumption. And increasing numbers of them, concerned about the future, hesitate to have children. In the poor world most people live in the rural areas, and, as far as food is concerned, they largely have to produce it for themselves. For them the labour of children is vital for family food output. And if one of them could be given the heavy educational investment that would lead to qualifications and a good job, their future contributions to family income might prove decisive. The intergenerational flow of wealth, in other words, is negative in the rich world and positive in the poor world. Hence the maintenance of higher fertility rates in the poorer parts of the world, even if that seems counter-intuitive from the economic point of view.

Germaine Greer in her book *Sex and Destiny* makes a few interesting observations about population.[225] Since rich world societies, with declining birth rates (such as Japan), are faced with declining populations with more old people and fewer young people, what are the likely consequences? One is of course the possibility of future labour shortages. But Greer focuses on the psychological profile of aging societies.[226] As people age, they become slower, less active, politically conservative, less productive and more dependent – or in Greer's words: more sclerotic. Political and environmental problems are shelved or not faced directly. Politicians in these societies reflect this lack of energy, and tend to pander to the aging electorates and their wishes. There is fear of change, and an inability to take risks. Greer writes: 'Aged nations, wedded to their own comfort, fearful of change, clinging to an ever-dwindling treasure, tend to commit suicide anyway.'[227] Globally, driven by rich world politics, that is what we are doing.

In the poor world it is the other way round. People do not live so long, so the populations have a lower average age. But, as Greer notes: 'A child is never an encumbrance to a beggar.'[228] So more children are born, and the population not only increases rapidly, but its average age decreases, and is weighted more and more towards the young. Extended families are normal. There is more psychological vitality, but there is also more poverty. Poorer countries are vulnerable both to their own kleptocratic ruling elites and to blackmail from rich world grain exporters. Disputes among the elites can lead to civil war, or, in the worst case, genocide, as in Rwanda in 1994. As population levels rise further there is more vulnerability to climatic or harvest crises, and the youthful populations of poor countries attempt to migrate to wealthier or more stable parts of the world. Africans attempt to cross the Mediterranean; Central Americans attempt to walk across the desert into the United States. Many of them are angry. The rich people become afraid, and seek to cling to their affluence by putting up barriers against immigrants. I am oversimplifying, but this is what is happening.

Inevitably the growth of population, coupled with our destructive production systems, combines to destroy the environment. Every year humans destroy around 150,000 square kilometres of forest, much of it tropical forest. Of the original 70 million square kilometres of forest that covered the planet about 2 million years ago, we had destroyed about 50% by 1970, leaving 35 million square kilometres. A further five million had been cut by the year 2000. At the current rate, all forest will be gone within 150 years. Just one example: since the arrival of Europeans in Australia in the 1780s 40% of the forests there have been cleared, another 35% partly logged, and only 25% are still intact. Trees endangered include the Victorian and Tasmanian mountain ash, among the largest trees in the world.[229]

Trees function to remove carbon from the air. On the natural death of a tree, its carbon is then buried underground (sequestered). The sequestering of carbon has cooled average planetary temperatures – a natural process that has been of decisive influence in stabilising the combination of life forms that have evolved on Earth.

Destruction of forests has also meant the destruction of the habitats of animals, birds, reptiles and insects. Gorillas, the ivory-billed woodpecker and the Philippine eagle are some of the many species threatened with extinction.[230] As George Schaller reminds us: 'Use a cell phone that contains the mineral coltan, and somewhere in the eastern Congo a coltan miner kills a gorilla for food.'[231] Forest soils are thin, and once tree cover is gone they are easily eroded. Although new trees may be planted, they are invariably industrial crops for harvesting.

Much damage is being done as well to rivers and lakes across the planet by human activities. Many of the great rivers have their flows reduced by dams, such as the Kariba and Cahora Bassa dams on the Zambezi, which were built for hydroelectricity. Downstream, water flow is often disrupted, affecting both human and animal habitats. The drying up of rivers can eliminate species, such as the magnificent Beluga sturgeon in the Amur River that divides China and Russia.[232] In North America salmon populations have been adversely affected by river blockades or low depths of water. Water in rivers is further polluted by human sewage and fertilizer run-off from farms. Fertilizer run-off from the Mississippi River has produced a dead zone at the river's mouth in the

Gulf of Mexico. Lake Chad, the huge expanse of water between Nigeria, the Central African Republic and Gabon, is rapidly drying up, with loss of fish life, and the elimination of habitats of many species.

The most catastrophic man-made water crisis is that of the Aral Sea in central Asia. This giant inland sea is, or rather was, fed by two rivers, the Syr Darya and the Amu Darya, which flow down from the western Himalayas. The water of these rivers gave life to orchards, gardens and fields along their courses in Uzbekistan, and provided flourishing fishing enterprises in the Aral Sea itself. During Khrushchev's rule in the 1950s, Soviet Union planners decided to grow cotton on a large scale in what was in effect desert. The cotton was to be watered from canals which were diverted from the two rivers. The loss of water from the rivers led to the shrinkage of the Aral Sea, slowly at first, then rapidly. Worse was to come: the soaking of water into the desert ground that was given over to cotton led to sequestered salt rising to the surface. Soon the whole region turned into a salt desert in which nothing would grow. The two rivers began to dry up, and ceased to reach the Aral Sea. According to Ryszard Kapuscinski, of the 178 species of fish in the sea only 38 remain. The once flourishing port of Muynak in Uzbekistan is now over sixty kilometres from the sea. Kapuscinski writes: 'Near the settlement, where the port once was, rusting carcasses of trawlers, cutters, barges and other boats lie in the sand....The place is deserted; there is no one around.'[233]

The oceans too are being damaged. In the 1940s, the total global fish catch was around ten million tons per annum. This doubled in the 1950s, when factory fishing with on-board refrigeration became possible. By the 1980s the total global fishing catch had reached 80 million tons per annum. After this the catch declined rapidly. Cod and herring catches collapsed, as did the catch of skates, rays and sharks, the latter all too frequently being unintentionally ensnared in nets. Whales, dolphins and porpoises are also endangered. The great white shark is still being hunted for shark fin soup. As the fish disappear, the food they once ate proliferates, and we see a rise in 'slime' and jellyfish. One dangerous slime is *Lyngbya majuscula* or fireweed, which affects the waters off southern Australia.

We pollute the environment in other ways – to our own harm and that of other species. In 2019 around 460 million tons of plastic were produced globally, including 6 quadrillion plastic bags. There are 5,000 plastic bag factories in India alone. Much of this plastic is thrown away, or escapes from dumps and is washed into the sea. The world's ships dump 650,000 plastic bottles and containers into the oceans every day. The oceans have turned into a vast human rubbish dump. A well known example is the North Pacific Gyre, where at least three million tons of plastic have accumulated, as Alan Weisman relates in his book *The World Without Us*. Trillions of plastic nurdles are washed into the sea every day. Some are consumed by fish and birds, resulting in many dying.[234]

In addition we have devised various methods of poisoning ourselves and other animals. Rachel Carson, in her ground-breaking 1962 publication *Silent Spring*, gave innumerable examples. She wrote: 'The most alarming of all man's assaults upon the environment is the contamination of air, earth, rivers, and sea with dangerous and even lethal materials.'[235] The 1940s saw the mass production of pesticide chemicals called chlorinated hydrocarbons, the best known being DDT, or dichloro-diphenyl-trichloro-ethane.[236] Even more dangerous are the so-called organophosphates such as Parathion, Malathion and Dieldrin, which are deadly to humans. Carson warned: 'the chemists' ingenuity in devising insecticides has long outrun biological knowledge of the way these poisons affect the living organism.'[237]

Carson documented what happened in Clear Lake, California, during the 1950s. In 1949 the lake was sprayed with one fiftieth part per million of DDT to get rid of gnats. There occurred what is called 'upward potentiation': the gnats were consumed by small fish, and they in turn by larger fish. Each level of consumption concentrated the poison further. By the time the larger fish were eaten by the lake's predominant water bird, the western grebe, the grebe's body fat contained 1,600 parts per million of DDT, and this killed them. Similarly for the peregrine falcon which also consumed the fish. The poison imbibed by the falcons thinned the shells of the eggs laid by the female, and the falcons were unable to breed. Although the spraying had stopped and DDT had disappeared from the water, it had not gone – merely been transferred 'into the fabric of the lake supports'.[238] Similar upward potentiation happens in food chains that involve humans. DDT and other poisons are increasingly present in human female breast milk, and have crossed the placenta into the foetus.

*Silent Spring* is nowadays regarded as the book that initiated the global environmental movement. In the early 1960s Carson was subjected to a vicious attack by chemical companies whose profits would be affected by the campaigns she inspired to ban chlorinated hydrocarbons. By the 1970s some of these poisons had been banned for sale in the United States. They were however permitted to be exported to poor world countries, and the manufacturers employed amenable 'academics' to propagandise the advantages of spraying DDT in Africa.

By the 1980s pesticides appeared to be having unexpected effects within the rich world. Several of the poisons mimic oestrogen, adding to the oestrogen in the water supply from contraceptive pills both directly or through urine. These have become linked to testicular and prostate cancer in the human male. Combinations of the chemicals have also been reducing sperm counts in men, and increasing the incidence of non-descending testes. Deborah Cadbury's book *The Feminization of Nature* relates how through excess oestrogen intake alligators and other water-inhabiting animals are becoming ambiguously male/female, unable to breed.[239]

In recent decades various ways of measuring our impact on the natural environment have been developed. One way is by assessing the proportion of the 'planetary photosynthate' the human species consumes. Like all animals, we are dependent on photosynthesis – which combines the sun's energy with water and carbon dioxide to create proteins and oxygen. This is achieved by bacteria on which all life forms depend. Most of the photosynthetic 'product' of bacteria is in green plants; the total mass of green plants produced in this way is called the planetary photosynthate, which is measurable as the annual photosynthate. Today, one species, *Homo sapiens*, consumes between 40% and 50% of the available annual photosynthate. Should our population continue to expand at present rates, the annual photosynthate we consume will increase to around 80% by the 2070s. At that level, no other large animals will be viable in the wild.

Another way of measuring the unsustainability of our activities is by the Living Planet Index, devised by the World Wildlife Fund. This index examines and assesses the viability of the planet's three basic ecosystems: freshwater, seawater and forests. It uses as a baseline the year 1970, with each basic system starting at 100 for that year. In the fifty years that we have been eliminating or damaging these three systems, the 1970 index of 100 has been reduced to 40.

A third method was devised at the University of Toronto in the early 1990s by Mathis Wackernagel, who sought to calculate the planet's annual sustainably replenishable ration of food and energy output consumed by humans. This is calculated by a complex mix of resources both on land and in the sea that is available to humans in a year, and comparing it with the actual resources consumed. The ratio of resources consumed to resources available in a specific year he termed our Ecological Footprint. Prior to 1980, we as a species had consumed under 100% of the output per annum. Around 1980, when our global population passed 4 billion, we were consuming 100% of the ration. Today, with nearly 8 billion of us, we consume 190% of the ration. We are in effect consuming future rations.

This can be expressed in planet hectares available per person per year: in 2022 this was 1.6 hectares, whilst human consumption averaged 3 hectares. At present we require 1.9 planets for sustainable existence. Again, the average conceals large differences between the rich and the poor world. The average African consumes one hectare per annum, whilst the average North American consumes between 9 and 12 hectares. If everyone consumed like a North American, we would need six planet earths.[240]

Our population growth and our over-consumption of the planetary photosynthate is obviously unsustainable. Yet our political leaders preach continued economic growth. The attitude of contemporary capitalism is that the environment can be plundered indefinitely. In 1991 Larry Summers, later to become US president, Bill Clinton's secretary of the treasury, stated: 'There are no limits to the carrying capacity of the Earth that are likely to bind in the foreseeable future. There isn't a risk of an apocalypse due to global warming or anything else. The idea that we should put limits on growth because of some natural limit is a profound error and one that, were it ever to prove influential, would have staggering social costs.'[241] As indeed it would.

In the same year that Summers was speaking, Thomas Berry, in his book *Befriending the Earth,* wrote with a different perspective: 'The difficulty with our use of industrial technology is that we have the cunning to use it to subvert the basic biological law. The basic biological law is that every life form should have opposed life forms or conditions that limit each life form so that one life form or group of them would not overwhelm the others. Technology enables us to get round these limiting conditions. We can overpopulate; we can tear the Earth to pieces in a devastating manner.' He continued: 'No generation that I know of has ever done such damage to its children as my generation has done. My generation, through the major part of the twentieth century, has shaped a world of ruins. Our children will live amid the ruined infrastructures of the industrial world and, indeed, amid the ruins of the natural world itself. We are making everlasting ruins. We are ruining the atmosphere, the forests, the mountains, and the rivers for the indefinite future. We are ruining the biosystems of the planet and handing them on to the next generation. saying, "Well, we had our fun, now you have yours."'[242]

In a talk to children in a New York school, Berry added that his generation had been an autistic one: 'That I think is what has happened to the human community in our times. We are talking to ourselves. We are not talking to the river, we are not listening to the river. We have broken the great conversation. By breaking the conversation we have shattered the universe. All these things that are happening now are consequences of this infantilism.'[243]

If we are to think seriously about solutions, we must ask from whose point of view? From that of *Homo sapiens?* Or from the perspective of the myriad animals and plants that *Homo sapiens* is destroying in our career of cancerous expansion? But the two perspectives are in fact one. Rachel Carson understood this. In 1962 she wrote: 'Man's attitude towards nature today is critically important simply because we have now acquired a fateful power to alter and destroy nature. But man is part of nature and his war against nature is a war against himself.'[244]

The Native American chief, Seattle, had reached the same conclusion over a century earlier: 'Whatever befalls the Earth befalls the sons of the Earth. Man did not weave the web of life, he is merely a strand in it. Whatever he does to the web he does to himself.' He added: 'This we know. The Earth does not belong to man; man belongs to the Earth. This we know. All things are connected like the blood which unites one family. All things are connected.'[245]

The corollary is provided by James Lovelock: 'If we lose our habitat, the system of life and its environment on Earth, Gaia, will go on. But humankind will no longer be a part of it.'[246]

# 18. Heating the Planet with Oil

Today we face two linked crises of our own making: a prospective energy crisis, as oil supplies run down; and a survival crisis as the planet heats up because of our burning of oil and other fuels. George Monbiot sums it up well: 'We seem to be in trouble. Either we lay hands on every source of fossil fuel, in which case we fry the planet and civilisation collapses, or we run out, and civilisation collapses.'[247]

Let us start with the oil problem.[248] The rise of capitalism and today's affluence have depended entirely on extracting, over a short 200 years, the carbon energy that the planetary life system spent millions of years removing from the atmosphere and burying underground. Trees and other plants take carbon out of the atmosphere and convert it into wood, which, over long time spans, is buried ('sequestered') to become coal, liquid oil, or gas. Without this removal of carbon, the atmosphere would have heated up and made the continuation of life impossible, and the Earth would have become a dead planet like Mars or Venus, with an atmosphere containing over 90% carbon dioxide.

Our entire modern civilization has been built on consuming this buried carbon energy, and returning it into the atmosphere. For the first several thousand years after agriculture began, the carbon energy we extracted came mainly in the form of wood from trees. From the 1600s, when wood in Europe became scarcer, there was a switch to the mining of coal. Beginning first in Western Europe, coal, via the steam engine and the coal-fired power station, was converted into the human cultural and economic advances of the nineteenth and twentieth century. From the later 1800s coal was supplemented by the mining of oil, which, via the petrol/diesel engine, made possible the economic accelerations of the twentieth century. The population explosion – from one billion humans on the planet in 1830 to today's eight billion – has depended on petrol driven machines and the fixation via electricity of nitrogen fertilizers. The human consumption of coal (burned in power stations for electricity) soared globally from around an annual 760 million tons in 1900 to an annual 5,000 million tons in the early twenty-first century.

We also 'eat' coal and oil since all commercial agricultural production depends on oil for fertilizers, farm machines, transport and manufacturing. In the United States, ten calories of oil are used to produce one calorie of food energy in the form of grain (a calorie of beef, however, requires 35 calories of oil, and a calorie of pork 68 calories). The rising affluence of the past century has been entirely dependent on oil.

At the time oil extraction began in the nineteenth century, the quantity of easily accessible oil across the entire planet was around two trillion barrels. Consumption was slow in the late nineteenth and early twentieth century, but rose rapidly with the discoveries of new oil wells in the United States (Texas), the Middle East (Iran, Iraq and Saudi Arabia), Russia and Indonesia. As global population increased dramatically in the latter half of the twentieth century, so too did the output of oil. From the end of the Second World War to around 1973 the global per capita increase in oil output was about 3.24% per annum. In the latter half of the 1970s this figure had reduced to a 0.64% increase per annum. In the last twenty years of the twentieth century average oil output per person per year became negative. By 2010 there was 0.75% less oil per person per year, and at the turn of the 2020s it was 3% less. This is because, while global oil production has still been increasing, global population has been increasing more rapidly. Because oil production is so tied to food production, this has led to a decline in the average human food production, from 340 kilograms of grain available per person globally in 1980 to 275 kilograms in 2020. Reduced to its simplest terms, one could say that our planetary human species crisis consists of this differential between the population increase per annum and the oil energy decline per capita per annum.

Why then can't we simply produce more oil? The answer is: because the amount of reachable oil is finite. Of the two trillion barrels of fairly easily accessible oil available in 1900, we have already consumed about 50%. Our contemporary oil consumption is about 33 billion barrels a year. Only 35 years of easily available oil is left.

The idea of 'peak oil' was first put forward by an American, M. King Hubbert, in 1956, at a time when national economies were almost drowning in cheap oil following big discoveries in Saudi Arabia.[249] Hubbert stressed the important distinction between oil discoveries and oil production. He noted that in the United States oil discoveries had peaked in the 1930s. Though oil was still being discovered in the US in the 1950s, these discoveries were fewer than twenty years earlier. Hubbert predicted that US oil production would peak in 1970-71, after which annual production would decline, slowly at first, then more rapidly.

Hubbert's predictions proved spot on. Oil production in the United States did peak in 1971. At the planetary level, global oil discoveries were still shooting up in the late 1950s and early 1960s, but dropped off between 1965 and 1967. Global production in turn duly peaked around 2010-12, which was when half the original two trillion barrels was surpassed. In response, prospectors for new oil reserves have turned increasingly to shale sands, oil tars, and the 'fracking' of oil available in underground rocks. The uncertainty over oil availability has led in turn to wild speculative swings in the price of oil, as occurred in 2008. A record price of US$ 150 a barrel was reached in June 2008, and its subsequent collapse to US$ 30 was interlinked with the global stock market crash after September that year. The Russian invasion of Ukraine in early 2022 in turn led to the price per barrel shooting above US$ 100 for a second time, after it had briefly fallen to US$ 14 a barrel during the early phase of the Covid-19 pandemic in April 2020.[250]

It is difficult to make precise predictions about when oil will run out. There have been intense debates between the early and late 'peakers' – late peakers believe annual global production will continue increasing until the 2030s, while early peakers insist that the peak point has been passed already. One of the difficulties is establishing how much oil is left underground, especially given the refusal of Saudi Arabia to reveal the level of its reserves. But nobody disagrees that reserves are diminishing. These issues have become central in the macro-politics of power. Control of Iraq's oil was the primary objective of the George Bush administration in 2003. In Africa competing moves are being made by the United States and China for access to Africa's oil in Sudan, Chad, Nigeria and Angola.

Whichever way you look at it, the 'oil party' is nearly over, well past midnight and into the early hours. The decline of oil is a major factor in the low economic growth rates of the post-2008 crisis years, and the lowering of average real incomes in much of the rich world, and the so far unsuccessful attempts by national reserve banks to get economic growth expanding again. The rising affluence of capitalism's golden years (1940s to early 1970s) is unrepeatable.

The Swedish scientist, Svante Arrhenius, writing in 1896, was one of the first to point out that the climate might be affected by the carbon rapidly being put into the air by humans, which would increase temperatures. For Arrhenius any raising of atmospheric temperature would be a good thing, as Swedish summers would be longer, and the country would be warmer.[251] Rising proportions of carbon in the air were noted by scientists in the late 1950s and 1960s, as carbon reached over 300 parts per million, although between the 1930s and 1960s the natural cycle of the planet was in a cool phase, and there was no particular concern. It was only in the early 1980s that scientists working in the Antarctic began to raise the alarm about rising temperatures. In 1988 the American meteorologist Jim Hansen briefed the United States Congress about the possible negative effects of a climate transformation brought about by rising concentrations of carbon in the air.[252] The United Nations set up its Intergovernmental Panel on Climate Change that same year, which drew on the researches of thousands of climate experts to assess the situation. The IPCC has since produced a series of six definitive Assessment Reports. The sixth, published in 2021, was signed by the world's top climate experts.

Total annual global carbon emissions by humans more than doubled between 1960 and 2000, from ten billion to 23 billion tons. Today the figure is around 31 billion tons per annum. The proportion of carbon dioxide in the air has risen steadily since the 1990s, by between 2 and 3 parts per million per annum. In 1850 the carbon dioxide level in the atmostphere was about 250 parts per millon; by late 2021 this had increased to 419 parts per million. This has produced an overall planetary temperature increase since the beginning of industrialisation of around 1.2 °C. By the 2050s we will be at over 500 parts per million, with a planetary temperature increase of over 2 °C unless decisive global action is taken. The failure of successive international conferences to get agreement since the first Rio conference in 1992 suggests this is unlikely.[253]

Let us look at some of the effects of the temperature rise.[254] First the ice. Three types of ice are monitored: massive ice layers of many kilometres in depth on the Antarctic subcontinent, as well as on Greenland; sea ice, around the North Pole and around Antarctica; and high altitude ice on mountain ranges such as the Himalayas, the Andes, and the Alps where water freezes into great glaciers. Bear in mind that the melting of land ice raises sea levels, whereas that of sea ice does not. If all the land ice of the Antarctic and Greenland were to melt, sea levels would rise by over 100 metres. Since the nineteenth century melted ice and the thermal expansion of water as a result of global heating have between them raised ocean levels by around 24 centimetres, with a third of that coming in the last two and a half decades.

Ice reflects the sun's heat back into space, so that temperatures are always lower over areas of ice than they are over dark land or sea, which reflect the sun's rays less. Loss of ice thus creates darker surfaces which leads to more warming, which leads to more ice melting – a positive feedback process which eventually becomes irreversible.

Ice provides a long and important historical record. As layers of snow are converted into ice during the winters, they are compressed and overlaid by later layers, building formations of annual layering that can reach many kilometres in depth and reflect thousands of years of ice formation. These layers of ice contain air that is trapped in bubbles, and analysis of this air gives us a record of the state of the atmosphere at the time, including levels of carbon dioxide.

This record shows that air temperatures around the Antarctic have risen by around 3 °C since the mid-nineteenth century, which is a much greater rate than the planetary average of 1.2 °C. In February 2020 a temperature of 17.75 °C was recorded at the Esperanza Base, the highest ever for Antarctica. The sea ice around the Antarctic is melting at a noticeable rate, affecting the life of fish and animals that inhabit those waters. For example there have been significant reductions in krill populations at the edges of the Antarctic sea ice, which have been attributed to warming waters; and this in turn has reduced the populations of Adele penguins which depend on krill.

In 2002, the Antarctic's 3,250 square kilometre Larsen B ice shelf broke up. As the sea ice broke away, land glaciers on the continent, no longer impeded by the sea ice that had acted as a sort of dam wall, began to flow more quickly into the sea. In 2017, a 5,000 square kilometre ice block weighing 1.1 trillion tons broke off from the Larsen C shelf. In 2021 another 1,276 square kilometre mass of the Brunt ice shelf 'calved' off into the Weddell Sea. The one kilometre thick Thwaites glacier, nicknamed the 'doomsday glacier', is also melting. It is a land glacier – the widest on the planet – that is blocked by sea ice in the Amundsen Sea. Water under the glacier has warmed by 2 °C, and the front of the glacier is breaking up. Should it break up entirely, global sea levels would rise by 64 centimetres. The Thwaites glacier is already responsible for 4% of the rise of global sea levels. Though ice break-ups of this sort are not unprecedented, they have occurred more frequently in recent decades, probably because of the thinning of ice shelves caused by the waters below warming rapidly. Tim Flannery wrote in 2005: 'a great domino effect – wherein the destabilisation of one ice field leads to the destruction of a neighbour – is playing itself out at the southern extremity of the world.'[255]

In just two months of 2019 Greenland lost 600 billion tons of ice, which raised sea levels worldwide 2.2 millimetres. Because warmer water expands, the rise caused by the volume of melting ice is doubled. In the Arctic temperatures are now over 2 °C higher than in the mid-twentieth century, and in Alaska and western Canada, 3 to 4 °C higher. As temperatures have risen, so the extent of Arctic sea ice has declined, especially in the summer months. In 2007 the North West Passage was for the first time ice free in September. Satellite pictures show drastic reductions in sea ice in the Arctic between the early 1980s and 2020. By 2010 the ice loss in the area was around 10% per decade. In the Arctic Circle, on 20 June 2020, a temperature of 38 °C was recorded for the first time ever. Prediction of the date when the entire North Pole region would be ice free in summer was once 2100 – it is now expected some time between 2030 and 2070. As far as the oil and gas industry is concerned this is good news, since the exploration of under-ice oil fields is now becoming possible in Greenland, northern Canada and Alaska. Houses in these areas built on permafrost are already collapsing as the permafrost melts.

Everywhere that they exist, glaciers are receding – in the Alps, the Pyrenees, Alaska, Greenland, the Himalayas, the Andes and Mt Kilimanjaro on the Tanzanian-Kenyan border. Some, such as the Chacaltaya glacier in Bolivia, have entirely disappeared. The ice on the Furtwängler glacier on the summit of Mt Kilimanjaro has been reduced in area by over 50%, and some of Mt Kenya's glaciers have shrunk to nothing over the past four decades. The Himalayan glaciers, which supply water to 1.4 billion people, are shrinking at an average of 20 metres a year. In the short term this can enhance downstream river flow, as has already happened in the Ganges, but in the longer term a decrease in river flow is inevitable.

Lakes that form behind moraines as a consequence of glacier melt are liable to burst through their constraining barriers and destroy settlements. The city of Huaraz in Peru, downstream from the glacial Lake Palcacocha, is such a threatened settlement. Thawing permafrost undermines rock faces, and can trigger rock avalanches. Landslides collapsing into glacial lakes can cause tsunamis.

A further environmental stress arises from the fact that the oceans are absorbing much of the carbon dioxide being added to the atmosphere by fossil fuel burning. This makes the sea water more acid, which is dangerous for many species of fish. Warmer surface waters can also transform the water mix between ocean levels, with damaging effects on sea life. The warming waters affect both the planet's flow of ocean currents, and its wind systems. There is a limit to what the oceans can absorb of our carbon dioxide output. Once that limit is reached, all our emissions will go into the atmosphere, accelerating its heating up.

One likely outcome will be the disruption of ocean currents in the north Atlantic, with adverse effects on climate in North America and Europe. Although some climatologists regard this as something for the distant future, in the shorter term it means that the previously stable climate of the US and Western Europe could become capricious and unpredictable, with much colder weather.

A minimum further rise in ocean levels of at least 90 centimetres is predicted for the twenty-first century, with some predictions as high as 200 centimetres. The oceans respond very slowly to temperature increases, and it is calculated that each 1 °C rise in temperature will lead to a rise of 2 to 3 metres in sea levels, though over several centuries. This slow increase is the good news. The bad news is that the oceans will be rising for centuries, irrespective of any success we may have in cutting carbon dioxide emissions.

Rising sea levels will inevitably lead to more frequent and more damaging flooding of low-lying coastal areas. Surges up major rivers will threaten the flooding of cities such as London and New York. The river Thames has been protected with a flood barrier, but it is not designed for a serious rise of water levels. For New York, an ambitious US$ 119 billion plan to protect the city from flooding was scrapped in 2018 by the federal government after the then president, Donald Trump, called it 'foolish' and advised New Yorkers to 'get mops and buckets ready'. Many coastal cities have already designed sea walls, surge barriers, water pump systems and overflow chambers to keep the water out. Hundreds of cities in East Asia are especially vulnerable, as are cities in the Netherlands and Spain. In Italy, Venice is sinking measurably already. Shanghai has built 520 kilometres of protective sea walls across Hangzhou Bay. Jakarta in Indonesia is building miles of sea wall, and Bangkok in Thailand is building a 2,600 kilometre canal network with integrated parks and an underground water storage system. Whether such preparations will be sufficiently protective only the future will tell, but it is doubtful. Low lying islands in the Pacific Ocean are already vulnerable to disappearing altogether under raised ocean levels. Kiribati, Tuvalu and the Marshall Islands are especially endangered, and already their governments' top priority is how and where to move their entire populations.

Added to the dangers for humans are changes in the atmosphere itself as a result of anthropogenic warming. Carbon dioxide and methane emissions warm the atmosphere, but a variety of positive feedback mechanisms worsen their effects. As the oceans warm, for example, more and more water vapour is produced, which itself is a potent greenhouse gas. The warmer the air, the more water vapour, and the more water vapour the warmer the air, in another vicious circle which roughly doubles the warming caused by carbon dioxide and methane emissions alone. Warmer air provides fuel for more frequent and more powerful hurricanes. In 2020 there were 29 major hurricanes off the Mexican Gulf and east coasts of the United States; many of them grade 4 and grade 5, causing flooding and massive damage when they struck land.

For each line of latitude away from the equator greater temperature increases are being found. Isotherms are shifting northwards in the northern hemisphere and southwards in the south, changing climate patterns over land and sea, and creating havoc in the living conditions of plants, animals and fish. For example the quiver tree, a giant aloe found in southern Africa and Namibia, is shifting its distribution, with those in the heating up northern regions dying, while others are moving south into areas that were once too cool. Similar shifts occur on mountains as warmer air moves higher, allowing lower vegetation bands to move upwards, and the higher altitude vegetation, along with its life forms, becoming unable to survive. Animals in the higher zones are seeing their environments and habitats collapse. The world's smallest plant kingdom, the fynbos of the southern Cape in South Africa, is threatened, as it cannot relocate southwards into the Indian Ocean.[256]

Well might one speak of 'climate change' as human populations throughout the planet are being made aware of the impact of the heating up of the atmosphere. Southern Canada is experiencing warmer and longer summers, allowing grain to be grown in previously inhospitable areas. In July 2021 an unprecedented 'heat dome' over south west Canada sent temperatures soaring to the upper 40 °C. Much of the frozen Siberian tundra is warming up. In Britain, winters are beginning later, and spring flowers appearing earlier, whilst in the southern parts of England the growing of grapes is being reintroduced. In southern Europe, summers are becoming hotter, with temperatures of over 40 °C now common. In northern India, maximum summer temperatures are breaking new records, with 53 °C being recorded near Delhi in 2020. Northern California has been subject to devastating forest fires as a consequence of drought and higher temperatures. Higher temperatures have led to drought conditions in parts of South Africa, where the cities of Cape Town and Gqeberha (Port Elizabeth) have had to introduce drastic water rationing. And in 2022, unusual drought conditions were experienced over much of Western Europe, leading, for example, to the near drying up of the River Rhine. Along the east coast of Australia massive rainfalls around Brisbane and Sydney led to unprecedented flooding in the winter of 2022. In early July 2022 parts of Sydney received 880 millimetres of rain in three days, the average rainfall for an entire year, whereas in the early summer months of November and December parts of New South Wales experienced dreadful droughts.

In the Gaian system the function of the forests and woodlands is to take carbon dioxide out of the air, which cools the atmosphere. Mists above the forests further cool the air. As humans destroy forests, for example in the Amazon, these carbon reducing and cooling effects are removed. And much of the wood harvested is burnt, returning to the atmosphere carbon taken out of the air by the Gaian system over millions of years. Once gone, the forest soils, hitherto kept moist and cool by the tree cover, dry out and heat up, releasing vast amounts of carbon stored in the soils as bacteria get to work more energetically. This is another positive feedback loop: green forest cover once reflected back the heat; dark soils now absorb heat, accelerating the heating process. The view of the planet from space shows green turning to brown. Green plants on the forest floors that used to absorb carbon dioxide can no longer do so. As weather becomes hotter, mosquitoes extend their range, bringing with them malaria and yellow fever to places that have never seen them before.

Our tragedy is that contemporary human civilisation, and our ability to feed 8 billion people, depends on a system of industrial production that depends on the burning of coal and oil. We *have* to heat the atmosphere for our way of life to continue. At the Asia-Pacific Partnership for Clean Development and Climate held in Australia in January 2006 the dilemma was summed up by the then Australian prime minister, John Howard: 'Our societies require of us that we find solutions to these issues that maintain the momentum of economic growth.'[257]

International meetings to discuss ways of reducing carbon emissions have been held regularly since the first at Rio de Janeiro in 1992. In the early 1990s a United Nations negotiating structure was established called the Framework Convention on Climate Change. This involves several high level international meetings, the main ones being the COP (Conferences of the Parties) meetings. One of the first COP meetings, in Kyoto in 1997, involved 'protocols' that were sent back to the parliaments of the countries attending to agree on and sign. Others followed: at Milan in 2003, Montreal in 2005, Durban in 2011, Paris in 2015, and Glasgow in 2021.

The first problem with the COP meetings is that some countries, such as the United States and Australia – among the worst carbon emitters – refuse to sign up to cutback agreements, or do so reluctantly with no follow-through back at home. A second is that the reductions in output that are agreed upon cannot be enforced and are not properly monitored, so that not only are emissions reductions not met, but emissions actually increase. A third is that it seems only fair that countries chronologically behind in their industrialisation should be allowed to emit more carbon for the time being compared to countries that industrialised much earlier. This has led to various schemes for 'carbon credits' in which heavy polluters pay not-so-heavy polluters to continue as they are.

The more fundamental problem is the lack of acceptance of the crisis and the lack of political will to carry out the commitments agreed upon. There are now, it is true, innumerable public and private initiatives to do something about global heating. Greenpeace and Extinction Rebellion do their best. The media are full of suggestions about how individuals can lower their personal carbon footprints (although right-wing media invariably label those who fight against climate change as leftwingers). Groups organising action to combat climate change are up against corporate interests allied to the oil and coal producers who pay think tanks and front groups to push the other way. Such groups include BP's Global Climate Coalition, dedicated to oil exploration in regions freed up from ice, for example in Alaska and northern Canada. Amongst climate scientists virtually 100% say the situation is critical; but when the issue is discussed in the corporate-owned media, it is framed as a 'debate', with about 45% of participants claiming there is no climate problem. Right-wing governments deny global heating is happening.

As one of the lead authors of the 2018 IPCC report, Raymond Pierrehumbert, wrote in August 2019: 'Let's get this on the table right away, without mincing words. With regard to the climate crisis, yes, it's time to panic. We are in deep trouble...There's no plan B. We must move to zero-net carbon emissions, and fast.'

Yet an effective global alliance of the planet's nations to carry through a species response to a species crisis is difficult to imagine.[258]

## 19. The Current Mass Extinction

There have been six major extinction events in the 3.8 billion years since the beginning of life on Earth.[259] The first was the decimation of single cell life as a result of the oxygen crisis around 2 billion BP. Since multi-celled life started around 700 million BP, there have been a further five extinctions in which high percentages of the Earth's life system were wiped out. The first was the Ordovician extinction around 440 million BP, the second the late Devonian extinction around 370 million BP, and the third, the most brutal, the Permian-Triassic extinction around 250 million BP, which destroyed around 90% of the planet's marine life and 70% of land-dwelling vertebrates. The fourth, the Triassic-Jurassic extinction, of around 200 million BP, killed off high percentages of both marine and land life. All these extinctions were rooted in natural causes – still being debated – such as falling sea levels or volcanic eruptions. The fifth, the Cretaceous-Paleogene event around 60 million BP, which destroyed 30%-40% of life, is thought to have been caused by the planet being hit by an asteroid. This coincided with the extinction of the dinosaurs and enabled the evolutionary rise of small mammals from which we are descended.[260]

The extinction we are now experiencing, the sixth, is the first to be caused by the activities of a single species within the life system. Humans are now a 'geophysical force, the first species in the history of the planet to attain that dubious distinction,' writes E.O. Wilson. 'How much extinction is occurring today?' he asks: 'Researchers generally agree that it is catastrophically high, somewhere between one thousand and ten thousand times the rate before humans began to exert a significant pressure on the environment.' And it is happening at unprecedented speed, faster than all the other extinctions.[261]

There are various drivers of the current extermination.[262] First, our population increase. As the human species reaches eight billion, we occupy huge swathes of the environment for our cities, roads, mines, plantations, and fields for cultivation and cattle. That is, we destroy the habitats of other animals and insects. Secondly, we kill other animals on a giant scale for food, the pet trade, sport, and 'to get them away'.

Thirdly we introduce alien species from one part of the world to another, frequently with deleterious effects; alien plants, trees, ants, rats, pigs, cats and snakes have devastated life on islands in particular. Jared Diamond refers to a fourth driver, what he calls 'ripple effects'. For example, if you get rid of wolves in a national park the deer will proliferate and destroy the woodland on which other animals depend. Amphibians are particularly vulnerable to being killed unintentionally by the ripple effects of pollution, drought, global heating, chemical pollution and fungi.[263]

The onslaught of *Homo sapiens* on the natural environment and wildlife, at least the multi-celled organisms, is so massive it is difficult to know where to begin to describe it. Our species' career as a killer, both of other animals and ourselves, goes back the whole two hundred thousand or so years since we evolved.

The growing consensus of specialists is that 'man' brought about the megafaunal (large animal) extinctions in the 50,000 thousand years before agriculture, especially around 11,000 to 9,000 years BP – the Pleistocene epoch at the end of the last glaciation. Initially it had been thought that the end of large animals, such as the mastodon and mammoth, was linked to the advances and retreats of the ice, but the ample evidence of the slaughter of large animals left in human middens suggests otherwise. In the thousands of years after humans moved into Australia around 70,000 BP, 85% of the large marsupial animals disappeared, with plenty of their bones found in human middens. This included giant kangaroos and a type of lion. Among the large animals that disappeared at the time of the human expansion into central and southern America were the deinotherium, the platypus-like glyptodont, and the woolly mammoth. E.O. Wilson comments: 'Humanity, when wiping out biodiversity, eats its way down the food chain. The first to go among animal species are the big, the slow, and the tasty. As a rule around the world, wherever people entered a virgin environment, most of the megafauna soon vanished.'[264]

In New Zealand, many of the big animals went extinct in the three or four hundred years after the arrival of the Maoris around 1000 CE. The first European arrivals in the 1770s found only their bones, including the bones of several species of ostrich-like moas ranging from three to ten feet high and from 40 to 500 pounds in weight. Not just the moa had disappeared: also a large duck, a giant coot, a giant goose, a massive eagle, a pelican and a raven. Diamond writes: 'It would have been an incredible coincidence if every individual of dozens of species that had occupied New Zealand for millions of years chose the precise geological moment of human arrival as the occasion to drop dead in synchrony.'[265] Maoris killed, cut up, and ate 'prodigious numbers of moas', using their egg shells as water containers. The number of moa skeletons found at Maori encampments has been estimated at between 100,000 and 500,000. The rats that accompanied the Maoris to New Zealand undertook their own massacres of smaller species, including snails, crickets, wrens and bats.

Similar events took place in Hawaii in the years after the arrival of Polynesians around 500 CE.[266] At least fifty species of birds disappeared between then and the arrival of Europeans in the later eighteenth century. Hawaiian geese were hunted for food; other bird species had their habitats destroyed by human agriculture, and once again rats added to the carnage. Wilson writes: 'What we celebrate in the colonization of Polynesia as a grand historical epic for humanity, was for the rest of life a rolling wave of destruction.'[267] The same themes occur throughout the Pacific after human arrival: in Tahiti, Fiji, the Solomon Islands, the Bismarck Archipelago. Even the very remote Henderson Island in the eastern Pacific had Polynesian settlements whose members killed off at least six island bird species for food: '[they] evidently subsisted mainly on pigeons, seabirds and fish until they had decimated the bird populations, at which point they had destroyed their food supply and either starved or else abandoned the island.'[268]

On the Indian Ocean island of Madagascar we find a similar story. On this large island, separated from Africa by a 200-mile sea channel, there had evolved very different animals and plants from the African mainland. Among them were several species of gigantic ostrich/moa-like birds up to ten feet tall, the largest birds ever known to have lived, whose enormous eggs and bones led to their being termed elephant birds. Also on Madagascar there were several species of giant tortoise, a dozen species of giant lemur, a species of miniature hippo, an aardvark, and an enormous mongoose almost as large as a small leopard. After the arrival of the Malagasy humans around 2,000 BP these all disappeared. The once-held opinion that this was an evolutionary coincidence is absurd. The elephant birds were butchered for their meat; their giant eggs were eaten, and the shells used by humans for containers. 'Certainly some and probably all of Madagascar's vanished giants were somehow exterminated by the activities of the early Malagasy,' Diamond writes. He adds: 'By the time that the Portuguese arrived, Madagascar's once abundant elephant birds had all been reduced to eggshells covering the beaches, skeletons in the ground, and vague memories of rocs [in the tales of Sinbad the Sailor].'[269] Destruction of the forests for crop fields finished off other species, including several species of tortoise. Human-introduced cattle, dogs, pigs and rats completed the destruction.

The musket, and its development into the rifle, was a disaster for large animals. After 1500, wherever Europeans arrived with firearms, the destruction accelerated. European explorers, after shooting food for the pot, became addicted to the pure fun of hunting and shooting. 'Scientific' expeditions from the 1700s also demanded the shooting of specimens of both birds and animals.

But even more destructive than hunting has been the destruction or alteration of habitats. Agricultural activity, along with the building of towns and cities, destroys habitat. Human introduction of predators and viruses has also contributed to the destruction. By the 2060s, human population expansion will have consumed virtually the entire planetary photosynthate and animal species will be confined to zoos. By that time, Wilson warns, we will be living in profound regret, 'an age of loneliness', because of the extinctions and near extinctions we have and will have brought about.[270]

Let us look at some individual species that have been wiped out by humans, starting with birds. I mention a few examples here, but there are many more. Dutch mariners arrived in Mauritius for the first time in 1598 to find a flourishing dodo population. The dodo was a large, flightless bird, unwisely tame to intruders. By the 1640s the dodo had been virtually wiped out after being hunted for food by humans, and the rats, pigs and monkeys they introduced. By the 1660s it was extinct.[271]

Another flightless bird that inhabited islands in the North Atlantic in their breeding season was the great auk. Its large size made it a target for food for Europeans as they sailed across the Atlantic in the seventeenth and eighteenth centuries. The huge colony of auks off the coast of Newfoundland had been virtually wiped out by the end of the eighteenth century, the remaining birds retreating to a few islands off the coast of Iceland. 'Hungry sailors feasted on the defenceless creatures and discovered that not only did they provide a handy food source, but also their feathers and the oil from their bodies were very useful commodities.' The last birds were killed by sailors on the island of Eldey during 1843 and 1844. In subsequent decades, the feathers, skins and skeletons of the great auk were much sought after by collectors and museums.[272]

It was not just island birds. The story of the destruction of North America's passenger pigeon is almost unbelievable. This columbine dove occupied the deciduous woodland regions of North America, and its flocks of millions would cut out light from the sun for two or three days. It may well have been the most numerous bird on Earth. According to a writer in 1759: 'big as well as little trees...sometimes covering a distance of 7 English miles, became so filled with them that hardly a twig or a branch could be seen which they did not cover...when they alighted on the trees their weight was so heavy that not only big limbs and branches were broken straight off, but less firmly rooted trees broke down completely under the load.' Apparently these flights made the birds so easy to shoot with guns that hunters established shooting competitions based on quantity – for a prize one had to kill 30,000 birds. The trees supplying the pigeons with food – beechnuts, acorns and chestnuts – were reduced as farming spread, and the scouting capacity of the birds declined as their numbers were shot out. There was a massive decline in the 1870s (the same time that Native Americans were being wiped out by the US army), and an outbreak of Newcastle's disease hastened the end. The last individual, a female passenger pigeon named Martha, died in the Cincinnati Zoo on 1 September 1914.[273]

Other species of bird have been eliminated as a result of habitat destruction. One example is the ivory-billed woodpecker. This magnificent bird inhabited the deciduous forests of Louisiana, Florida and Cuba. It nested in large dead trees, feeding on wood-boring beetles. 'Destruction and fragmentation of its habitat caused massive decline in numbers,' notes the *Handbook of the Birds of the World*, and by the 1940s very few were left. The last confirmed sighting was in the 1950s, although birders are still dreaming of coming across survivors.[274]

Other birds to suffer from the reduction of their habitat and environment include the Philippines eagle, the largest eagle on the planet in length and wingspan, and the harpy eagle, the largest in weight and bulk. The Philippines eagle has declined drastically as its forest habitat has been destroyed by logging companies. Despite being named the Philippines' national bird and appearing on the nation's stamps, it is critically endangered, with only around 600 remaining in the wild. The harpy eagle inhabits the rain forests of central and northern South America. Along with the Philippines eagle and the African crowned eagle it is one of the most powerful of all eagles, with monkeys and macaws amongst its prey. Although it is the national bird of Panama, most of its range is threatened by logging, cattle ranching, agriculture and prospecting. Its large size and fearless behaviour around human settlements make it an irresistible target for hunters. The CITES (Convention on International Trade in Endangered Species) organisation lists it as 'threatened with extinction'.

Globally the whole family of fifteen crane (*Grus*) species faces difficulties, four of them facing imminent extinction.[275] The shallow water areas needed by most cranes are damaged by human settlement, dams, sewage and other pollution, as well as drought. In southern Africa wattled cranes, which depend on shallow waters for their feeding, have been severely reduced in number. The most threatened cranes are the Siberian crane, the red-crowned crane of the far east, and the whooping crane of North America. The beautiful Siberian crane's migratory patterns have made them vulnerable to being shot by hunters when flying over Afghanistan to avoid the high Himalayas. Encroachments on their breeding grounds by farmers worsen matters. Similarly, the red-crowned crane, which has its wintering grounds in Hokkaido in Japan. It is Japan's national bird, but as we have seen with other countries, this status does nothing to halt its decline. The red-crowned crane and other species of crane have created a temporary reprieve for themselves by discovering the region abandoned by humans in the demilitarized zone between the two Koreas.

The whooping crane was down to its last dozen or so birds before being at least temporarily saved from extinction by keen crane enthusiasts. Its long migratory flights from central-north Canada to the gulf coast of Texas and Louisiana exposed it to being shot by hunters, along with losses from egg collectors and the draining of marshland habitats for rice cultivation. Crane preservation organisations in the US have tried everything to keep the species alive, including, in the past two decades, taking 'spare' eggs from breeding pairs and giving them over to the relatively more common sandhill crane.

The same fate is overtaking the family of albatrosses. Of the twenty-two species three are 'critically endangered', five are 'endangered', seven are 'near threatened', and seven are 'vulnerable'. These magnificent, legendary birds have the longest wing spans of any birds, and roam the oceans looking for krill and other fish. Early sailors hunted them for food, and also for their wing bones, which they turned into tobacco pipes or flutes. Towards the end of the nineteenth century, demand for their thick coats of feathers led to breeding colonies being raided and slaughtered.

Over a million short-tailed albatrosses were killed in the northern Pacific by plume hunters between the 1880s and the early twentieth century. Their main breeding grounds were off Japan, where despite prohibition by the Japanese government, the killing continued into the 1930s, when only around 1500 birds remained. This number dropped even lower after one of the islands on which the birds bred experienced volcanic eruptions in 1939 and 1941, until the short-tailed albatross was thought to be extinct. But a few survived, and by the 1980s numbers had climbed to three or four hundred. In 1957 Japan declared the bird a Special National Monument.

Despite international efforts to sustain albatross populations, the overall situation worsens year by year. Many albatrosses are killed as a result of collisions with aircraft, and many that nest on remote islands have their nests raided by human-introduced cats, rats and mice or destroyed by fires. The major threat in the past half century has been long-line fishing, with an estimated 100,000 birds a year getting hooked and drowned after ingesting fishing hooks and plastics. This includes many of the largest species of albatross, the wandering albatross and the southern royal. Although legal commercial fisheries do their best to sink the fishing lines, increasing numbers of illegal fisheries off southern America take no precautions and kill a lot of albatrosses and other birds. Laysan albatrosses are killed every year in Japanese gill nets.

Let us turn now to the large mammals, again mentioning just a few examples. Among those threatened by a combination of human encroachment and poaching are the five species of rhinoceros. The Javan and Sumatran rhinos are both down to below 100 individuals left in the wild, and the Indian rhino down to under 4,000. In Africa the black (or pointed-nose) rhino is today reduced to about 5,000 individuals, whilst the white (or square-lipped) rhino, once on the verge of extinction, has recovered to around 20,000 individuals after intensive conservation efforts.[276]

Throughout the penetration of Africa by Europeans, rhinos were shot for food and as trophies by hunters, traders and missionaries. Rhino horn powder fetches high prices in the Far East because of the belief that it has aphrodisiac and other medical properties, although the keratin which forms the rhino horns has no medicinal value. A systematic attempt is now being made to remove the horns of rhinos to help ensure the animals' safety. Africa's rhinos, once shot in large numbers by European explorers and missionaries, are increasingly confined to game reserves, and even here park ranger teams do not always have the manpower to head off highly paid and well equipped poachers who shoot a rhino and hack off its horn, leaving the animal dead or dying. Despite armed guards, individuals are regularly killed. In Kenya the last remaining individual of the northern white rhino subspecies has to be guarded around the clock by two armed rangers. Local politicians are often found to be linked to the international syndicates and gangs organising the poaching. The African civil wars of recent decades have given rise to guerrilla groups who shoot rhinos and elephants routinely to help finance their arms supplies.[277]

Indian and African elephants are similarly threatened by a combination of human population expansion, ivory poaching, and political breakdown. Indian elephants are down to around 50,000 individuals and are listed as endangered. The African elephant (both the savannah and forest subspecies) once roamed the continent in huge numbers, estimated in the early 1930s at 10 million. In recent decades their numbers have collapsed catastrophically, by over 95%, to just over 400,000 individuals. They remain best preserved in the game parks of South Africa, Namibia and Botswana. Their main attraction for poachers is for their ivory tusks, which command big money on international markets.

Richard Leakey in Kenya took up the directorship of the Kenya Wildlife Service in 1991 in order to do something about the killing of Kenya's elephants. He writes: 'I had seen countless corpses of poacher's victims: great, grey bodies lying bloated under the hot sun, the white excreta of vultures spelling the story of death on their backs...Worst of all was their faces, transformed from majestic visage into bloody pulp within a few seconds as poachers ripped off their tusks with axes or chain saws. It was a truly sickening and emotion-roiling sight. Add to this the common occurrence of an emaciated, perplexed infant pathetically trying to arouse its murdered mother, and the rational urge to put an end to the slaughter became an emotional obsession.' In July 1989 Leakey was able to get President Moi of Kenya to stage a publicity event with the setting alight of 2,500 elephant tusks, rather than selling them off for US$ 3 million to help finance Kenya's Wildlife Conservation Department.[278]

The problem of ivory poaching is compounded by the confining of elephant herds into reserves such as Tsavo in Kenya, Hwange in Zimbabwe, or Kruger Park in South Africa. Though large, these reserves are inadequately sized. Experts have different views on how to keep elephants safe. Many 'realists' advocate regular culling programmes, whilst those who disagree, such as Leakey, argue they should be left to roam without any interference. Elephant habitat in Africa has been reduced by 50% since the late 1970s (in India by 85%). The 'great elephant count' in 2016 found only around 352,000 African savannah elephants left. The increasing incidence of drought in Africa has made things more precarious, as the animals are driven to starvation.[279]

Another endangered mammal is the largest animal ever to have existed, the blue whale, *Balaenoptera musculus*, which can grow to over 30 metres long, and weigh up to 170 tons, in separate northern and southern hemisphere populations. Because of their size and speed they were difficult for whalers to kill. This changed with the invention of the exploding harpoon gun by the Norwegian, Svend Foyn, in 1864, and the development of the California whaling rocket by the American, Robert L. Suits, in 1877. Thereafter blue whale populations began to be decimated. Around 350,000 were slaughtered in the first half of the twentieth century, at least 29,000 in 1931 alone. Their survival became precarious after the development of factory ship whaling in 1954. In 1966 the International Whaling Commission banned all blue whale hunting, but, despite the ban, the Soviet Union and Spain continued blue whale hunting well into the 1970s. Norwegian whalers still kill blue whales in the guise of 'scientific research'. In the late twentieth century global numbers recovered partially to 20,000, but by 2015 blue whale numbers had again declined to somewhere between 5,000 and 15,000 individuals worldwide. They are now formally recognised as endangered under the Endangered Species Act, and as 'depleted' under the Marine Mammal Protection Act. Their only natural enemies are killer whales (orcas) – many blue whales have scars from killer whale attacks.

Even though hunting blue whales is banned, population attrition still takes place due to strikes by ships, especially in busy shipping channels like off the western coast of the United States, and off Sri Lanka in the Indian Ocean. Eleven blue whales were killed by ship strikes off Sri Lanka between 2010 and 2012, and another two in 2014. Others have been killed off the coast of Chile. It is hoped that these killings can be reduced by better 'predictive models of whale distribution' and 'dynamic management of shipping lanes'. But there are other threats. Blue whales feed mainly on krill – a single whale is able to take in over 200 tons of krill-laden water in one lunge. Climate change is affecting krill availability as oceans warm, and become more acidic. Another problem (for all whale species, indeed all marine life) is plastic pollution. Whales ingest plastic, particularly plastic bags, and every year around 300,000 whales, dolphins and sharks die a slow death after becoming accidentally entangled in nets and lines. Similar attrition is happening to the populations of Fin, North Atlantic and Bow whales, all of which are critically endangered.

And the tiger? The number of tigers left in the wild has been reduced from an estimated 100,000 around 1900 to between three and four thousand today (with two or three times that number alive in zoos and other forms of captivity). Tigers once ranged from the Turkish Caucasus in the west, through Afghanistan and Tibet, much of India, Burma, Thailand, Laos, China, southern Siberia and the Amur region, as well as Indonesia. Today the tiger has become extinct in southern China and is found only in parts of India, and patches of territory in other regions. The dignitaries of the British Raj together with the Indian princes used to hold regular tiger shooting parties. The British civil servant Jim Corbett wrote a popular series of books on hunting man-eating tigers. He relates his disgust at the huge numbers of the animals shot by wealthy Indians in the 1930s, which led him to giving up his rifle for a camera.

Tigers can turn on humans if injured or unable to tackle their normal prey, which happens increasingly, given their shrinking territories. In India only about 11% of the tiger's original territory remains, mostly confined to wildlife reserves. With its natural prey reduced, the tiger will turn to killing livestock, provoking drastic retaliation. In the 1970s, the Indian prime minister, Indira Gandhi, set up *Project Tiger* for the preservation of tigers. This effort increased the number of Bengal tigers from around 1,200 in the 1970s to over 3,000 in the 1990s, but by 2007 the numbers had declined to 1,200 again. Any breakdown in human politics is bad news for the tiger. In Soviet Siberia concerted attempts to raise the decimated tiger population above 100 at first seemed to be succeeding, but the small numbers declined further after the collapse of the Soviet Union in 1991. The Chinese communist administration only slowly came round to supporting efforts to conserve the tiger, and had by the 1990s banned trade in tiger body parts, and signed the CITES treaty. In China there are now a number of tiger farms where the animal is bred for profit, to meet the continued (although now illegal) demand. Despite this, the black market trade in tiger body parts continues, and poachers are actively killing wild tigers.

Another two prominent mammal species facing extermination are our closest evolutionary relatives, gorillas and chimpanzees.[280] Two species of gorilla – the western and eastern (each with two subspecies) – inhabit areas in western and eastern Congo, and both are under considerable threat, with all four subspecies designated 'critically endangered'. The primary cause is a deadly combination of huge human population increase and political breakdown. Forests are destroyed as human settlements increase. The expanding road systems built for loggers enable hunters with guns to move in, and gorillas are killed for 'bushmeat'. Although the hunting, trading and eating of gorillas is illegal, breakdown of political authority and corruption often render the laws useless. Gorilla meat is openly sold in urban markets, and is regarded as a delicacy, and authorities turn a blind eye to illegal poaching. Infant gorillas are also captured for sale to zoos. The mountain subspecies of the eastern gorilla is the most threatened, its numbers having shrunk to about 700 individuals inhabiting only eight Virunga volcanoes on the borders of Uganda, the Congo and Rwanda, as well as the Bwindi Impenetrable National Park in Uganda. Park rangers protecting gorillas are occasionally killed by poachers.

The number of chimpanzees, in 1900 thought to be one million, had been by 2020 reduced to below 250,000 and the chimpanzee is now officially an endangered species. As with gorillas, the combination of human population increase, the quest for bushmeat, and the opening up of the forests of central Africa by logging companies has led to their mass slaughter. Road building fragments chimpanzee social groups, and human penetration brings diseases. Chimps are also taken for the pet trade and zoos. Federally funded medical research units in the United States use chimpanzees in medical experiments, in which many die. Notes Jared Diamond: 'The ethical dilemma posed by animal experiments is compounded for chimps by the fact that they are endangered as a species. In this case medical research not only kills individuals but threatens to kill the species itself.'[281]

One last list in this tragic litany of extinction is that of marine and river animals. 'It is time,' writes Ellen Pikitch, 'to replace the old myth of the sea's inexhaustibility with understanding of the fragile and limited nature of ocean dwellers. Already, dozens of marine animals have been pushed beyond the point of no return, gone for all time. Still more are critically endangered.'[282] As for the fish, which our species hunts remorselessly, Jared Diamond notes: 'Sadly...the majority of the world's commercially important marine fisheries have already either collapsed to the point of being commercially extinct, have been severely depleted, are currently overfished or fished to the limit.'[283] The ocean cod is an example. It was once assumed that the populations of cod were infinite, yet, after the 1950s, the coming of the factory ship and the development of motorised fishing nets, had reduced their numbers by 90% by the year 2000. In the 1990s severely reduced fishing quotas were imposed. Populations by that time had plunged, and traditional fishing expeditions became pointless. It was the same for haddock, mackerel and other fish.

All large fish eaten by humans are being hunted to virtual extinction.

Another casualty has been the sturgeon as a result of the popularity of caviar – the eggs of a single sturgeon can command a price of over $1 million. Various species of croaker fish are now protected by the CITES treaty. The swim bladders of these fish, known as 'soft gold', are used in traditional Chinese medicine.[284] Around a quarter of the global species of sharks are also threatened. The great white shark, for example, is killed as a potential man-eater, and for its jawbone, which can command up to US$ 50,000.

One consequence of the destruction of fish has been the rapid rise of jellyfish in the oceans. Some of the species, such as the box jellyfish, are deadly to humans, and are flourishing as a consequence of warming waters, pollution, and a reduction in the fish that compete with them for food. With around 90% of the oceans' fish gone, jellyfish are flourishing. Species that feed off young jellyfish, such as sea turtles, are fast disappearing. Perhaps this is a harbinger of the Gaian system fighting back. A lethal combination of predator collapse, fertilizer run-off from rivers to the sea and warming waters has created dead zones, for example at the mouth of the Mississippi River, where even jellyfish are absent.

One could continue this list of threatened species indefinitely. Amphibian extinctions continue to increase every decade, such as the Golden Toad of Costa Rica, whose populations have disappeared as a result of habitat destruction and drought. Dozens of species of frogs, toads and salamanders are extinct or threatened. Endangered snakes include the Albany adder of South Africa's eastern Cape. The short-nosed sea snake is critically endangered. The Antiguan racer snake, once common on the islands of Antigua and Barbados, has been driven to near extinction by the introduction of rats, cats and mongooses by humans.

How should we conclude? Our species, *Homo sapiens*, has the dubious distinction of being the first animal species to bring about a mass extinction. Given our likely growth of population to 11 billion by the 2060s, as well as the likely further development in our technical ability to destroy forests, expand cities, and consume a greater proportion of the planetary photosynthate, it is difficult to see how this extinction is going to stop. E.O. Wilson warns that we are about to enter a new geological era: the eremozoic – 'the age of loneliness'.[285]

An optimistic conclusion is impossible, much as it is our human nature to want it. One of the few writers to face the reality has been Derrick Jensen in his book *A Language Older Than Words:* 'As a long-time environmentalist, I am deeply acquainted with the language of loss, and have grown accustomed to carrying the daily weight of despair. When it comes to our relationship with nature, there is little to feel good about. A happy reckoning of this relationship would not only be dishonest, it would be unworthy of the subject matter, of the great runs of salmon we're destroying, of the billions of chickens forced to live miserable lives, of the beautiful forests our children will never see. If the salmon or the forests could write a book, what would it be like? More to the point, if we were to take the time to listen to what they might already be saying, do you think their stories would be cheery or bright? Yet that is precisely what the public discourse demands. I cannot count the number of times I've been commissioned to write environmental pieces, and the editors have said to me, "Make sure it's positive". Never once has an editor said, "Make sure the piece is honest". Before we can fix our troubled relationship with nature, we must be willing to look at it...If I were to be honest, it could only be a cry of outrage, a lamentation, and at the same time a love story about that which is and that which was and is no longer.'[286]

## 20. Genocides

*Homo sapiens* not only kills other animals but, more than any animal, indulges in frequent acts of self-killing on a very large scale. Although our evolutionary relatives, chimpanzees and gorillas, occasionally kill their own species, human self-killing is on an altogether different scale and is a regular and central feature of our behaviour. Especially during the twentieth century, as global populations increased and our technological capacity for killing improved, incidences of mass self-killing increased, and so did the number of people killed in each 'event'. Yet historians have never made it the central theme in any overview of history. My well-taught courses in Military History at King's College, London University, in the 1960s looked at warfare from every conceivable angle except the angle that its central activity is the organised killing of humans. It is often implied that killing one another is an embarrassing abnormality – but one that we can educate or moralise ourselves out of.

Nevertheless, 'wars' and 'self-massacres' have been central features of our behaviour throughout history, and it is unlikely that we will stop. Some self-killing episodes are definable as 'wars' whilst others are definable as 'genocides'. Reviews of Martin Shaw's *War and Genocide* characteristically note: 'the generally legitimate business of war and the monstrous crime of genocide are closely related.' The distinction, however, given the results – mass slaughter and reduction of population – is problematic. Until the Nazi massacre of Jewish people during the Second World War, indeed, no distinction was made,[287] and there is still no clear formal definition that clarifies the difference between a 'war' and a 'genocide'.

A genocide, though, is when a state orders the massacre of a group of people, whether its own population or foreign people under its control, because they belong to a group that the state for one reason or another has made it a policy to eliminate and kill. In certain cases a genocide may be part of a war (as in the Armenian massacres of 1915), whilst in others, a war or civil war may be integral to a genocide (as in the 1994 Rwandan case). Whether a genocide, a war, or the two combined, however, we are dealing with the systematic and organised killing of one group or state's people by another, and such events are integral and normal aspects of human behaviour

There are innumerable examples in the historical record. A mass grave north of Vienna near Schletz indicates that early Neolithic groups engaged in mass self-killing around 5,000 BP. In the fourth century CE a civil war in China, the Wei-Jie war, led to the massacre of over 100,000 of the Jie. In the early thirteenth century the Catholic pope ordered the extermination of religious dissidents known as the Cathars in southern France – 'one of the most conclusive cases of genocide in religious history', according to Raphael Lemkin. Also in the thirteenth century groups of Mongols were massacred during the depredations of Genghis Khan. Around 20,000 people were killed in Magdeburg in 1631 when the Catholic army of Tilly broke into the Protestant city, and slaughtered and burnt the citizens, including cutting off the heads of over fifty women.

During the European colonial conquests there were innumerable acts of deliberate massacre of 'native' peoples, such as the wiping out of Tasmanians by Australian white invaders in the early 1800s, the hunting down of San (Bushmen) by Boer and British invaders in southern Africa also in the early 1800s, the slaughter of Xhosa groups by the British army in the eastern Cape in the frontier war of 1852, the wiping out of large percentages of North America's 'Indians' in the later decades of the nineteenth century, and the massacres of Herero in Namaqualand by German colonists in 1905-06 (the Germans finally apologised in 2021). European colonial writers referred to genocidal attacks as frontier 'wars' or Indian 'wars'.

The twentieth century saw such massacres increase both in frequency and in the number of victims: some defined as wars others as genocides.[288] The First and Second World Wars between them saw at least 100 million deaths. During the First World War the massacres of the Armenians by the Turks in 1915 is definable as a genocide, whereas the slaughter of men at Verdun and the Somme in 1916 is regarded by historians as part of a war. Mass killings in the interlude between the First and Second World War included those in the Spanish civil war of 1936-39, and the Japanese massacres of Chinese in Nanking in December 1937. With the development of the atomic bomb it became possible to kill 100,000 people with a single order from the US president, killings that were then and subsequently justified as being militarily necessary. Was that an act of war, or part of a genocidal onslaught on the Japanese people?

Stalin's killings in the Soviet Union during the 1930s and 1940s included at least three million famine victims in Ukraine during the forced collectivisation of 1932-33, when Soviet military and NKVD troops rounded up peasants who refused to hand over their farms, and shot them or deported them to regions in Siberia. Millions of people died in the gulag camps after being rounded up for forced labour in mining, the digging of canals, or the cutting down of forests: they were deliberately worked to death and starved in appalling conditions. Many other Russians were killed in the purges of the later 1930s.[289] An estimated 25 million more Russians, mostly men, died in the 1941-45 war against the Nazis, amongst whom were many taken prisoner by the Germans and starved to death in camps. Hitler's regime made no secret of their intent to depopulate Ukraine and replace Ukrainians with Germans. By the 1950s there was a noticeable shortage of men in the Soviet Union compared to the number of women. Some of the victims were casualties of war, others of genocidal state policy, whether Nazi or Stalinist.

The mass killing of Jewish people of Europe by Hitler's Nazis, that reflected the centrality of antisemitism in Nazi thinking, is unambiguously a genocide. The death camps at Treblinka, Sobibor, Auschwitz and Chelmno were factories for the killing of certain defined groups of people, something new in history. The methods had been pioneered in asylums inside Germany where, after 1939, the mentally ill and those with certain types of hereditary illness – who were 'a financial burden on the state' – were killed. Noteworthy in these genocides is the overall acquiescence of the German people despite all their education and culture.[290] Many Germans approved of the killings, and many benefitted from the redistribution of Jewish property. Those who disapproved, or were not terribly aware, found themselves living in a modern militarised state with an efficient secret police; what could any individual actually do? The same applied in Soviet Russia during the 1930s, where the entire population lived in fear of arrest by the NKVD. Christopher Browning notes: 'Everywhere society conditions people to respect and defer to authority. In every modern society the complexity of life and the resulting bureaucratization and specialization attenuate the sense of personal responsibility of those implementing official policy.'[291]

In the seventy years since 1945, there have been innumerable genocides and mass killings. Some took place during the cold war, in which the United States and its allies backed anti-communist groups against governments attempting social-democratic policies (Indonesia 1965; Chile 1973). Other genocides were linked to the United States' disastrous war in Vietnam (Cambodia 1975-78). Others were partly or wholly rooted in the unthought-through decolonisation policies of the British, French and Belgians (Uganda 1983-85; Rwanda 1994). Massive killings in Mao's China in the 1950s and 1960s, while not strictly speaking genocides, were the outcome of absurd and utopian economic strategies that failed.

Some of Mengistu's actions in Ethiopia between 1975 and the mid-1980s verge on the genocidal, including the deliberate starvation of peasantry and the massacre of political opponents. The killing of thousands of 'leftists' by Pinochet's regime in Chile after 1973 and the military junta in Argentina between 1976 and 1983 are further examples. The slaughter of many thousands of Ndebele people in south-west Zimbabwe by the Shona armies of Mugabe's ZANU-PF was a genocide in which a majority ethnic group slaughtered members of a minority ethnic group. In 1995, during the civil wars that engulfed the disintegrating Yugoslavia, the murder of 8,000 Bosnian male Muslims by Bosnian Serbs with the support of the Serbian army in and around Srebrenica was genocide. The massacre of two or three hundred thousand Christian Africans by the Muslim Sudanese army and Arab Janjaweed forces in Darfur from 2003 onwards is sometimes referred to as the first genocide of the twenty-first century.

Whether other recent events can be called genocides or wars with genocidal aspects, is arguable. The fact is that hundreds of thousands of people have lost their lives during the United States' operations in Iraq and Afghanistan in the two decades since the 2001 attacks on New York's twin towers; unknown numbers of people have been killed in Russia's military operations in the Caucasus region to prevent the secession of various groups and in the ongoing invasions of Ukraine; and China has been responsible for the killings of Muslim groups in its far western regions, including the use of sophisticated torture and 're-education' techniques. Clearly mass killing episodes have been and continue to be routine events in human history.

The five mass killing events of the twentieth century that I focus on in this chapter are usually classified as genocides: the Ottoman massacres of Armenians in 1915; the massacres in Indonesia in 1965; the massacres in the eastern section of Pakistan in 1971; the massacres in Cambodia 1975-78; and the Rwandan mass killings in 1994. Between them, these examples illustrate the often complex causes of genocides.

The first 'pure' genocide of the twentieth century is usually regarded as the massacre of the Armenian people by the Turks in 1915. It was linked to the emergence of the modern Turkish state out of the older Ottoman Empire, which had been collapsing over many decades. Armenians occupied large areas of the Caucasus in the east and north-east of Turkey, but also lived throughout Turkey both in rural and urban areas. Unlike the Turks who were Muslim, the Armenians were Christian, and were distrusted by both the successive Ottoman and Young Turk leaderships. In the mid-1890s the Armenians had been subjected to a series of pogroms. In 1908 the Young Turks seized power and set about building the national Turkish state, which led to further friction with the Armenians. The Turks, who were mainly Muslim, entered the First World War in October 1914, fighting the Russians along the Caucasus border, and being defeated at the battle of Sarikamish in early 1915. Russian troops moved in, invading much of the region occupied by the Armenians, some of whom welcomed the Russians as liberators.

In March 1915 the Young Turk government made the decision to eliminate the allegedly pro-Russian, Christian Armenians, seize their land, and deport their populations under military escort into the deserts of today's Syria and Iraq, still then under Ottoman rule. Large scale killings of Armenians began to take place, with men and boys being shot, and women being starved, raped and sent on forced marches into the desert. The Young Turks set up a 'Special Organisation' to form killer squads to eliminate the 'Christian element' throughout the country, including in the cities. Between 1915 and the early 1920s the two million Armenians in the wider Turkish area were reduced to about 400,000.

After the surrender of Turkey in September 1918, leaders of the genocide argued that the elimination of the Christian Armenians was a necessary act in the establishment of the new Turkish state. When the exact borders between Turkey and Soviet Russia were thrashed out in complex negotiations in the early 1920s, the bulk of the Armenian area remained in Turkey, whilst the north-eastern slice was refashioned under Stalin into Soviet Armenia. The horror of the events of 1915-16 was only slowly pieced together by historians. Details, when they emerged, shocked the world.

Successive Turkish governments have refused to recognise the events as genocidal, stating that the killings were exaggerated and/or legitimate wartime actions against internal Armenian treachery for their support of Russia. Only in 2021 did the United States presidency assert unequivocally that what happened was a genocide. At its root were a combination of religious differences, the reorganisation of the Turkish state, wartime emergency, and fear of Armenian disloyalty. The Armenian mass killings were what gave rise to the term 'genocide' as coined by Raphael Lemkin in 1944.

For our second example, the mass killings in Indonesia during 1965,[292] let us briefly examine the political currents that led up to it. In the early 1960s, the various constituent islands of Indonesia were under the unstable regime of President Sukarno. The 'West' saw Sukarno as unreliable, and regarded his support for the Indonesian Communist Party, the PKI, as dangerous. It was during the heart of the cold war, when the United States government, in the context of the expanding Vietnam war, believed that states could fall under communist rule one after the other. In September 1965 there was a failed coup attempt by some communist-linked soldiers in the Indonesian capital, Jakarta, which involved the assassination of a dozen army generals. The head of the army, General Suharto, with the United States and Britain's backing, used this as a pretext for a full takeover of power. Mass killings took place across the Indonesian islands of Java, Sumatra and Bali throughout October 1965, mostly of poorer people and known leftists. President Sukarno was deposed, and Suharto set himself up as a dictator. He remained in power for thirty years, a period in which killings of communists and the establishment of a dictatorship were welcomed both by the US and Britain. The British ambassador in Jakarta, Andrew Gilchrist, reported to London: 'I never concealed from you my belief that a little shooting in Indonesia would be an essential preliminary to effective change.'[293]

Estimates of the number of victims vary, but scholars today calculate a minimum of 500,000 and possibly as many as a million deaths. Most of the killings were carried out with hand weapons such as knives, machetes, and swords, rather than firearms. Bodies were thrown into rivers, and victims' houses were seized and handed over to the military. In Bali, death squads roamed the countryside for victims, given a free rein by the army. Around 80,000 Balinese were murdered in the latter months of 1965. Chinese immigrants were targeted as well, and in Sumatra immigrants from Java were killed. Devout Muslims massacred members of the communist party (the PKI) at the instigation of the army. Hundreds of thousands of political suspects were detained, and many were tortured. Women prisoners were beaten, subjected to sexual violence, and had their genitals and breasts mutilated. At the end of 1965, the United States embassy in Indonesia informed their government in Washington that the events had enabled foreign capital to return to the islands and regain control of estates, companies and mines. As for the killings, the US State Department official Howard Federspiel wrote: 'No one cared, as long as they were communists, that they were being killed.' At the United Nations only Albania issued a formal protest. In 1975 Indonesian forces repeated further genocidal operations when they invaded the East Timor islands to prevent an independent East Timor being established following the departure of the Portuguese the previous year.

Another genocidal event took place in East Pakistan during 1971, again with the tacit support of the United States.[294] The historical roots of this went back to the years 1946-48 when the British abandoned India, and India had plunged into a civil war, involving massacres of Muslims by Hindus and vice versa. Seeing their country taken over by Hindus, some Indian Muslims fled west while others fled east. The result was the creation of Pakistan in two geographical parts, separated by 1,200 miles of Indian territory. Although West Pakistan had a smaller population than East Pakistan (around 70 million compared to 120 million), its ruling Muslim elites held influence over both parts of the recently created country, and tended to look down on the Bengali Muslims in the east. The first Pakistan leader, Ali Jinnah, declared Urdu the national language, despite the fact that in the east, where Bengali and Hindu were the dominant languages, Urdu was hardly spoken.

In December 1970, when democratic elections were first held in Pakistan, the impracticality of a nation state divided into two parts a long way from each other became apparent. In the east the elections were won by the Amani League, headed by Sheik Mujibur Rahman, which demanded greater autonomy from the western part. The president, Yahya Khan, refused to accept the election results, and on 25 March 1971 the Pakistan army was sent into the east to begin a war of reconquest, which they assumed would be over quickly. The cities in East Pakistan were subdued, but the resistance continued strongly in rural areas. The city of Dhaka, the east's capital, was set alight, and fleeing citizens were machine-gunned. Hindus and Bengali speakers were shot, Hindu males being identified as anyone who was uncircumcised. Over a million Bengalis fled west across the Ganges into India. *Time* magazine reported the shelling of cities where opposition held out and quoted a United States official saying: 'It is the most incredible, calculated thing since the Nazis in Poland.' Intellectuals, students and teachers were massacred. Hospitals and places of refuge were shelled and women rounded up and herded into camps, where they were made available to the troops. An Australian doctor brought in to carry out abortions on raped women said: 'Some of the stories they told were appalling. Being raped again, again and again. A lot of them died in those rape camps.'[295]

Nixon and Kissinger in Washington saw Pakistan as an ally and distrusted India. They feared that the Indian government, led by Indira Gandhi, could align with the Soviet camp. Gandhi had called the massacres in East Pakistan a 'genocide'. Nixon is reputed to have said that the people of the US were not 'stirred up' much by the Pakistan events 'because Pakistan, they're just a bunch of brown goddam Muslims.' The Indian government strengthened troop concentrations along the borders with Pakistan, and as tensions mounted in the latter months of 1971, the Pakistan military took preemptive action and declared war on India on 2 December. This was suicidal: the war was over by late December, after which East Pakistan was established as the independent state of Bangladesh. Debates over the number of victims still continue, but the consensus is between 400,000 and one million deaths, or 0.5-1.5% of the East Pakistan population.

In Cambodia, our fourth example, an even higher proportion of the population was to die between 1975 and 1979 during the disastrous regime of the Khmer Rouge.[296] Again, the genocide had long historical roots. Cambodia had been a French colony since the 1860s, and was briefly occupied by Japan in 1944-45. It was internationally recognised as independent in 1953, when a superficially democratic system was set up in the capital, Phnom Penh, headed by the sovereign monarch King Sihanouk. For most of the next fifteen years Sihanouk spent considerable time and energy running a fake democratic system in which his own party took most of the vote and all of the seats in parliament. Right wing and leftist groups were balanced off against each other, and foreign policy steered between the US and China. Most of the country's population was rural and poor, with a small class of capitalists and traders in the towns, and echelons of intellectuals. Some of the intellectuals studied abroad, especially in France, and became leftists, strongly influenced by the ultra-Stalinist French communist party. On their return home, several became school teachers. An attempt to absorb them into the national government failed, and some of them set up the Communist Party of Kampuchea (CPK) in 1961, and began insurrections in the rural areas. Sihanouk called the CPK the red Khmers, the Khmer Rouge in French.

In early 1970 General Lon Nol seized power from the monarchy in Phnom Penh with the backing of the United States. The deposed King Sihanouk travelled to Beijing, talked with Mao's people, and formed an alliance with the leaders of the Khmer Rouge. New guerrilla actions were initiated by the Khmer Rouge, accompanied by North Vietnamese and Viet Cong incursions into the east of Cambodia in the later phases of the Vietnam War, which in turn provoked Nixon and Kissinger to authorise heavy bombing raids on east Cambodia. The United States bombing persuaded many of the eastern population of Cambodia to support the Khmer Rouge. Things were going from bad to worse for the Americans in Vietnam during the early 1970s, so any idea of sending US troops to Cambodia was not entertained. Khmer Rouge fighters gained control of most of the north-east and large areas of west and south-west Cambodia. In April 1975, just after the last US troops had left Saigon, Lon Nol's regime collapsed and Khmer Rouge guerrillas entered Phnom Penh.

The Khmer Rouge brought with them their mysterious administration known as Angka Loeu ('high organisation'). Their leaders: Saloth Sâr (known as Pol Pot), Ieng Sary, Khieu Samphan and others were middle class school teachers who had spent some of the 1950s in Paris learning Stalinist and Maoist theory and revolutionary tactics. Their aim was to smash the 'old society' and turn the country into a classless peasant society, with the poorer peasants held up as the ideal 'old people'. The 'new people' (meaning everyone else) were to be re-educated along Stalinist and Maoist lines. The Khmer Rouge troops, many of them young children with Kalashnikovs, were ordered to round up the entire population of Phnom Penh and herd them out of the city.[297] Over the next few days three million people were driven into the rural areas. At the same time the Khmer Rouge carried out massacres of civil servants, Lon Nol's soldiers, teachers, doctors, intellectuals – in fact anyone who wore glasses was killed. Hospitals were emptied out, and patients who could not move were shot. Capitalists, shopkeepers, traders, bankers, as well as students, teachers, aristocrats and property owners were killed. About 90% of the country's Buddhist priests were killed, as were most of the Vietnamese and Chinese minorities in Cambodia. A large Muslim sector of the population, the Chams Khmer, were also murdered. The stated object of all the killing was to create a new society and begin economic development afresh.

Those allowed to live were herded into camps and ordered to begin agriculture collectively, without proper equipment.[298] Medical facilities collapsed; people suspected of not working or theft or sabotage were taken to killing sites and, to save bullets, battered to death by young Khmer Rouge cadres with picks, knives, spades, and bludgeons. The wives and children of victims were forced to watch, and were then themselves killed, small children being battered against a tree. Here is the evidence of IthThain, a refugee drafted to drive a Khmer Rouge truck:

'At Mongkol Borey, the local Khmer Rouge commander ordered a squad of young Communist soldiers to punish a group of civilian officials of the fallen government. The fifteen Khmer Rouge rounded up ten former civil servants and their wives and children – about sixty people – tied their hands behind their backs, and drove them to a banana plantation. Scattered about the place were the bodies of people killed one or two days earlier. The Khmer Rouge thrust each official forward one at a time and forced him to kneel between two soldiers armed with bayonet-tipped AK-47 assault rifles. The soldiers then stabbed each victim simultaneously through the chest and back. As each man lay dying, his anguished, horror-struck wife and children were herded up to the body. The women, forced to kneel, also received the simultaneous bayonet thrusts. The children, last to die, were stabbed where they stood. Of the sixty or so executed, only about six were spared the bayonet. These were very small children, too young to fully appreciate what was happening. In a killing frenzy now, the two executioners each grabbed a limb – one an arm, the other a leg – and tore the infant apart.'[299]

The objective was totally to destroy religion, the family, patterns of landowning, and the aristocracy. To survive one had to conform to a collective ideal with no place for individualism. Without doctors or medical treatment, and forced to work throughout the day with minimum rations, only the strong or lucky survived. One of the top cadres, Kang Kek Lew, who took the pseudonym Brother Duch, was appointed head of an interrogation centre established at Tuol Sleng secondary school near the Phnom Penh city centre, which came to be called S21. Here those arrested for 'crimes' were taken and tortured to make confessions of real or (mostly) fictional deviationist/individualist behaviour. Once confessions had been secured, they were taken to a killing site outside the city and battered to death. Meticulous records were kept, and each victim photographed. Tuol Sleng is today a museum of the genocide.

The Angka Loeu leadership looked to China for support, and Saloth Sar paid several visits to Beijing. China sent much material support, including food, which helped disguise the collapse of the Cambodian economy that was taking place. Saloth Sar and his colleagues' other idea was to force a collective Cambodian nationalism on the country and get rid of all minorities. This brought them into conflict with the new Vietnam government that was establishing itself to the east after the departure of the United States, and which objected to the killing of Vietnamese living in Cambodia. During 1976 and 1977 Khmer Rouge troops entered Vietnam and perpetrated several massacres of Vietnamese villages near the border (which helps explain the support of the United States for the Khmer Rouge). China became reluctant to get more involved in overt support for the Khmer Rouge in case Vietnam's major ally, the Soviet

Union, might step in and trigger a wider war.

Inside Cambodia, the Khmer leaders became increasingly paranoid, and turned on their own cadres, some of whom were sent to Tuol Sleng. Others fled into Thailand or went east and linked up with Vietnam forces that invaded Cambodia in 1977 and 1978. Finally, on 25 December 1978, Vietnam mounted a full-scale invasion, and its troops easily took Phnom Penh in January 1979. The Khmer Rouge leaders went back into the jungle, and resumed guerrilla operations. Throughout much of the 1980s they and other dissident groups received the financial backing of the United States, Britain and China against the new Cambodia now under socialist Vietnamese communist guidance.[300]

Over 1.3 million dead have been discovered in Cambodia in more than 23,000 execution sites. Total deaths in the three and a half years after April 1975 are estimated to be between one and a half and two million people, about 15% of the country's women and 20% of the men, in a country with a population of eight million: the highest proportion of a national population of all genocides. Only much later were some of the Khmer leaders arrested and tried for their crimes. And only with the collapse of the Soviet Union in 1991 did the United States begin to admit that a genocide had taken place.

Two African examples show how different types of conflict and tension can lead to genocidal mass-killing. The first was in the British colony of Uganda, which received its independence in 1962. Uganda's Westminster-style democracy had by the late 1960s deteriorated into Milton Obote's single party presidency, which was corrupt, nepotistic and fixated on 'socialism'. Britain and Israel were concerned, and tacitly supported a coup by the head of the army, General Idi Amin, in January 1971. In the next few years Amin carried out a series of massacres against two ethnic groups in the northern part of Uganda, the Acholi and the Lango, who had been among Obote's supporters. He also expelled from the country the Asian commercial and trading classes, leaving Uganda's weak economy in tatters.

Amin was a colourful though brutal dictator whose rule led to over 300,000 deaths. Foolishly declaring war on Nyerere's Tanzania in 1978, Amin's forces were defeated by the Tanzanian army, and Obote was returned to power. Obote's rule again proved unpopular and by 1981

Yoweri Museveni, a Bugandan, had taken up arms against the Lango and Acholi groups, who were once more at the centre of the Obote administration. Between 1982 and 1985 the fighting intensified, and massacres of Bugandans took place in the Luwero Triangle just to the north of the capital, Kampala, where Museveni had his stronghold. Obote, and his successor General Okello (an Acholi), were finally driven out when Museveni's National Resistance Army entered Kampala in January 1986. Between 200,000 and 500,000 people were massacred during the fighting between 1981 and early 1986, and piles of human skulls lined some of the roads in the Luwero triangle. In 2022, thirty-eight years later, Museveni was still president of Uganda, having established a comparatively stable country after the disasters of 1971-85.[301]

The African genocide in Rwanda had a very different history.[302] Originally a colony under German administration after the 1884 Congress of Berlin, it passed to Belgian rule after Germany's defeat in the First World War. Rwanda is a fertile, hilly country, heavily populated. The two major ethnic groups, Hutus (the majority) and Tutsis, speak the same language; however the distinction between them was exaggerated by Belgian administrators for divide and rule purposes. Hutus and Tutsis had always intermarried, cultivated their fields and lived together in the rural areas, even though Belgium ruled through a Tutsi monarchy. The Belgian colonial government emphasised the Hutu-Tutsi 'differences' when in 1935 they compelled each inhabitant to have a passbook in which they had to state their tribal group. By the late 1950s, as the Belgians were leaving Africa, rule was transferred to the Hutu majority, who promptly overthrew the Tutsi monarchy, and began purges against the Tutsis. Confusingly, these tensions and killings were mirrored in Belgium's companion ex-colony of Burundi to the south of Rwanda, where the Tutsis dominated over the Hutus. In 1972 the Burundi Tutsis organised mass killings of between 100,000 and 200,000 Hutus to ensure their continued domination – echoing events in Amin's Uganda at that time.

With the establishment of a Hutu military dictatorship under General Habyarimana in 1973, Rwanda entered a relatively stable and peaceful decade and a half. He ruled through the only party permitted: the Mouvement Révolutionnaire National pour le Développement, the

MRND (to which was added 'et pour la Democrati' after the insistence of the World Bank in 1991). Rwanda came increasingly under French influence and French remained the language of the elite.

Rwanda's economy was based on the export of coffee and tin. Industrialisation was minimal, and based on import substitution. In the late 1980s a debt crisis and drying up of loans forced Habyarimana's government, as with so many other African countries, into the arms of the International Monetary Fund and the World Bank, which insisted on comprehensive 'structural adjustment'. Industries were to be privatised, government expenditure cut, repayment of interest on debt prioritised, the currency devalued, and democratic elections to be held. The devaluation (against the US dollar) led to high inflation, including higher prices of fuel, which in early 1990 brought the taxi drivers in the capital Kigali out on strike. To make matters worse, drought in 1988-89 caused a famine, exports of coffee collapsed, and unemployment in the towns soared. In October 1990, Tutsi opponents of the Hutu regime, under an organisation called the Rwandan Patriotic Front, invaded northern Rwanda and demanded a say in government. The Hutu ruling group faced an unprecedented economic and political crisis.

Other African countries, like Kenya, had faced similar problems but had finessed them away, displaying a facade of democracy for the benefit of the international community. In Rwanda, by contrast, some very poisonous developments now took place. While Habyarimana was trying to gain time at various conferences, also attended by the Rwandan Patriotic Front, extremist Hutu power groups began to organise a longer-term 'solution' to their problems. Killings of Tutsis took place in several regions during 1992-93, and militia known as Interahamwe and Infutamingi were formed from the young unemployed. The Hutu army was increased in size and was trained by the French military. Big business, the army and a group around Habyarimana's wife, 'le clan du madame', began to prepare for larger scale killings of Tutsis as well as any Hutus who supported democracy. The extremist Radio-Television-des-Milles-Collines poured out anti-Tutsi vitriol, and Hutu intellectuals issued poisonous pamphlets and newspapers, such as *Kangura,* which characterised all Tutsis as 'cockroaches' fit only to be exterminated. A *Kangura* editorial of 9 February 1991 advised: 'Let us learn about the Inkonyati [supporters of the Rwandan Patriotic Front] and let us exterminate every last one of them.'[303] Gérard Prunier notes: 'In Rwanda, all the preconditions for genocide were present: a well-organised civil service, a small tightly controlled land area, a disciplined and orderly population, reasonable communications, and a coherent ideology containing the necessary lethal potential.'[304]

In the early morning of 6 April 1994 the aircraft carrying Habyarimana back from a conference in Arusha in Tanzania was shot down over Kigali airport, killing everyone on board. Whoever shot down the plane has never been identified. Within hours the genocide, well prepared in advance, began. During the following hundred days between 500,000 and 850,000 Tutsis and some Hutus were murdered. The United Nations Mission in Rwanda, UNAMIR, was given orders just to help Europeans leave Kigali. Belgian soldiers were among the first to be killed. Both Tutsi and Hutu members of parliament, including the Hutu prime minister, were murdered. As waves of killing expanded in the days after the shooting down of the plane, and it was plainly apparent that a genocide was taking place, the UNAMIR troops withdrew, and neither the United States nor the French governments did anything. At the same time, the Rwandan Patriotic Front resumed their invasion of northern Rwanda, and began to inch their way towards Kigali.

In Kigali and other towns, people were stopped at roadblocks by the Presidential Guard, the army or the Interahamwe, and those identified as Tutsis were murdered on the spot. In the rural areas, in the villages, Hutus everywhere dutifully carried out killings, having been persuaded that this was their patriotic duty. They murdered neighbours and friends with whom they had lived their entire lives. The instigators and organisers of the killings included officials, teachers, and even Roman Catholic priests. Seeking refuge in churches, groups of Tutsis were slaughtered. Thousands of bodies were thrown into rivers. As in all genocides women were raped and mutilated before being killed. Countless schoolchildren were killed, their bodies strewn all over the classrooms. A few Tutsis managed to hide in attics, or were able to cross into the Congo, Tanzania or Burundi, but they were a small minority. A French army unit arrived in Cyangugu in the south-west of Rwanda in late May to help stabilise things, but were misled into believing that the victims were the Hutus, who were in fact carrying out the murders. The French were suspicious of the English-speaking Rwandan Patriotic Front leadership, and only slowly came to understand what was happening. The killings only abated as the Tutsi RPF advanced, taking Kigali on 4 July 1994, and securing the rest of the country by 18 July.

Much of the world's media initially falsely portrayed Paul Kagame, the RPF leader, as being somehow behind the genocide. And it is true that RPF reprisals did take place in the following months, during which 50,000 Hutu genocidaires (a Rwandan coinage for people guilty of genocide) were murdered. A most extraordinary mass exodus now took place as about two million Hutus fled Rwanda, either west into the Congo or east into north-western Tanzania. There they were assembled into refugee camps set up by the international community. The refugees included leaders and organisers of the genocide. It was weeks before the true nature of what had happened was understood in the capitals of the world. Gradually what had been viewed as just another African 'tribal war' was understood to have been a genocide.

Analysts have placed different stresses on the causes of the Rwandan killings. Was it inter-ethnic, springing from Belgium's 'tribalisation' policies? (Hutu Power had been an ideological reaction to Belgium's earlier sidelining of the Hutus in favour of a Tutsi monarchy.) Or were the killings the outcome of a straightforward political crisis within the Rwandan kleptocracy in the late 1980s as the pork barrel shrank and the threat of democracy loomed? Another view was that the genocide was a reaction to the very unwise structural adjustment programme imposed by the IMF at a time of economic deterioration, which led to inflation, high petrol prices, unemployment, and angry young people on the streets of Kigali. Or was it primarily a genocide orchestrated by the media? The poisonous, incendiary incitements of Hutu extremists in the Hutu gutter press and on the RTLM TV/radio station cannot be left out of a full explanation. Even the Nazi press in 1930s Germany appears moderate compared to the filthy ravings in the newspaper *Kangura*. (A nowadays quite common though baseless view is that everything should be blamed on the invading RPF and President Museveni of Uganda who gave them support, along with the tacit support of the United States for their fellow English-speakers.)

Other writers stress the rapid population growth, and the shrinking of the size of the average farm in Rwanda. Jared Diamond refers to the research of Belgian economists who worked in Kanama commune in north-western Rwanda in the early 1980s and again in the years following the genocide.[305] They showed that the population in the commune had soared to 2,040 people per square mile, which made it possibly the most densely populated rural area on the planet. Farm sizes had shrunk to an average 0.75 of an acre, but with large variations in acreage between the relatively well-off and the poor. Food production per person had plummeted, so that, by the early 1990s, hunger and near starvation were common. Many poorer people were compelled to sell what little land they had to richer neighbours. Rivalries between the generations intensified: fathers conflicted with sons. The younger men in particular, the ones who later joined the Interahamwe, often had nothing. 'Those land disputes undermined the cohesion of Rwandan society's traditional fabric,' writes Diamond.[306]

The Kanama commune was atypical in that the entire population was Hutu, and during the genocide, apart from a single Tutsi woman, it was Hutu killing Hutu. The land, cows and other possessions of the victims were distributed amongst those without. A Tutsi teacher in another part of the country, whose wife and four children had been killed, said: 'the people whose children had to walk barefoot to school killed the people who could buy shoes for theirs.' Such statements lead Diamond to conclude that it was a Malthusian event, where 'population pressure was one of the factors behind the...genocide.' He warns: 'Severe problems of overpopulation, environmental impact, and climate change cannot persist indefinitely: sooner or later they are likely to resolve themselves, whether in the manner of Rwanda or in some other manner not of our devising, if we don't succeed in solving them by our own actions.'[307]

Whilst the causes of the various genocidal events I have described were complex, in just about every case it is clear that governments holding power ordered the killings, frequently at a time of real or perceived national crisis. Targets of these and other mass killings have been minority ethnic groups, religious minorities, groups with the 'wrong' political orientation, or the relatively wealthy. The Indonesian and Cambodian killings were inter-involved with the cold war policies of the

United States to combat the spread of communism. In some cases (Stalin's Soviet Union, Cambodia) communists massacred those perceived to be on the right; in other cases (Indonesia, Argentina, Chile) it was the right wing ultra-capitalists who murdered leftists. In several African cases, the artificiality of colonial borders combined with drought, economic crisis, and politically threatened kleptocracies to bring about decisions to wipe out opponents. However, in nearly every genocide, armed forces were central to the killings, whether it was the armies of recognised national governments, as in the Pakistan case, or guerrilla units that had seized power, as in Cambodia. Real or perceived pressures of excess population are another driving force, as in the quest for Lebensraum of Hitler's Germany, and in the Rwandan case. Racist ideas underlay many of the policies of killing, as in the United States during the massacres of Native Americans, the killings of Jews by the Nazis, and the massacres of Tutsis by Hutus in Rwanda. In virtually every case the majority of the population was propagandised, often quite easily, into accepting the regime's characterisation of a vulnerable group as enemies of the state. Pseudo-scientific concepts were sometimes invoked to justify the killing of physically or psychologically handicapped groups, as in Germany after 1939.[308]

Once war has broken out, military leaders lose all inhibitions about genocide. The Armenian massacres in 1915 were partly a response by Muslim Turks to counter the threat of Russia. Roosevelt's plea to war leaders not to harm non-combatants in September 1939 had turned by 1945 into US air-force commander Curtis LeMay's: 'We knew we were going to kill a lot of women and kids when we burned a town. Had to be done.'[309] Diamond writes: 'Modern push-button weapons bypassed these inhibitions by enabling us to kill without even seeing our victims' faces. Technology thus created the psychological prerequisites of the white-collar genocides of Auschwitz and Treblinka, of Hiroshima and Dresden.'[310] But, as we have seen, limited technology is not necessarily an inhibiting factor either. Mass killings can be done at close distance, of neighbour by neighbour, with the crudest of weapons: pangas, nail-studded clubs, or knives.

One can only conclude that under certain types of stress, humans under a particular type of leadership turn on each other in killing frenzies that are a central and regular mark of us as a species. Any organised state with an executive elite is capable of deciding on a policy of mass killing, with the support of the requisite proportion of elected or non-elected politicians and other leaders. The historical record shows that the military or police will obey whatever orders they are given, civil servants, lower rank bureaucrats, officials, and soldiers will carry them out, and the mass of the untargeted citizenry will look the other way.

# 21. The Nuclear Shadow

After the quarter-million deaths and long-term destruction at Hiroshima and Nagasaki, there were mixed reactions amongst politicians in the United States. President Truman was unapologetic about his reasons for giving the go-ahead to the bombings: showing the Soviet Union what the US was capable of; saving the thousands of US troops that would have been lost if it had come to an invasion of Japan; and retribution for the 1941 Japanese attack on Pearl Harbour. (According to his Commerce Secretary, Henry Wallace, Truman balked at ordering the dropping of a third bomb: 'He didn't like the idea of killing all those kids.'[311]) For a general such as Curtis LeMay there was no real problem: atomic bombs were simply more powerful weapons than those already destroying Japanese cities.

The scientists had more qualms. Robert Oppenheimer felt 'a little bit scared of what I have made', but also: 'If you are a scientist you believe that it is good to find out how the world works.' Others were much more worried. Joseph Rotblat called the Hiroshima bombing a 'wanton, barbaric act'. Leo Szilard posited a scenario – what if the Germans had dropped some atom bombs on Europe or the USA but had then lost the war? 'Can anyone doubt,' wrote Szilard, 'that we would have defined the dropping of atomic bombs on cities as a war crime, and that we would have sentenced the Germans who were guilty of this crime to death at Nuremberg and hanged them?'[312]

Although the US public were mostly delighted by their nuclear power, the publication in the August 1946 edition of the *New Yorker*, of a series of essays by John Hersey (later published as *Hiroshima*) on the effects on individual Hiroshima victims led to sobering doubt. A Manhattan Project scientist, after reading Hersey, wrote: 'I was filled with shame to recall the whoopee spirit...announcing the bombing of Hiroshima...at the same moment the bomb's victims were living through indescribable horror.'[313]

Soviet physicists during the war years had been too preoccupied by the fight against Nazi Germany to have much time left over for atomic research, and Stalin was not enamoured with scientists, who were regarded as likely to have liberal opinions. But they had been working on the theoretical calculations since 1941, aided by information sent them surreptitiously by inside agents on the US project. Klaus Fuchs, one of the central group of physicists at Los Alamos, was feeding facts to the Soviets about the design of the US bombs as they progressed. Fuchs was a communist who had escaped Hitler's Germany for Britain in 1933 and had been among the British participants in the team building the bomb. Via a line of spies, who included David Greenglass and Julius Rosenberg, information was passed along to the Soviet diplomatic bag in Washington, and then on to Moscow. When Truman boasted of a new type of weapon of unusual power at the Potsdam conference in July 1945, Stalin already knew about it, but feigned polite lack of interest.[314]

In fact the Russians were still waiting to be fully impressed. This changed a month later when the Soviet leaders saw what happened to Hiroshima and Nagasaki. By September 1945 Stalin had recruited the Soviet's top nuclear physicist, Igor Kurchatov, to collect a team and get to work. Physicists and other scientists recruited were taken by train to an old Christian monastery at a place called Sarov on the Sarovka River. Here they were sequestered under guard and, aided by thousands of slave labourers from the gulag, they got to work under the control of the NKVD. The NKVD man in political charge of the project was Lavrentiy Beria. Among the scientists were Kurchatov's close confidants, Yuli Khariton and Yakov Zeldovich. Stalin told the physicists they only had to ask, and whatever finances or materials were necessary would be provided. The project leaders were given spacious dachas and more than adequate food.[315]

Detailed information about bomb design, materials and construction techniques continued to be forwarded from the United States by Fuchs and associated spies. Although Stalin knew that the US was building more atomic bombs (by 1949 they had fifty, mostly plutonium), he calculated Truman would not use them against Russia. Even though friction was developing between the two ex-allies, the Soviets knew that a few bombs, even if they were atom bombs, would not make much of an impact on a country as large as the Soviet Union. Unlike with Los Alamos, no information was allowed to go beyond the gates of the Sarov compound – the NKVD police had learned much about information containment from the camps.

By the end of 1946 the first Soviet nuclear reactor had been completed and had gone critical. Shortly afterwards the first plutonium producing reactor was built near Kyshtym in the Ural Mountains, and plutonium was being extracted from uranium rods by August 1948. Kurchatov, trying to meet Stalin's demand to get the Soviet bomb completed and tested as soon as possible, decided to imitate the Los Alamos 'Trinity-Nagasaki' plutonium bomb design as closely as was feasible. (One of the key Soviet physicists, Peter Kapitsa, later to win a Nobel prize, was arrested for arguing too strongly for a better Soviet design.)

The components of the bomb were brought together in late August 1949, and the two hemispheres of plutonium integrated to await implosion. The test site was on the river Irtysh north of Semipalatinsk. The bomb detonated with a flash reminiscent of the Trinity test and the 1946 United States tests on the islands of Bikini in the Pacific, according to Soviet observers. The yield was an estimated 20,000 tons (20 kilotons) of TNT, similar to the Trinity and Nagasaki bombs. Beria, the disbelieving Soviet commander, phoned Stalin at 6 a.m. Moscow time, and was told curtly that he had already got the news. In the US the surprise was total when a few days later radioactive fallout was picked up from the test by a patrolling B29. One of the Soviet scientists, Igor Golovin, remarked: 'The Soviet physicists knew they had created the weapon for their own people and for their own army which was defending peace...they had knocked the trump card from the hands of the American atomic diplomats.'[316] They were rewarded with Hero of Lenin and Order of Lenin medals.

Shocked, hawkish US scientists now urged that the United States develop the hydrogen bomb. Conceptualised at the same time as the fission/uranium bombs, the hydrogen bomb would use a fusion reaction detonated by a fission reaction. President Truman supported the proponents of this bomb because he felt the United States could use it to block Soviet aggression and its (alleged) aims to turn Western Europe communist, as well as future communist threats on the southern half of Korea. In any case, after August 1949 Truman assumed the Soviets would go ahead with the hydrogen weapon, so in January 1950 he gave the go-ahead for the infinitely more powerful fusion bomb, which physicists as yet understood only sketchily.

The US physicists got to work.[317] The calculations were unbelievably complex, and only when the mathematician John von Neumann had access to one of the first computers (the ENIAC) did they become possible. The main designers of the first thermonuclear weapon were Edward Teller, Stanislaw Ulam and Hans Bethe, with von Neumann's support. Early design proposals focussed on alternating layers of fissionable uranium and fusionable deuterium-lithium, but this design did not work. The problem was how to get the explosive force from the plutonium explosion to the deuterium at sufficient speed. The solution came with the discovery that radiation from the exploding plutonium would get to the deuterium more quickly than the explosive blast itself. This design sequence was now possible: a sequence of fusions and fissions between the plutonium, deuterium and uranium that could, for a very short instant, exceed the temperature at the centre of the sun.

The first test of a fusion bomb (nicknamed 'Mike') took place on 1 November 1952, on the island of Elugelab in the Marshall Islands, a US possession in the Pacific Ocean. The force of the explosion dwarfed the atom bomb's, producing a fireball over three miles across (Hiroshima's was a tenth of a mile), and evaporated the island of Elugelab, leaving a crater a mile in diameter and nearly 200 feet deep. At its maximum the cloud widened to a thirty mile stem that formed a canopy over a hundred miles wide. The shock waves of the blast registered twenty minutes later at Berkeley campus in San Francisco 5,000 miles away, where Teller and scientists were listening. Uranium and plutonium bombs had yielded up to 20,000 tons TNT equivalent, whereas the 'Mike' bomb yielded 10.4 million tons (10.4 megatons). It was 500 times more powerful than the Hiroshima bomb.

Unlike atomic devices, which fission only up to a certain size, thermonuclear devices have no size limit. Our species now had the capacity to destroy the entire surface of the planet. As Martin Amis commented: '[Nuclear weapons] are remarkable artefacts...Their size, their power, has no theoretical limit. They are biblical in their anger. They are clearly the worst thing that has ever happened to the planet, and they are mass produced and inexpensive.'[318]

An escalating race for who could build the biggest bomb now took off between the Americans and the Russians. The Soviet physicist,

Goncharov, said: 'We were always told we must not lag behind...we must have everything the Americans have.'[319] Four months after 'Mike', in early March 1953, Stalin died. In commemoration the Soviet team quickly got their first thermonuclear device ready and detonated it in Kazakhstan on 12 August 1953, to the consternation of the recently elected Eisenhower administration in Washington. It was not a full thermonuclear design, but it yielded a mighty 600 kilotons (thirty times the Hiroshima bomb). Worryingly for the Americans it was, unlike 'Mike', a 'dry' bomb, one that could actually be used in bomb form. From a certain point of view, the Russians were ahead.

President Truman had in 1953 briefly contemplated using atom bombs against the Soviet and Chinese supporters of the North Korean communists to conclude the Korean War, thoughts that were no longer sensible. Eisenhower wanted 'to find a way by which the minds of men, the hopes of men, the souls of men everywhere can move forward to peace and happiness and well being.' Be that as it may, the United States exploded its first deliverable thermonuclear bomb on 1 March 1954 at its Pacific Ocean territory of Bikini Islands. It delivered a staggering 15 megatons (15 million tons) explosive force, twenty-five times more powerful than the Soviet hydrogen bomb. It also was what would come to be called a 'dirty bomb', since it spread clouds of radiation over a vast area of several hundred square miles, including casualties on a Japanese fishing boat 80 miles away. The United States had to pay the Japanese government US$ 2 million compensation. But they were ahead in the nuclear bomb race.

Khrushchev in Moscow urged his scientists to do something about the developing gap. They had (apparently) independently discovered the 'radiation-implosion' method the US had used in 'Mike'. On 22 November 1955 the Soviets detonated the next bomb at Semipalatinsk. It only yielded 1.5 megatons, but had the advantage that it was small enough to drop out of an aeroplane. The test had caused damage to towns fifty miles away. A soldier and a child had been killed. The windows and doors had been blown out of the scientists' hotel. 'We started celebrating immediately,' noted Goncharov. 'We took out all our supplies. Someone brought alcohol. There was a sense of fulfilment.'[320] (Apart from Edward Teller in the US, most of the world's nuclear physicists were tormented by the implications of their discoveries.)

The next eight years, from 1955 until after the Cuban missile crisis of October 1962, was a time when the big powers began incautiously to think about the new military paradigm they had created. The problem was how to fight a war with the new weapons. Until 1963, politicians and high military generals in Russia and the US furiously studied how they might win a war in a way that von Clausewitz, or Hitler for that matter, would have approved. The object was to break the enemy's will to continue fighting before he did the same to you. The generals debated how many men, women and children would be worth sacrificing: five million, ten million? As the availability of thermonuclear bombs increased, US generals thought of a surprise first strike against the Soviets. Gerard DeGroot relates how the US strategist William Kaufman suggested that the nuclear focus should be limited to military targets in order to save civilian lives. The response from the head of the General Staff, General Thomas Power, was: 'Why are you so concerned with saving *their* lives? The whole idea is to *kill* the bastards!' Power said that if, at the end of the war, there were two Americans left alive and one Russian, the war would have succeeded. 'Well, you'd better make sure that they are a man and a woman,' Kaufman replied.[321]

The US objectives for such a war were often changed, though they always included preventing Soviet communism overrunning Western Europe. The Russians thought less in terms of overrunning Western Europe than of defending themselves against imperialist nuclear attack. Both Eisenhower and Khrushchev spent much energy keeping their more aggressive top military in check, while trying to maintain a plausible facade of defensive capability and at the same time denying any aggressive intentions against anyone. In the late 1950s and early 1960s the selection of deadly weapons available to the politicians, supplied by the peace-loving scientists, increased menacingly. They included nuclear missiles (which could leave and re-enter the atmosphere), and also small atomic 'tactical' weapons, such as the United States' Davy Crockett hand weapon (discontinued 1971) which could fire a mini-yield nuclear bomb a few hundred metres.

The nuclear powers increased in number. The United Kingdom became the third country to develop 'the bomb' (atom bomb in 1952;

hydrogen bomb in 1957), mainly to try to sustain its unsustainable self-image as a great power. It took a few years for the British to realise that their nuclear policy could not be independent of the United States. De Gaulle's France was the fourth nuclear power (atom in 1960; hydrogen in 1968). And in 1964 came China's atom bomb, followed in 1968 by its thermonuclear bomb. The nuclear strategists nervously pondered Mao Zedong's assertion that China would win a nuclear war because they had so many more people who they could afford to let die compared to the capitalists.

The publics in the bomb-toting countries began seriously worrying around 1957, when campaigns for nuclear disarmament took off against the spread of the new weapons. The civilian men and women who went on the marches protested that the risks of a nuclear war were too large. If everyone disarmed, they said, the survival of the species would not be threatened. Marches were made on nuclear power stations where plutonium was being created, on weapons centres where the bombs were put together, and, later on, on the military bases where the weapons were kept in readiness for action. The protesters were depicted by the establishment press as left-wing softies who had little influence on events. In Britain the issue split the Labour Party, with the unilateral disarmament wing briefly taking control of the party, and retaining influence even when Hugh Gaitskell's realists outvoted them in 1960 – a divide that was politically beneficial to the Conservatives.

By the 1960s, evidence was mounting that the radiation fall-out from the increasingly frequent atomic tests was causing high incidences of cancer amongst populations that were near to or downwind from the test grounds. Soldiers, who had been ordered to observe atomic explosions, and then advance towards ground zero, were similarly afflicted. The testing grounds in the Nevada desert (US), Semipalatinsk (Russia) and Australia (conducted by Britain) became the most heavily polluted places on Earth. Medical warnings were contradicted by military posturing about the harmlessness of the tests. In the United States in the late 1950s there were even attempts to sell atomic bomb tests as a tourist attraction. Families were encouraged to witness tests and enjoy the whole atomic theme, with dedicated atomic hotels, where they could drink atomic liquors with their atomic dinners. Miss Atomic Bomb beauty contests were staged and films were made on heroic atomic themes.[322] Edward Teller suggested that thermonuclear blasts could be used to excavate harbours, or save the labour on widening the Panama Canal. Pro-bomb enthusiasts attacked the medical doubters on the grounds that an atomic war would be good for morale: a bit of destruction always brought out the innovative best in a nation.

Dangerous competitive posturing continued between the United States and the Soviet Union. When the Russians launched Sputnik into space in 1957, it was as if the United States had been humiliated. Some in the United States recommended exploding an atom bomb on the moon in response. The bomb and space programmes were seen by both the United States and the Soviet Union as parts of a technological duel. The need to be seen to be technologically ahead drove the new Kennedy administration to push the US programme to land men on the moon (achieved in 1969). The politburo in Moscow used their technological advances to boast how communism would beat capitalism and the proletariat would rule the world. Conversely, the US White House and Pentagon saw reds under every bed, and vowed to expand their military arsenal to defend capitalist Western Europe from being overrun by the Soviets. In the United States the 'military-industrial complex', as Eisenhower called it in his final presidential speech in January 1961, grew large and powerful, using Khrushchev's threats to justify massive expansion of the US's thermonuclear capacity. By 1960 American U2 spy planes were photographing Soviet missile sites. When a U2 was shot down over Russian territory, Khrushchev angrily stalked out of an arms control meeting mouthing nuclear threats.

In 1961-62 there were two dangerous flashpoints which could have led to war between Moscow and Washington. The first concerned Germany. After the defeat of the Nazi regime in 1945, Germany had been divided into what became West Germany (the American, British and French zones) and East Germany (the Soviet zone). Berlin was isolated geographically in East Germany, but it was part of the post-war agreement that the American-British-French sector of Berlin should have a road and rail safe access across East Germany through to West Germany. In the city itself there was relatively easy movement from one zone to the other. During the 1950s West Germany began to prosper compared with East Germany, and many people in East Germany used Berlin to get through into West Germany. The desire of many people to move to the West (both West Germany and other countries) threw doubt on the East German claims that communism was paradise on Earth. In August 1961 the East German regime decided to stop the flight, and, with Moscow's encouragement, threw up a wall across Berlin.

Relations between Moscow and Washington grew tense. In October 1961, to impress the world, the Russians detonated a 50 megaton device over Novaya Zemlya island in the Arctic. This bomb, nicknamed 'Tsar Bomba', yielded 50 million tons of TNT equivalent -- more explosive power than all the bombs dropped in World War 2. Its designer, Andrei Sakharov, proclaimed: 'Let this device hang over the heads of the capitalists, like a sword of Damocles.' With the technical successes of Sputnik and Tsar Bomba it wasn't wise to mess with Moscow, even though the West heavily outnumbered the Russians in useable thermonuclear missiles. In early 1962 the Americans responded by placing Jupiter nuclear missiles in Turkey and Italy, putting Russian cities under direct nuclear threat.

The second flashpoint, Cuba, very nearly led to a nuclear holocaust.[323] In 1959 Fidel Castro's communists had seized control of the island, which is just ninety miles off the coast of Florida. In April 1961 President Kennedy, in an attempt to evict Castro's regime before it became established, ordered the Bay of Pigs invasion. The failure of the invasion prompted Khrushchev to put nuclear missiles on the island in order to deter further US aggression, protect Castro's people, and bring the United States within range of Soviet missiles. Khrushchev's action was also a response to the US missiles in Turkey and Italy. He was working on the assumption that Kennedy would protest, but in the end do nothing. He further hoped to use the presence of missiles on Cuba to get the Americans and British out of west Berlin.

From August 1962 contingents of Soviet troops and technicians began building the missile sites, and by mid-September both medium and intermediate range nuclear missiles were being offloaded and taken to the launch sites. For reasons that are still obscure, Kennedy only received proof of this upon receiving photos from a U2 flight on 14 October. In Washington a fourteen man executive committee was immediately convened to decide what to do. They decided that the US would tell Khrushchev to remove the missiles or there would be war. Khrushchev blustered to gain time for the missiles to be made ready for use and lied that no missiles were in place. The United States military put Kennedy and the executive committee under intense pressure to bomb Cuba and invade. Generals Power and LeMay wanted to seize the opportunity not just to get rid of the missiles and the Castro regime from Cuba but to get rid of the Soviet Union as a threat once and for all. By 22 October nuclear-armed US planes were ready for take-off. Kennedy was not prepared to take such a risk. He finally decided to place a blockade around Cuba, preventing further missiles and supplies reaching the island. Because the blockade was technically a formal act of war, the US warships were described as a 'quarantine'.

The American public was only told of developments on 22 October, from which moment the world held its breath. Khrushchev realised the Americans were serious – it was either nuclear war or removing the missiles. He made two conditions for withdrawal: the removal of the US missiles from Turkey and Italy, and an undertaking from Kennedy not to invade Cuba. Moscow was looking for a way out without losing face. But the danger was that a war could be started by some unauthorised action. A United States U2 plane was shot down over Cuba on 25 October. The Americans responded by saying the next one shot down would mean war.

The US military wanted to provoke hostilities, and they nearly succeeded. They fired off test missiles and sent U2 planes to stray 'accidentally' over Soviet territory. Nuclear-armed US bombers circulated just outside the Soviet Union's borders. Meanwhile on Cuba the missiles were in position, armed, and ready to fire, as also were tactical nuclear weapons that the United States did not know about. The Castro people pleaded with Khrushchev to begin hostilities. Most dangerously of all, on 28 October, US ships dropped depth charges on a Soviet submarine armed with nuclear torpedoes that was in the ocean near Cuba, to force it to the surface. Soviet naval regulations required three officers in charge of a submarine crew to agree before firing the torpedoes: two said yes, one, named Vasily Arkhipov, said no. Khrushchev frantically called to Kennedy to explain what he had and had not authorised.

After this, the crisis began to simmer down. The Soviet missiles on Cuba were dismantled in the first half of November, and the United States lifted the blockade on 22 November. On the surface the Soviet Union appeared to have suffered a political defeat, but this was not so. Kennedy had publicly agreed not to invade Cuba again, giving Castro's communists a right to a safe existence that they would not otherwise have had. Kennedy also agreed to remove US missiles from Italy and Turkey (Khrushchev agreed not to make this public). The Soviets had not achieved the eviction of the Western powers from Berlin. In retrospect the stand-off led to roughly equal concessions on both sides, though at the time and in most US history texts it was described as a victory for Kennedy.

Also in retrospect, the weekend of 27-28 October 1962 was the most dangerous two days in the history of our species. That Saturday I was a 17-year-old at the Olympic Motor Show in London viewing the E-type Jaguar, unaware that the US Chief of General Staff, Curtis LeMay, was shouting at Kennedy to start Armageddon. We owe a lot to submarine officer Vasily Arkhipov[324] and the young US president.

Both Washington and Moscow were so unnerved by the fact that a thermonuclear war had been averted by sheer good fortune that they agreed to go more carefully in future. A telephone hotline was established between the White House and the Kremlin, and in 1963 the first serious nuclear negotiations were held between the two superpowers. They agreed to restrict the testing of weapons to under the ground. The British signed up as well, whilst insisting on keeping 'the bomb' so as to maintain their illusory great power status. (France refused to sign on the basis that they were not yet a proper nuclear power.) The realisation had finally dawned on all sides that nuclear weapons meant an entirely new military paradigm. Von Clausewitz's textbook on war could be thrown in the dustbin.

In 1968 a Non-Proliferation Treaty was signed, which went into force in 1970. Designed ostensibly as a first step towards eliminating nuclear weapons, the treaty morphed into a means by which the established nuclear powers could prevent smaller powers from having nuclear weapons. Those who signed the treaty made a tacit agreement to go on building nuclear weapons but not to use them. Issues, such as non-proliferation, test bans, and having enough weapons to deter the enemy, were set out in the treaty in quantified combinations. The crux of the agreement was Mutually Assured Destruction (MAD, as it was soon nicknamed). This was defined by the US secretary of defence, Robert McNamara, as 'an understanding that if either side initiates the use of nuclear weapons, the other side will respond with sufficient power to inflict unacceptable damage.' By that he meant a minimum of several or more million of a population would be killed. For a quarter of a century this was to keep the nuclear strategists on both sides preoccupied.

By 1980 the global stockpile of nuclear weapons numbered 55,000, half of them in the United States. India began the 'peaceful' development of atomic capacity in 1974, and carried out its first explosive tests in 1998. India had the Chinese nuclear capacity to worry about, but more dangerous was the rivalry over Kashmir between India and Pakistan. In response to the start of the Indian nuclear tests the Pakistan prime minister, Ali Bhutto, in 1974, asserted: 'If India builds the bomb we will eat grass or leaves, even go hungry, but we will get one of our own.' The Pakistanis achieved that by 1998.

The Chinese had built their weapon because great powers had to have them, but also, dangerously, with an eventual eye on Taiwan. The Israelis have built, it is believed, between 80 and 400 nuclear bombs for use against any serious allies of the Palestinians whose land they have taken. By the end of the twentieth century eight countries had nuclear weapons: the United States, Russia, Britain, France, China, Israel, India and Pakistan.

The arrival of Ronald Reagan as US president in 1980 revived the war rhetoric against the Soviet Union. New MX missiles were developed with multiple warheads, each independently targetable. American missiles were installed in Britain and Germany that could 'cruise' close to the ground and evade Russian radar. The US military spent billions of dollars attempting (unsuccessfully) to develop a satellite defence system against incoming intercontinental ballistic missiles, a programme known as 'star wars'. The atmosphere harked back to the early 1960s and led to new protests, such as the women-led movement to surround Greenham Common, the American missile base in Britain. Jonathan Schell's 1982 book *The Fate of the Earth* made the point: 'The choice is really between two entire ways of life. One response is to decline to face the peril, and thus go on piling up the instruments of doom year after year until, by accident or design, they go off. The other response is to recognise the peril, dismantle the weapons and arrange the political affairs of the earth so that the weapons will not be built again. We do not have two earths at our disposal – one for experimental holocausts and the other to live on.'[325]

In 1985, when Gorbachev became leader of the Soviet Union with his policies of 'perestroika', the hostilities between Moscow and Washington thawed slightly. Gorbachev and Reagan got on quite well; and in any case the Soviet Union was collapsing. Reagan verbally agreed to disarmament, throwing his military advisers into a panic. His disarmament pronouncement was overruled, but the rhetoric was toned down, and US military budgets cut back a little. With Yeltsin, and after 2000, Putin, the Soviet Union returned to being Russia, and the seeds of Russian capitalism were replanted. With communism gone, the need for a cold war faded. On both sides thousands of missiles were destroyed or put into storage. From the 1990s the US's nuclear strike capacity has relied increasingly on its fleet of 14 Ohio Class nuclear submarines, each with 24 Sea Launched Ballistic Missiles, and each of these with five warheads (1680 warheads in total).[326]

Let us now turn to the 'positive' side of uranium: nuclear reactors that generate electricity without the carbon emissions associated with coal-fired power stations. Since the first peacetime reactors began operating in 1954, various designs of reactors have been devised. By the mid-1980s nearly 500 were operating worldwide, and nuclear-generated electricity was seen as the future. A blow to this rosy picture has been a number of serious nuclear reactor accidents that have led to the release of radiation and, in the case of the Chernobyl disaster in the Soviet Union in 1986, the necessity to evacuate the population from a wide area. Other serious accidents occurred at Windscale in Britain in 1957, at Three Mile Island in the United States in 1979, and at Fukushima in Japan in 2011.

Nuclear power generators are incredibly complex and, if an accident leads to a 'meltdown' of their uranium rods, they can cause massive radiation damage, with the possibility of making large areas uninhabitable for hundreds of years. Following the Three Mile Island accident, Charles Perrow posited the idea of 'Normal Accident Theory' which refers to scenarios 'in which an accident occurs, resulting from an unanticipated interaction of multiple failures in a complex system'. Such accidents are 'unexpected, incomprehensible, uncontrollable and unavoidable'. In other words humanity should accept the likelihood of a nuclear disaster every so often, since 'such modern high-risk systems are prone to failure however well they are managed.'[327]

The 1957 accident at the Windscale reactor on the coast of Cumberland, north-western England, illustrates Perrow's point. Windscale consisted of two reactors whose main purpose was producing plutonium for Britain's nuclear weapons. When one of the fuel rods in Pile 2 overheated and caught fire, the operating teams misdiagnosed what had happened, and by following the textbook on what they thought was the problem, they made things worse, and caused a meltdown of the reactor. When uranium melts, deadly radiation is given off in the form of iodine-131, iodine-137 and caesium-137. At Windscale the radiation was spread by prevailing winds south-easterly towards the urban populations of the English midlands. It is estimated that at least 100 deaths from cancers occurred as a result. The reactor had to be sealed off and decommissioned; the uranium rods were still giving off heat over fifty years later.

Windscale was an old-design reactor with graphite moderators, but the reactor at Three Mile Island was a more modern pressurised water reactor. In March 1979 a stuck-open relief valve was misdiagnosed, leading to counter-measures that made matters critical. A crucial indicator light was hidden from the operators, who, with inadequate training, were misled as to what was happening. Radiation escaped into the surrounding area, eventually costing over a billion dollars to clean up. As with Windscale, the reactor was not repairable and had to be sealed off. Anti-nuclear groups in the United States campaigned to have all nuclear reactors decommissioned, and few new reactors have been built in the US since 1979.

A more serious nuclear disaster occurred in 1986 at the Chernobyl reactor No. 4 on the edge of the Ukrainian city of Pripyat in the then Soviet Union. It reached grade 7 (the most serious) on the International Nuclear and Radiological Event scale (Windscale and Three Mile Island were both grade 5.) Everything that went wrong underscored Perrow's point about the inevitability of systemic accidents in complex systems: a combination of poor reactor design, inadequately trained operators, poorly thought-out tests on the cooling mechanisms, and a still-disputed sequence of meltdown events in the uranium tank.[328]

On 25 April 1986 a tricky, complex test was scheduled to be run by the Chernobyl day-shift team, which then had to be postponed until later that night because of an unanticipated demand for electricity from the city of Kiev. The evening team continued the test preparations, then went off duty at midnight, handing over to the night team. The reactor was an older design with a graphite moderator and graphite-tipped control rods that operated in water, and did not have the thick concrete roofing or the proper concrete foundations necessary to contain a meltdown. The purpose of the test was to establish whether, during the shutdown, the reactor could be cooled for about 45 seconds using steam from the turbines, while the electricity-operated diesel engines that pumped coolant water got going. Earlier stages of the test had, unbeknown to the nightshift operators, built up dangerous levels of caesium-137 within the reactor, but the team leaders' requests to halt the test were overruled by the deputy chief engineer. There were strange surges of power in the reactor, first going low, then, as attempts were made to raise the power, uncontrollably high. The control rods were hastily re-inserted to stop the reaction process, but were blocked when the heat expanded their graphite tips. The coolant water turned to steam. At 1.26 a.m. the build-up of steam exploded, destroying the roofing of the reactor. Half a minute later a second explosion took place. Radioactive gases were exploded hundreds of meters into the air.

Firefighters were on the scene within twenty minutes, and residents of Pripyat came out to watch the firework display. The firemen had no idea of what was happening, and handled pieces of burning graphite. Water was hosed onto the burning reactor. About twenty-eight of the firefighters died of radiation poisoning within the next two weeks, as did two of the night team managers. In the following days around 5,000 helicopter flights dropped sand and boron on to the burning reactor in an attempt to quell the expulsion of iodine-131, caesium-134, caesium-137 and strontium-90 radiation to which the pilots were exposed. Teams of miners dug under the burning reactor to construct a sandwich foundation that consisted of a pair of two-meter thick concrete layers separating a group of water pipes so as to prevent nuclear meltdown into the earth below the reactors. The fact that this under-layer had not been part of the original structure was another design shortcoming.

After some delay, and keeping a tight lid on the news, the Soviet authorities evacuated the entire population of Pripyat. They were told it would only be for a few days. Eventually over 100,000 people were evacuated and an area of 1,200 square kilometres is still abandoned, and likely to be uninhabitable for decades, perhaps centuries. Many animals died in the first weeks from radiation poisoning, and Soviet police and volunteers spent days shooting abandoned pet dogs and cats. Radiation spread over much of Western Europe, extending as far as Norway, Britain and Ireland. By the end of 1986, a massive concrete structure had been built over the still burning reactor. Its gradual disintegration in the early twenty-first century led to an international team-effort to build a stronger sarcophagus. This was completed in 2016 and is expected to remain viable into the 2060s. By 2001 the three other reactor units at the Chernobyl complex had been closed down. The wider region of north-western Ukraine and southern Belarus that had to be abandoned by humans has been slowly resettled by wildlife – including wolves, moose, elk and lynx. A few people have since returned into the contaminated zone. One can today book tourist holidays to the Pripyat region and wander among the abandoned buildings.

In 2006 the last Soviet leader, Mikhail Gorbachev, suggested that the Chernobyl nuclear disaster had been decisive in leading to perestroika and to the collapse of the Soviet Union in 1991. Throughout much of Western Europe Chernobyl led to an intensification of the anti-nuclear protest. In 2003 the Schröder government in Germany decided to set up an environmental ministry and to end the use of nuclear-generated electricity. The Belarusian writer, Svetlana Alexievich, summed up the impact of Chernobyl: 'Military nuclear power meant Hiroshima and Nagasaki, whereas peaceful nuclear meant an electric light in every home. Nobody had guessed yet that military and peaceful nuclear power were in fact twins. Accomplices. We grew wiser, the whole world grew wiser, but only after Chernobyl. Today, like living black boxes, Belarusians are recording information for the future. For everybody.'[329]

The other INRE (International Nuclear and Radiological Event) level 7 catastrophe occurred in 2011 at the Fukushima Daiichi reactor complex in Japan, in reactors owned and run by the Tokyo Electrical Power Company and supervised by the Japanese Ministry of Economy, Trade and Industry. It started at 2 p.m. on 11 March 2011 with an unprecedented level 9 earthquake off the coast. Of the six reactors at the plant, two were already closed down, and the other four were immediately switched off in response to the earthquake. The reactor complex was protected by a sea wall 10 metres high which had been constructed in case of high waves from earthquakes. However the tsunami caused by this earthquake, which hit the shore around 45 minutes later, was 15 metres high.

The earthquake destroyed the electricity supply that cooled the reactors, but diesel generated power was set to switch on automatically to maintain the cooling. However, the tsunami wave overwhelmed the reactor foundations and flooded the diesel generators. The effects of the combined earthquake-tsunami meant that access to the plant for rapid repair was not possible. Within hours, three of the reactors had overheated, and meltdown had begun. A fourth reactor, initially unaffected, was subsequently flooded and also melted down. Hydrogen explosions in each reactor destroyed the reactor roofing. By the evening of 11 March the Japanese government had ordered the evacuation of residents from a 20 kilometre radius inland from the shore, and eventually over 150,000 people were forced to relocate. Coolant water emitting radiation flooded into the sea.

Years of self-blame followed. The other Japanese reactors were shut down. *The Japan Times* reckoned that 'by shattering the government's long-pitched safety myth about nuclear power, the crisis dramatically raised public awareness about energy use and sparked strong anti-nuclear sentiment.' In the short term, the country's use of coal for power generation increased by around 30%, and in 2012 the Japanese government announced a policy of making the country nuclear-free by the 2030s. Between 2016 and 2018 eight new Japanese coal-fired stations were operational, with thirty more planned for the 2020s.

There were few, if any, deaths from the Fukushima Daiichi disaster, none from Three Mile Island, and a few hundred from Chernobyl. These fatality rates are insignificant when compared to deaths from road accidents or smoking. In his 2007 book *Revenge of Gaia,* James Lovelock called for an increased reliance on nuclear fission as an interim measure, to give us time to develop a safe energy based on nuclear fusion. He wrote: 'In several ways we are unintentionally at war with Gaia, and to survive with our civilization intact we urgently need to make a just peace with Gaia while we are strong enough to negotiate and not a defeated, broken rabble on the way to extinction.'[330] In his 2020 book *Novacene: The Coming Age of Hyperintelligence,* Lovelock, according to a review in the *Financial Times,* insists that 'our reluctance to embrace nuclear power is an act of "auto-genocide".'[331] As the examples of Germany and Japan show, however, the weight of public opinion in the world today is away from nuclear-generated electricity and towards solar and wind energy. In the meantime more coal-fired carbon goes into the air.

The threat of atomic bombs and hydrogen bombs will not go away. North Korea joined the nuclear club in 2006 and now boasts that its missiles can reach New York. Iran is suspected of wishing to enrich uranium, not just to generate electricity, but to make bombs. Israel will not tolerate a nuclear-armed Iran. There have been periodic tensions and crises, made worse in 2018 when President Trump tore up previous agreements with Iran. Big powers attempt to prevent the spread of nuclear weapons to regimes they disapprove of. This destroys the basis on which the Non-Proliferation Treaty of 1970 was signed, and ensures that smaller powers become even more determined to go nuclear. This hollowing out of the 1970 treaty is made worse by the US's repeated threats to pull out of it altogether.

There is also the danger that non-state or terrorist groups will one day be able to construct effective uranium fission devices. Joseph Cirincione writes: 'The danger comes from apocalyptic or messianic groups that believe that mass destruction can bring about the global conflict they seek, helping achieve their day of reckoning in this world or the next.'[332] There is also the danger of an unauthorised official firing of missiles, and the danger that a president or prime minister could order a nuclear attack as a result of mistaken information. This nearly happened in 1995 when the Russians mistook a Norwegian weather rocket as the start of a nuclear attack.[333] Even a single nuclear detonation as an act of war would plunge the global economy into depression. The complex system of human political, psychological and technical interaction ensures that one day nuclear weapons will be used. Fission and fusion bombs cannot be uninvented. They will be with us always.[334]

## 22. Financial Crises

The economic crisis of 2008 nearly brought down the world's financial system. Such crises – a periodic feature of modern human history – may have profound political and economic consequences, amongst other things reducing our capacity to react adequately to global heating. Before examining the factors that led to the 2008 crisis, it is instructive to examine the causes of the Great Depression of the 1930s with its disastrous consequences. Emergency financial policy in response to the 2008 crisis was designed to avoid the mistakes committed by the Americans during the early 1930s which made the depression worse, helped bring Hitler to power in Germany, as well as usher in the Second World War.

Throughout the nineteenth century, the major world economies had been relatively stable. Britain's currency, the pound sterling, then the world's strongest currency, was tightly linked to the gold standard – the amount of gold in its vaults. However by the beginning of the First World War in 1914, the British economy was being outpaced and challenged by that of the United States. The drastic costs of the 1914-1918 war led Europe's nations to break the link with the gold standard, and finance the war's costs by printing money. When money is printed without being linked to gold it tends to be inflationary; and in the aftermath of the war there was inflation, especially in Germany. This was to be accompanied by political destabilisations in Europe that opened up the way to the Second World War.

By the 1920s economic power had swung decisively to the United States which had boosted production for the First World War. New motor cars and household appliances were coming on to the market and Americans were buying things. The Wall Street stock market began to rise. The feeling of prosperity gave rise to an unrealistic optimism that the market would go on rising indefinitely, and this induced people to borrow money to buy shares. These buyers only needed to pay a proportion of the cost of the value of the shares. In stock market jargon, this is known as buying shares 'on margin'. If the shares go up in price, that is good. If they go down, the borrowers must either put in extra cash to keep the borrowed amount at an agreed percentage of the value of the shares, or sell the shares. When too many people have bought shares on margin and have to sell, this can lead to a spiralling down of share prices, which is what happened in 1929-30.[335]

That led to very negative consequences for the wider US economy. The United States banks, for example, which mixed lending money to people with speculating in the stock market, had to sell shares in large amounts. As banks were threatened with bankruptcy, and their account holders had no guarantees on their money, they withdrew the money in their bank accounts. By 1931 many of the banks were indeed going bankrupt. As people were threatened with the loss of their money, they stopped spending. Millions of people lost their jobs as the collective national purchasing power dwindled and people became unemployed. Those who retained their jobs were relatively secure, especially as prices were dropping; but they tended to wait for further price drops before spending, which led to further price drops and, in turn, a drop in wages – a process known as deflation. The absence of government benefits for the unemployed made a drastic situation worse.

By 1932 the unemployed in the United States were taking to the streets, and soup kitchens run by charities were feeding those without means. The wealthy, with an eye on Stalin's Soviet Union, began to fear a communist revolution. The administration of President Hoover unwittingly made matters worse. They stuck by the gold price of the US dollar, which was then valued at US$ 22.67 an ounce. Rather than devalue the dollar against gold, which would have increased (by cheapening) US exports and helped the economy, the Hoover government raised interest rates and cut government spending. Raising interest rates reduced exports, meant borrowing was made difficult and debt burdens made heavier; and the cuts in spending worsened unemployment. These policies further reduced spending. Then, with the Smoot-Hawley Act of 1930, the government unwisely imposed duties on foreign imports. Foreign countries retaliated, and in turn cut imports from the United States, which increased US unemployment. Trade wars between countries hugely reduced international trade. US farmers' grain exports were cut, and many farmers dependent on grain exports lost their mortgages and farms. The negative impact on European economies, particularly in Germany, led to cutbacks in government spending, mass unemployment and political destabilisations which led to the Nazi takeover in early 1933.

Some sensible measures to stimulate the US economy were taken by the administration of Franklin Roosevelt inaugurated in early 1933. First, Roosevelt devalued the US dollar against the price of gold, with an ounce of gold valued at US$ 35 rather than the former value of US$ 22.67. This increased the dollars in circulation. Second, interest rates were cut, making it cheaper to borrow money. The money hitherto used for interest payments could now be spent. Thirdly, government spending was increased, particularly on social security benefits and government work projects (such as the Tennessee Valley Dam), which helped increase spending and aided the unemployed. Critically, fourthly, through the Glass-Steagall Act of 1933, the banking system was made more secure by separating street operating bank branches from their investment sections. This increased confidence in the banking system; a confidence that was further increased when people's bank accounts were given some protection. And fifthly, government income was augmented by taxing the wealthy at higher rates, enabling money to be diverted to the poorer sections of the population and increasing spending power. Even with these measures, collectively known as the New Deal, the economic recovery was slow and incomplete, and there was further recession in 1937 when the Federal Reserve (established in 1913) raised interest rates prematurely. Only the spending on war after 1941 ended the depression decisively.

The post-war golden years of the 1950s and 1960s were underpinned by a strong US dollar, an explosion of industrial production, low fuel prices and money spread more fairly through progressive taxation, thus encouraging spending. The dollar was tied to gold at US$ 35 dollars to an ounce of gold, and capital movements between nations were restricted. This underpinned 'the golden age'.[336] But then the massive US spending on the Vietnam War from the mid-1960s led to a loss of confidence in the dollar. Foreign central banks sought to convert dollar balances into gold, which compelled Nixon to break the dollar's link to gold in August 1971. From then on the dollar, and all other currencies, became 'fiat' currencies: worth only the paper on which they were printed. There was now nothing to hold back government spending. In response the dollar value against gold fell heavily throughout the 1970s reducing to US$ 800 to an ounce of gold in 1980. This was the leading cause of the inflation of the 1970s. From 1914, when the First World War triggered the beginning of financial instabilities, to the early twenty-first century, the dollar was to fall 96% in value.[337]

The floating value of the dollar gave large economic power to the investment banks which, now that capital controls had been abolished, were able to manipulate currencies for speculative purposes. With the abolition of the Glass-Steagall Act by the Clinton administration in 1999, the speculative sections of the banks were once more combined with their loan sections, as in pre-1933. Bad speculations could once again threaten the entire bank. The potential dangers were obscured by rising stock markets after 1982 and cheap imports from a rapidly industrialising China. Chinese administrations deliberately kept their currency, the Renminbi, undervalued so as to keep their exports cheap.

What resulted from cheap Chinese imports in the United States and other rich countries was a dangerous development.[338] Inflation was reduced, despite strong spending and mounting debt. Inflation, as measured by the Consumer Price Index, was kept low at around 2% a year during the 1990s and 2000s. In contrast 'asset' prices – shares and property – were rising rapidly, especially on the New York stock market. The trend in rich countries was for people to borrow money at a low interest rate and invest in the stock market with 10-20% returns. The years 1982 to 2006 witnessed the longest stock market boom in history. By the early twenty-first century teachers and office workers were discussing their latest stock exchange purchases in the same way that taxi drivers and shoe-shiners did in the 1920s.

Banks fell over each other to loan people money. As the interest charged on borrowed money was very low, people with low (or even non-existent) incomes were able to borrow money to buy property, and there was a speculative rush to buy homes that sent house prices rising rapidly. As long as house prices were rising, the increase in value of property more than compensated for the interest payable on the loan. The result was both a housing market bubble and a stock market bubble.

Canny banks found a way of reducing the risk that loans might not be paid back. Mortgage loans they made were bundled together, with strong borrowers' loans (those of people with good incomes), combined with those of people with low incomes. The mixture of good and bad loans was termed 'collateral debt obligations' (CDOs). These were issued as if they were government bonds, but with higher rates of interest, and marketed as a new type of 'security'. Banks and other financial organisations all over the world bought them with enthusiasm as safe investments. To make them even safer, they insured these investments with 'credit default swaps', the rational being that if those who had invested in CDOs defaulted, an insurance company would compensate them.

The sale of CDOs was huge – around US$ 45 *trillion* worth were sold as good investments. The risk that the purchasers of the 'bonds' would default (stop paying the interest) was regarded as slim to non-existent, especially as the three rating agencies (Moody's, Standard and Poor's, and Fitch) had each given them AAA ratings. But this rise in asset prices, financed mostly by borrowed money, was unsustainable.

While interest rates were low, the dangers were obscured. When, however, the Federal Reserve under the chairmanship of Ben Bernanke raised interest rates in 2006, and again in 2007, and then again in early 2008, the speculative house of cards began to collapse. In September 2007 the British Northern Rock bank suffered a run on its assets, and had to be nationalised. In early 2008 the US Bear Stearns bank went bankrupt and was bought out by its competitor J.P. Morgan. More disastrously, in September 2008 the Lehman Brothers bank, one of the largest in the US, required rescuing from bankruptcy; but unlike Bear Stearns, no-one obliged. Unfortunately for Lehman Brothers, the US Treasury secretary, Henry Paulson, was a partner of the rival bank Goldman Sachs, and refused to bail them out.[339] The collapse of Lehman Brothers on 15 September triggered the global financial crisis. Two days later the American Insurance Group, holding all those credit default swaps, plunged into bankruptcy. A chain reaction of global company failures precipitately began, and Wall Street and the world's stock markets plunged. For a few days the whole world's financial structures teetered on the edge of collapse as banks stopped loaning to each other, and money markets froze.

The stock market collapse that accompanied the collapse of the banks exposed the poor condition of the balance sheets of many financial institutions. The years since the 1999 abolition of the Glass-Steagall Act had witnessed shady financial practices, with debts held off company balance sheets, and regulators turning a blind eye to dubious practices. However, Paulson and Bernanke in their respective capacities, as US treasurer and chair of the Federal Reserve, rode to the rescue of the money people. In October the US government spent over US$ 700 billion on buying up the 'poisoned' loans of banks faced with failure. This huge sum was to be paid for by taxpayers (of both the present and the future) and was in effect a transfer of money from the public to the banks. Meanwhile millions of 'little' people lost their homes to mortgage foreclosures, as they could no longer pay the interest on their loans.

The justification for bailing out the rich was to avoid the deflation which nearly set in, as had occurred in the early 1930s. Deflationary spirals are difficult to control since people either cannot spend, or they delay spending because things will be cheaper next year. So to avoid what happened in the Great Depression, the US treasury decided to prevent deflation by keeping the banks going whatever the cost. The initial bailing out of the banks with public money was followed by what was euphemistically called 'quantitative easing' – extra money printed and provided to the banks so they could continue loaning money and 'repair balance sheets'.[340]

The intentions may have been good and may have helped the economy limp along, but ultimately all these measures just fed the wealthy. When rich people and industrialists got the treasury money, rather than spending it producing jobs and getting people back to work, they tended either to repay their own debts or to put the money into the stock market. Little or nothing was passed on to 'ordinary' people whose spending might have kept the economy alive. The result was a deflationary trend. By 2016 negative interest rates were normal in both the US and Europe. This was accompanied by an asset bubble on the stock markets, and a growing contrast between the money assets of the super rich and the low incomes and savings of the majority of the population.

The global situation was not helped by the state of the European economy. The European Union has around 7.3% of the world's population, yet contributes 20% of the global GDP, making it the largest economy in the world. If it were to collapse economically or politically it would set off a global financial crisis that would make that of 2008-09 appear minor. A full monetary union had been established in 2002 in which national currencies such as the German deutschmark and French franc were scrapped and replaced by the euro – now the common currency for fifteen or sixteen independent nations. Unlike the United States, which is simultaneously both a monetary and a fiscal union, the EU is only a monetary union. The nations that make it up have retained their own national status, and their independent national fiscal budgets. There remains a large gulf between the financial strength of Germany and weaker economies of southern and eastern Europe such as Spain and Portugal.

The recession that hit Europe in the aftermath of the 2008-9 financial crisis hit the southern European states and Greece particularly hard.[341] If these countries had had independent currencies, the way out of recession would have been to devalue their currencies. This would have made their exports cheaper and imports more expensive, helping to repair the national balance sheet without too much unemployment. In the EU, with its single currency, this cannot happen. So in a recession the weaker countries are faced with a difficult choice: they can either leave the EU and return to their own currency, which they can devalue, or they can remain in the EU, keep the euro, and pursue a policy of ultra fiscal austerity. This means massively cutting back government spending, leading to more unemployment and less spending on social security, leading to a crisis for many poorer people, and especially for young people who find there are no jobs for them. This inevitably leads to the rise of political factions demanding to leave the EU, and a return to monetary and fiscal independence. This is what happened in the Greek crisis of 2015. We now have a situation where one part of the EU is doing well (for example Germany) while other parts are in deep recession, and having to pursue austerity reforms. In political terms this is surely unsustainable in the longer term.

There are three possible outcomes for the European Union countries over the next few years. The first is that the present policy continues, with the European Central Bank pursuing a policy of austerity. In this depressed situation banks and corporations will be reluctant to invest in new production, unemployment will remain high, and there will be cutbacks in state spending, particularly in the weaker economies. The second way forward, and in principle the best, is for there to be a move towards a full fiscal union – a United States of Europe with a single European treasury, a single budgetary policy, a single EU national debt, and a single taxation system for the entire region. Such a fiscal union would, however, mean the ending of each state's national sovereignty, and so far little enthusiasm has been shown for this by European governments. The third possible destiny is for the European Union to break apart and for the member countries to return to their national currencies. This is what extremist parties in every member country (for example the National Front in France) are advocating, and which was in fact the action taken by the United Kingdom with its 2020 'Brexit'.

The success of fringe groups in the UK in bringing about Britain's decision to withdraw from the EU illustrates the dangers. Although Great Britain retained the pound sterling, its membership of the EU after 1973 was an important contributor to its economic strength. But with its withdrawal from the EU in early 2020 – Brexit – both the UK and the EU have been seriously weakened. The people in Britain who pushed for the separation from Europe were partly driven by deluded nostalgic fantasies about the old British Empire, but mainly by the wish to separate from the rules the EU set for production, trade, and immigration and return to the ultra-competition of the 1930s. The British economy looks inevitably to be set back several percentage points in an act of pointless national self-harm. In 2022, tensions in Northern Ireland were also being provoked by the British government over how and where to draw the border with the Republic of Ireland, which remains in the EU. Border hostilities with France are being stoked by the British in the English Channel, particularly with the Home Office attempts to prevent refugees from crossing the Channel including plans to deport those that succeed to Rwanda. Should other countries follow the UK's self-harming strategies, the EU is unlikely to survive.

Ominous developments threatened after Russia invaded Ukraine in February 2022. Oil prices shot up to over $US 100 a barrel, and food, petrol and other prices rose in response. Poorer people especially were finding it difficult to live. The rapid inflation caught national banks by surprise and they were forced to raise interest rates from the extremely low levels in operation since 2008 – at a time when economies were still facing recession. By the end of 2022 the yield on 10-year US government bonds had risen from around 0,2% to over 4%, with other interest rates following.

In May 2023, just before this book was published, another period of stagflation (inflation combined with recession) had set in: a world with high levels of debt, and therefore particularly dangerous.[342] Local banks everywhere were taken by surprise. Many banks had overborrowed at the low interest rates of 2009-21, and, as rates exploded upwards, were finding it difficult to pay the higher interest on the debt. In response, deposit holders rushed to take their money somewhere safer. The US Silicon Valley Bank collapsed, and several other US regional banks were in difficulty.

## 23. The Gathering Storm

While our planetary population continues to rise, and the natural environment on which we depend continues to be unsustainably plundered, our political capacity to unite and attend to the dangers is waning. Many nations are controlled by kleptocratic oligarchies for whom environmental issues are secondary. Moneyed elites run down social services, reduce taxes for themselves, and hide their plundered wealth in tax havens. Russia, after the collapse of the Soviet Union, is ruled by oligarchic kleptocrats. In the United States the Republican Party is tearing up democratic norms and ignores Russia's blatant interference in the country's internal politics. Authoritarian regimes that focus on economic growth, such as China, centralise decision-making, and regard democracy as an enemy. The Russians, as they bid to reabsorb Ukraine, openly threaten the use of nuclear weapons should the US or EU intervene militarily.

There has been a merging of the interests of giant corporations and gangster regimes, which in turn merge seamlessly with criminal organizations. Increasing numbers of people rely for their information about the world on social networks that are all too frequently manipulated by right-wing governments to distort the truth, while independent newspapers and media are collapsing. A variant form of fascism, in some ways different from but in other ways similar to the Hitler fascism of the 1930s, is gathering strength in Russia and the US and many other countries, including Brazil. Race hatred and antisemitism are not only reviving but becoming central in the politics of many countries, including the United States. The multiple global crisis of climate change, environmental degradation and the Covid-19 virus epidemic, has needed united and urgent cooperation and leadership from all nations. This has not yet occurred, despite smooth talk from the world's politicians. Young people, even in the rich world, are growing up in incomparably worse psychic circumstances compared to the generation born after the Second World War. For them, the natural expectation of youth, that the future will be better than the present, has faded.

The waning of the global hegemony of the United States, despite its military strength, is increasingly evident, with China positioned to take its place. President Xi Jinping is effectively the most powerful politician in the world. Xi replaced Hu Jintao in 2012 as head of the Chinese communist party, and combined that position with the presidency the following year. The overwhelming strategy of the Chinese regime has been to accelerate economic growth, while brooking no threats to the rule of the communist party. Hong Kong, which China resumed control of from the British in 1997, is, in the 2020s, seeing its democracy dismantled. Xi has also made it clear that Taiwan is an integral part of China, implying future – possibly nuclear – conflict with the United States. Dissident movements in the western regions of Xinjiang and Tibet have been suppressed and many members have been tortured in prisons in brutal processes of 're-education'. In 2022 the Chinese Communist Party scrapped the norm that party leaders retire after two five-year terms and elected Xi for a third five-year term, making him the most powerful Chinese ruler since Mao Zedong. Xi and his family have amassed personal fortunes, while pushing anti-corruption strategies against perceived political opponents. Chinese economic growth has been phenomenal, with many United States and European corporations setting up operations in China because of its cheap, hardworking and controlled labour. The People's Republic Central Bank's policy of keeping the renminbi, the Chinese international currency, artificially undervalued, has led to exports skyrocketing, especially to the United States. The Chinese government now has over five trillion US dollars invested in US government bonds, leading to an effective intertwining of the two countries' economies. Should the Chinese sell their US bonds, the world's markets would collapse.

The population of China has soared to over 1.4 billion people, whilst at the same time it has an increasing proportion of aging people as a result of the 'one child policy' initiated in the early 1980s. To head off the dangers of too few young people, Xi's regime has relaxed the one child law, and urged families to have more children. Although population growth rates have slowed in the past three decades, the increasing affluence in the urban areas has led to smaller families, and hence a larger number of households, all of which aim for improved living standards. The environmental damage in China includes deforestation, drought, the drying up of river systems as a result of giant dams, poor air quality resulting from the burning of coal and other fossil fuels, and vast areas where rubbish, much of it imported, is accumulated. Although Xi and his colleagues are aware of the dangers of climate change, China continues burning coal for electricity because growth of the economy always remains their priority. Politically there have been growing clashes between China and the United States, leading to closer ties between China and Putin's Russian Federation.

In the 1980s Vladimir Putin was a mid-ranking operative in the Soviet KGB. He witnessed the sudden collapse of the Soviet Union during 1988-91 which destroyed the entire basis of the Soviet political and economic structures put together under Stalin after the mid-1920s. Parts of the Soviet empire, such as Ukraine, Kazakhstan and Belarus, were given independence. The Russian people were assured that capitalism would be quickly established. Instead, jobs were lost, industries collapsed or were bought at ridiculously cheap prices by entrepreneurs, and all the state supports of the Soviet era disappeared. A few clever and lucky entrepreneurs began to import Western capitalist goods and grew rich. McDonalds and KFC were soon visible. But as the currency collapsed, most people could not afford the new capitalist lifestyle.

One 87-year-old, who had been a member of the communist party since 1922, complained eloquently: 'We had a great empire – stretching from sea to sea, from beyond the Arctic to the subtropics. Where is it now? It was defeated without a bomb. Without Hiroshima. It's been conquered by Her Majesty's Salami! The good chow won! Mercedes Benz. The people don't need anything else, don't even offer it to them. Only bread and circuses for them. And that truly is the most important discovery of the twentieth century. The response to all the famous humanists and Kremlin dreamers. While we, my generation...we had great plans. We dreamt of worldwide revolution: "To the grief of all bourgeois, through the world, we'll spread the fire." We wanted to build a new world where everyone would be happy. We thought that it was possible.'[343]

Some high-up officials in the ex-Soviet empire were able to seize political power for themselves, for example, Nursultan Nazarbayev in the Kazakh Soviet Region, who became self-proclaimed president of the new Kazakhstan. Oil companies, iron and steel works, and banks were sold to cronies at low prices. Tom Burgis in his book *Kleptopia* describes how swathes of the Kazakhstan economy were given over to a trio of men whose company, The Eurasian Natural Resources Company, listed on the London Stock Exchange in 2007. This was effectively a criminal looting enterprise, with money siphoned off with the collaboration of UK lawyers and London-based banks. These so-called oligarchs quickly accumulated huge personal fortunes which they safeguarded by ingenious schemes of money laundering and tax evasion. All that was asked was loyalty to the 'big man', for whom an appropriate cut of profits was required. Workers in the towns and labourers in the rural areas were paid low wages and controlled by the police and the military. Strikes were ruthlessly suppressed, and the leaders imprisoned. United States and British judges tended to play safe, and side with Nazarbayev's regime. Burgis points to the central issue: 'For Nazarbayev the fundamental problem remained. Globalisation meant that rule by theft and rule of law were coexisting... Such tensions could not be maintained indefinitely. One system would have to dominate, leaving the other a facade.'[344]

The Russian Soviet, the largest of the Soviet Union's ex-components, became the Russian Federation in the early 1990s. In the turmoil accompanying the downfall of Gorbachev, Boris Yeltsin emerged the winner as Russian president. During his tenure a system in which there were elections and a parliament was established. Vladimir Putin rose in the ranks and was made prime minister in 1999. When Yeltsin retired in 2000, Putin played the strongman and took over as president as well. Restricted to two terms of the presidency, he had a colleague succeed him in 2008, and resumed the presidency for himself in 2012. Putin had by then evolved into the supreme kleptocrat out of the debris of the collapse of the Soviet Union, to whom other kleptocrats owed their position. He surrounded himself with advisers who were influenced by nationalistic and neo-fascist ideas. They had a hostility to all forms of democracy: as in Kazakhstan, protestors were arrested and their leaders imprisoned, murdered, or hounded into exile.[345] As the dissident Russian economist Boris Kagarlitsky put it, the global trend was not so much the weakening of the state 'but the rejection by the state of its social functions, in favour of repressive ones, and the ending of democratic freedoms'.[346]

Putin is unambiguously intent both on undermining the global authority of the United States and doing everything possible to weaken the European Union. He is the mastermind behind an emerging form of kleptocratic fascism which seeks to combat all democracy in whatever way possible.[347] Russia's comparative military and economic weakness is to some extent compensated for by its astute use of the internet and social networks to manipulate electorates into collectively irrational behaviour. As with Xi in China, Putin has changed Russia's electoral law so that he can remain president indefinitely; and he can disregard the Russian Parliament via rigged elections.

In 2012-13, secure in his third term as president, Putin turned on Ukraine, which had become independent in 1991 as the Soviet Union fell apart. Ukraine had been part of the Soviet/Russian empire since the 1780s, and for the Russian rulers Ukraine's strong democratic movement, embraced by the European Union and supported by the United States, was a red line. Russian troops were mobilised to put down Ukrainian democracy. Russia first invaded and annexed the Crimean peninsula in 2014; attempts were simultaneously made to invade the Donetsk region of south-eastern Ukraine.

Eight years later, in February 2022, the Russians again invaded Ukraine, aiming to overrun the entire country. By late 2022 the Russians had failed to take Kiev, and the war was being fought bitterly once again in Ukraine's south-east. The strong and growingly successful defence put up by the Ukrainians had by then demonstrated the relative weakness of Russia's military capabilities. The European Union was considering candidate membership for Ukraine, something that looked likely to provide fuel for the crisis. Russia seems to be settling in for a long struggle, and the outcome is uncertain. Putin has threatened to use nuclear weapons if sufficiently provoked.

Central to Putin's foreign policy has been the attempt to undermine the political strength of the EU and the US via methods subtler and more successful than military invasion. Russian propaganda distorts the truth, using the internet to plant false claims and stories – what Timothy Snyder calls 'implausible deniability, telling obvious lies and then daring the Western media to seek the facts.'[348] Putin has been supporting ultra-right and fascist allies throughout Western Europe, including Nigel Farage and his UKIP Brexiteers in Britain.

He was also able to help tilt the scales in favour of the failed businessman, Donald Trump, in the American presidential elections of 2016. 'Having used its Twitter bots to encourage a Leave vote in the Brexit referendum in June 2016, Russia now turned them loose in the United States,' writes Timothy Snyder. That same month Trump and his advisers got together with the Russian ambassador to the US in the Trump Tower in New York to define strategy. Trump's Democratic Party opponents were attacked with a tissue of false innuendoes and outright lies, and Trump was declared winner in TV debates in which it was clear he had lost. 'Trump's preference for Putin over Obama was not just a matter of racism or rivalry: it also was an aspiration to be more like Putin,' writes Snyder: 'American and Russian oligarchs have more in common with one another than they do with their own populations.'[349]

After his November 2016 victory, Trump appointed several men to important posts who had close connections with Russia. Neo-fascist organisations in the US – for example the Breitbart News Network, directed by Steve Bannon – pushed racist, anti-black, anti-Jewish, and anti-democracy propaganda. Trump, openly contemptuous of democracy, cosied up to Putin and the communist leader of North Korea.[350] His economic strategy was the usual neoliberal agenda – lower taxes for the rich and reduced spending on social services. Climate change, Trump claimed, was just a hoax. After the outbreak of the Covid-19 virus epidemic in early 2020 Trump downplayed its danger, with the result that many more thousands of Americans died than would have otherwise been the case.

The presidential elections of 2020, in which Democrats chose the 79-year-old Joe Biden as their candidate, witnessed another attempt by right-wing media to get the clearly unsuitable Trump re-elected. Biden narrowly won the election, although over 74 million Americans voted for Trump. Trump and the bulk of his Republican followers refused to recognise the election result, and called for an uprising against the result that on 6 January 2021 saw the storming of the US Congress building by an armed mob. Trump's subsequent impeachment, though passed by the House of Representatives, was blocked by a minority of Republican senators. It was the lowest point of democracy in the US since the civil war of the 1860s.[351] Right-wing and outright fascist organisations have proliferated throughout the country, continuing to push white supremacy. By around 2040 whites will become a minority in the United States.

Trump's US administration was openly hostile to the European Union, and allied with Putin's strategies to see the EU weakened. Although after the British Brexit the 27 remaining countries in the EU have given the impression of strengthening their unity, the EU's capacity to survive in the longer term is uncertain. In 2022 Poland and Hungary, both EU members, were in the grip of right-wing administrations with no affection for democratic norms or independent judiciaries, and they looked as if they might in the future lean politically and economically towards Russia and China. Ultra right-wing minorities exist in most European countries, represented by organisations such as the Front National in France and the Alternative für Deutschland in Germany, which push for secession from the EU. The political and military weakness of Europe compared to China and the US is apparent. The biggest problem for the EU remains the political inability to bring about a full fiscal union in which the budgets and finances of all the EU's members are merged, taxation is 'europeanised', and policies for social services and unemployment benefits are merged.

The activities of kleptocratic regimes increasingly straddle the line between corruption and outright criminality. Both kleptocratic regimes and criminal organizations engage in tax evasion and money-laundering. Whilst nation states focus on the local, criminal organisations and gangster regimes increasingly organise globally. They include the Sicilian Mafia (Casa Nostra), the US's Mafia, the Yakuza gangs in Japan, the mafias in Russia, the Colombian 'cartels', Turkish heroin traffickers, Nigerian 419 networks, and others. Their activities include smuggling (of anything[352]), money laundering, the drug trade, extortion and blackmail, gambling, loan sharking, 419 frauds, kidnapping, protection racketeering, the counterfeiting of money, killers for hire, prostitution, dealing in stolen goods, the supply of body parts and bodies to hospitals in need, and the supply of children, including babies, where required. Several of these criminal concerns intermesh with the activities of kleptocratic state groups. The globalization of crime, according to the Anti-Mafia Commission of the Italian Parliament, creates 'a genuine criminal counter power capable of imposing its will on legitimate states, of undermining institutions and forces of law and order, of unsettling delicate economic and financial equilibrium and destroying democratic life...and this on a planetary level.'[353] To the extent that vital figures in the state, such as police, judges, business people and politicians become corrupt, the democratic state is weakened. The international drugs trade – worth at least US$ 500 billion a year – often facilitated by corrupt police, is an example.

The weakening of democracy at the global level is not only attributable to the machinations of kleptocrats and gangsters. The masses of people who vote in elections puzzlingly appear often to put their faith in dubious candidates or parties which represent the super-rich and are contemptuous of the ordinary voter. Or they do not turn up to vote at all. To some extent this can be explained by the global economic downturn in the decade after 2008: the loss of jobs, static wages, the end of the idea of permanent progress. The wealthy have now accumulated such mountains of spare cash that they can control the media at a time when many independent newspapers are closing down. The internet can easily be manipulated by unscrupulous agencies to sow doubts about reality in the minds of those who rely on social media for their information about the world. In the 2010s the internet 'became an attack surface of the Russian secret services, who were able to do what they liked inside the American psychosphere', writes Timothy Snyder.[354] Social media, such as Facebook, Twitter, TikTok and Instagram, have facilitated this organised lying by dominant groups. Entire departments of kleptocratic regimes are given over to the manipulation of public opinion both at home and in other countries. The 'realities' that are put over in the social media are often constructed by agencies that wish to turn the truth on its head and create a state of mind in the 'masses' favourable to their own goals. Hannah Arendt had warned in 1972: 'The historian knows how vulnerable is the whole texture of facts in which we spend our daily life. It is always in danger of being perforated by single lies or torn to shreds by the organised lying of groups, nations or classes.'[355]

As the world's human population approaches eight billion, these political deteriorations coincide with mounting problems springing from human vulnerability to viral infections. Human history is punctuated by disease events that have brought about widespread death and economic dislocation. These include the bubonic plague of the mid-fourteenth century, the widespread transmission of syphilis after the Europeans invaded the Americas, the high death rates brought about by cholera and tuberculosis during the first century of industrialisation, and the spread of malaria after the European invasions of Africa. The First World War, in which over ten million men were killed, was followed in 1918-19 by our species' most fatal epidemic, the influenza epidemic in which over 50 million people died.[356] The spread of the human immunodeficiency virus (HIV-AIDS) is a more recent example of a virus disease event.

Today we are in the midst of another global epidemic. Covid-19 (the Severe Acute Respiratory Syndrome Coronavirus 2, SARS-CoV-2) was first picked up in China in December 2019. It rapidly spread throughout Asia, and by February 2020 was widespread in Italy and the United States. Within two months, by April 2020, there was no human settlement on the planet that was unaffected. By December 2022, there had been over 630 million confirmed global cases, and 6.6 million deaths.

Measures taken to minimise the spread of Covid led during 2020 to the worst global economic recession since the Great Depression of the 1930s. The interruptions to agriculture led to widespread hunger in the poor world, with famines threatening many populations. The cutting off of Ukraine's grain exports after the Russian invasion of February 2022 made matters worse. Education was badly hit, as schools and universities were closed, and increasingly students worked and studied alone at home. Each national government had to deal with infections in their own country, with varying successes and outcomes.

Some key leaders ridiculed the dangers of the virus, including Trump in the US and Bolsonaro in Brazil, two countries where the infection rates skyrocketed. Tourism was heavily hit, and unemployment in tourist sectors was high. Losses for insurance companies and other costs made the epidemic the costliest disaster in human history. New variants of the original virus appeared, such as those that first emerged in the UK, South Africa and India. The speed with which companies were able to produce effective vaccines by the turn of 2020/21 was commendable, but the focus of the rich world on the health of their own populations meant that the elimination of the virus became difficult if not impossible. On the brighter side, the collapse in the use of fossil fuels and human travel witnessed what has been termed an 'anthropause'. During 2020 carbon emissions were reduced by a quarter in China, and emissions of nitrogen oxide decreased globally – far more achieved by the Covid virus than by climate action of governments. However the rapid comeback of industrial production meant that the relief for ecosystems was short term.

While humanity is suffering its crisis of politics and greed, our once blue planet is suffering what can only be termed an all-out cancerous attack. Clive Ponting, in his *A New Green History of the World*, termed it 'the rape of the world'.[357] Over the entire land mass, humans are destroying both tropical and temperate forests at lightning speed. The oceans are polluted with vast accumulations of plastic and poisonous effluents from rivers, and are becoming more acidic because of the $CO_2$ absorbed from human industrial and other activities. The animals that inhabit the lands and seas are being killed off in what has been called the anthropogenic extinction – the sixth extinction in the history of multicellular life.[358] The atmosphere is being transformed by the addition of vast amounts of carbon dioxide from the burning of fossil fuels that the Gaian system buried underground, and which now fuel the destructive industrial growth of our species. The warming up of the planetary atmosphere, apart from the impact on all other living systems, is itself a threat to the continuation of our species' activities. Despite this, the preoccupation of the wealthy remains fixed on economic growth, which means irreversibly accelerating the devastation of the planetary life systems.

The onslaught on the planet's forests by human agriculture and cities accelerates. Today, only about 27 million square kilometres of the original 70 million square kilometres of total forest is still standing (this includes 6 million of the original 16 million square kilometres of tropical forest). Despite warnings from environmentalists, the destruction is accelerating: well over 2 million square kilometres of the planet's total forests were torn down between 2000 and 2020. Human agriculture already takes up around 50% of all habitable land on Earth, and, as populations expand, will take up more. Besides land for agriculture, forests are also destroyed to make way for human settlements, roads, mines and industrial areas. Much of the rest is turned over for humans to grow commercial crops such as tobacco, cotton, soya and palm oil, and rear cattle for beef and their hides. Much of the timber cut down is burnt, increasing carbon in the air. Vast areas of rain forest have already been destroyed throughout Central America, Indonesia, New Guinea, and the Philippines. On Madagascar, ninety percent of the original forest is gone. In Brazil 1,180 square kilometres of rain forest were destroyed in the month of May 2021 alone, a record for a single month. At the present rate of destruction all of the world's tropical forests will be flattened by 2050. The loss of tree cover accelerates soil erosion, reduces cloud formation, increases temperatures, and enhances desertification. The destruction of the forests releases around 1.5 billion tons of carbon into the air per annum, with devastating effects on global heating.

Animal populations are decimated as our destructive orgy continues. We have lost about 69% of all vertebrate wildlife populations since 1970, and around three quarters of all flying insects. As animal populations decline and their habitable areas shrink, animal viruses spread more easily. In the past fifty years, as our population expansion brings us more closely into contact with animals, animal viruses have frequently jumped species to humans. For example, the pig farms that replaced forests in Malaya led to the Nipah pig virus crossing to humans, and the loss of thousands of lives. The grasslands that replace forests are often ideal environments for mosquitoes, resulting in more malaria, as has happened in Kenya. David Quammen writes: 'We cut the trees; we kill the animals or cage them and lead them to markets. We disrupt ecosystems, and we shake the virus loose from their natural hosts. When that happens they need a new host. Often we are it.'[359] This may well be what happened with the Covid-19 virus, which is thought to have passed to humans from bats.

The oceans and the life they contain are also suffering badly. A key date in history that seldom gets mentioned is 1907, which saw the creation of the first artificial plastic by the Belgian-American chemist Leo Baekeland, following experiments in his garage in New York. It was a mixture of phenol and formaldehyde that he called Bakelite (and from which he made a fortune). It was soon in great demand as an electrical insulation material. By the 1930s new forms of plastic were resulting from various experiments such as nylon, polystyrene, polyethylene and polyvinyl chloride (PVC). By the 1970s just about anything could be made, or partly made, out of plastic, including the ubiquitous plastic bag.

When thrown away, much of the plastic eventually escapes landfills, and around 300 million tons is now in the oceans. Here it has a devastating impact on oceanic species. Global ocean currents herd the plastic waste into huge 'gyres', such as the North Pacific Subtropical Gyre, sometimes termed the Great Pacific Garbage Patch. Of particular danger to many oceanic species are so-called 'nurdles', tiny plastic pellets, 5.5 trillion tons of which are manufactured annually. These are mistaken by fish for food, and swallowed.[360] The plastics biodegrade only over hundreds of years, and are broken down into smaller and smaller particles, which sink to the depths, and are consumed by krill and other micro-species on which fish feed. Other plastic refuse in the sea is ingested by birds, often with fatal results. Whales and sharks may be trapped in plastic fishing nets, again with fatal results. Species that are caught in fishing nets, and die, are discarded as 'by-catch' by the fishing industry. These include seals, dolphins, sharks and sea turtles.

Human waste is also washed into the oceans via rivers, including poisonous wastes and faeces. Even the most remote islands in the eastern Pacific have beaches inundated with human garbage. In combination with global warming, micro plastics have led to the death of corals. Tim Flannery gives an example. In 1857 when the naturalist Alfred Russel Wallace sailed into Ambon Harbour in eastern Indonesia he saw 'one of the most astonishing and beautiful sights I have ever beheld. The bottom was absolutely hidden by a continuous series of corals, sponges, actinae, and other marine productions, of magnificent dimensions, varied forms, and brilliant colours.' In the 1990s when Flannery went into the same harbour he saw 'no coral gardens, no medusae, no fishes, nor even bottom. Instead, the opaque water stank and was thick with effluent and garbage. As I neared the town it just got worse, until I was greeted with rafts of faeces, plastic bags, and intestines of butchered goats.'[361]

The destruction of forests and pollution of the oceans, being far away, worry comparatively few people, but the changes in temperature and weather conditions are there for everyone to experience. In 1997, when I started the History course on which this book is based, there were around 362 parts per million of carbon in the air compared to about 250 parts per million in the mid-nineteenth century. The consensus in the early twenty-first century was that carbon had to be halted at 350 ppm to avoid runaway global heating. In 2022 carbon in the air amounted to 420 ppm, a 15.75% increase in less than a quarter of a century. If the same rate of increase continues, we will reach 485 ppm by 2045, and 560 ppm by 2069. Carbon dioxide and methane emissions from human activities are the cause.

A stream of warnings comes through the media and from the politicians. In 2021 Canada experienced its highest ever temperature: 46.6 °C at Lytton, a small town to the north-east of Vancouver in British Columbia. This was attributable to an unusual 'heat dome' over south-west Canada and Washington state that has also led to record temperatures in the US cities of Portland and Seattle. The US state of Oregon has been afflicted by unprecedented forest fires and temperatures several degrees higher than usual. A prolonged heat wave in Alaska during July 2022 triggered over 250 major fires following 40,000 or so lightning strikes. These are attributable to more vapour in the air across the state due to the relatively warm air. Death Valley in the western US registered over 53 °C in 2021, and the previous year a portion of Death Valley experienced the hottest atmospheric temperature ever recorded on Earth: 54.4 °C. In the land areas of the planet where high temperatures are accompanied by droughts, the combination of heat, dryness and winds has caused extensive forest fires, as in California and eastern Australia.[362]

Unfortunately the political and practical difficulties of retreating from our current situation make any possible solution difficult to imagine. Rich countries and their politicians are focused on growth, and given the pressures, will always be. They tend to say that the more recently industrialising countries, such as China, should do something about it. In response, China and countries, such as India, that took off industrially relatively recently say: 'You Europeans and Americans put all your carbon into the air during your industrialisation, and now you have the hypocrisy to point a finger at us!' The many international conferences over global warming have tended to produce fine words, but negligible effective changes in behaviour. 'Green' parties are making political progress in a few countries, such as Germany, but in general if people are worried about climate change, they do not decisively show it at elections. Their important concerns (shaped to a great extent by right-wing media) are with lower taxation, jobs, economic growth, and drum-thumping national pride. This is the strange gap in today's democracies between what people understand and their collective voting behaviour. Another gap is between the scientific understanding of the mechanisms of global heating, and the practical steps we have taken to change our economic and industrial systems in order to retreat from our present dangerous position. As recently as July 2022 the US Supreme Court (under pressure from corporate interest groups) turned down the US government's bid to phase out coal-fired power stations 'without clear congressional authorisation', which is unlikely to be given.

Meanwhile the concentrations of carbon and methane in the atmosphere continue to rise. The Greenland glaciers are melting faster than earlier predicted, and, along with the reduction in the areas of Arctic ice, are threatening to slow the Gulf Stream that keeps Britain and Europe warm. This may result, paradoxically, in a colder Europe. Melting land ice on the Antarctic continent, also accelerating beyond earlier predictions, is raising sea levels, an increase that will be added to by melting glaciers in South America and the Himalayas. At the moment much of the carbon dioxide given off by industrialisation processes is absorbed by the tropical forests and the oceans, but the current rate of destruction of the forests, and the finite amount of carbon dioxide that is absorbable by the oceans, will weaken these temporary safety valves. As the oceans heat up, more water vapour will evaporate into the lower atmosphere, and as water vapour is a major retainer of heat, this will mean warmer conditions, and more intense hurricanes and other weather events. And as the oceans warm, their water also expands, adding to the rise of sea levels. Greater heat over Siberia will mean more methane given off from the vast areas of peat, supplemented by the methane generated by the increasing herds of cattle in Amazonia. Greater heat and, in places, decreased rainfall, will reduce crop yields and make us vulnerable to food shortages. This will be experienced most painfully in the hotter parts of the poor world, much of which is already suffering drought and food shortages – my own country South Africa being one of them. This means that the gaps between the rich and the poor world will widen, at least in the short term. In the longer term, though, the comfortably off will have more to lose.

# 24. Will our Species Survive?

In the lifetime of a young person reading this book many dangerous changes seem inevitable. By the 2050s, human population on this planet will reach at least nine and possibly ten billion people. Average planetary temperatures will increase by at least a further one degree centigrade, as carbon in the air increases from its present 420 parts per million in the direction of 500 ppm.

After that point, a runaway warming will be irreversibly underway. The roughly one trillion barrels of accessible oil left in the ground will be consumed at around 30 billion barrels per annum, allowing oil supply to stretch to the 2040s and 2050s. And then? The outlook for grain production will be grim. Forests will be destroyed at well over 100,000 square kilometres a year, shrinking the currently surviving 27 million square kilometres of forest to about 23 million square kilometres. The proportion of the planetary photosynthate consumed by the human species will increase from its current 40-50% to 60-70%. As our population increases, the maximum sustainable, per person, ecological footprint will decline from today's 1.7 hectares to about 1.4 hectares, and the average consumption of grain per person per annum will decline sharply from its present 290 kilograms. The mass extinction event in the planet's life system now underway will gather pace, with large animals increasingly remaining only in zoos. There will be more famines, more capricious rainfall patterns, more inequalities, and more conflicts.

Any hope that there will be some sort of political transformation, some total change of heart by the world's rulers, seems slender. The corporate grip of the rich world, with its twin aims of economic growth and the appropriation of a larger part of the fruits of that growth by the wealthy, is likely to continue. While there will doubtlessly be some efforts to reduce industry's impact on the environment, the fixation on economic growth may even intensify as unemployment, population growth and stagnant consumption increase political tensions. Effective political policies to cut back population and production so as to avert environmental catastrophe will surely bring about the social, financial and economic crisis which politicians see as their duty to prevent. Put more bluntly: the stability of the current economic order depends on trashing the planet.

In 2021 Peter Kalmus summed up the dire scenario: 'Fossil fuels must be capped and rationed, and diverted to necessities as we transition to a zero-carbon civilization. If we fail, the planet will continue to heat up, creeping up past 1.5° C, then 2° C, then 3° C of global heating as we keep squandering precious time. With every fraction of a degree, the floods and fires and heat will get worse. Coastal cities will be abandoned. Ocean currents will shift. Crops will fail. Ecosystems will collapse. Hundreds of millions will flee regions with humid heat too high for the human body. Geopolitics will break down. No place will be safe. These disasters are like gut punches to our civilisation.'[363] Predictions of future events are risky, but history does show that when humans are placed under very great stress they fight and kill one another for survival. Given that the great powers possess nuclear weapons, it is not easy to visualise how future conflicts will play out: but it is certain there will be future – potentially genocidal – conflicts as environments collapse.

Jared Diamond at the end of his *Collapse* retains a vestige of hope: 'On the one hand, I acknowledge the seriousness of the problems facing us. If we don't make a determined effort to solve them, and if we don't succeed at that effort, the world as a whole within the next few decades will face a declining standard of living, or perhaps something worse...On the other hand, we shall be able to solve our problems – if we choose to do so...we are not beset by insoluble problems.'[364] Clive Ponting was less optimistic: 'The fact that a breakdown has not so far occurred does not guarantee that it will not happen...the scale of the environmental problems [modern societies] have created...is unprecedented and of a complexity that almost defies solution.'[365]

The warnings have been coming for decades. Here are four from the 1990s. Adam Hochschild, in *The Unique Ghost: Russians Remember Stalin*, noted how very few Russians in the 1930s made any attempt to flee from the NKVD. They assumed that the early morning knock on the door would only happen to people next door, not to them. If it did, 'that would mean the whole system had gone mad'. Hochschild continued: 'And today? If there is a greenhouse effect, a depletion of the ozone, a shrinking of ocean fish stocks and an expansion of the deserts, a steadily widening gap between the world's rich and poor, then that, too, means that the whole system has gone mad. But the analogy is imperfect. For we are free to read and write and talk endlessly about the greenhouse effect or the ozone layer or all the other problems, hence we do not feel the intense fear produced by the NKVD's knock on the door. That very lack of urgency is our form of denial, as foolhardy as the denials of the fellow travellers. For the knock, for all these things, will come.'[366]

The climate scientist James Lovelock wrote: 'In the world today there is a feeling like that before a coming war, or of the ominous calm that precedes a tropical hurricane. For the changes that threaten the world now, we have no detailed guide, we can only guess what they will be. Change may come gradually, but more often in stressed systems it arrives in a series of abrupt events...we are in for surprises, events that could not have been predicted.'[367]

The Buddhist writer Andrew Harvey warned: 'Our unwillingness to face the extremity of the situation is part of the problem. We are certainly at the end of a civilization, a whole cycle of history, and, possibly, at the end of the world. The facts of our global crisis – a crisis that is at once political and economic, psychological and environmental – shows us clearly that the human race has no hope unless it chooses to undergo a total change of heart, a massive, quite unprecedented spiritual transformation. Only the leap into a new consciousness can engender the vision, moral passion, joy and energy necessary to effect change on the scale and with the self-sacrifice necessary to save the planet in the time we have. The message we are being sent by history can be summed up: transform or die out.'[368]

The historian Eric Hobsbawm ended his history of the twentieth century with the caution: 'We live in a world captured, uprooted and transformed by the titanic economic and techno-scientific process of the development of capitalism, which has dominated the past two or three centuries. We know, or at least it is reasonable to suppose, that it cannot go on *ad infinitum*. The future cannot be a continuation of the past, and there are signs, both externally, and, as it were, internally, that we have reached a point of historic crisis. The forces generated by the techno-scientific economy are now great enough to destroy the environment, that is to say, the material foundations of human life. The structures of human societies themselves, including even some of the social foundations of the capitalist economy, are on the point of being destroyed by the erosion of what we have inherited from the human past. Our world risks both explosion and implosion. It must change...We do not know where we are going. We only know that history has brought us to this point and why. However, one thing is plain. If humanity is to have a recognizable future, it cannot be by prolonging the past or the present. If we try to build the third millennium on that basis we shall fail. And the price of failure, that is to say, the alternative to a changed society, is darkness.'[369]

The obstacles confronting any groups committed to environmental and political reform are formidable. As Tony Wood wrote recently: 'What kind of political agency, in any country, can assert control over capitalism run amok – and who is going to summon it into being?'.[370] The bulk of the world's media is controlled by corporate-funded opinion-makers who depict groups pushing for change as left-wing idealists or Marxists. The thousands of movements across the planet working for change are split into countless, often conflicting, agendas. Some, like the Swedish Ende Gelände, focus on reducing carbon in the air, for example by sabotaging peat mines in northern Europe. Their leaders view humanity as salvageable, endangered only by a corporate conspiracy to refuse to convert to carbon free forms of energy.[371] At the other extreme is the Deep Green Resistance movement which argues that our species is unreformable, and we should hasten its end so that animals and the natural system can recover from our onslaught. Others believe the only solution is a massive reduction of the world's human population from eight billion to around two billion, though without going into how this could be achieved. Any effective changes will require large scale political organisation between nations, but this will be difficult given the massive corporate influence on governments, disunity in the goals of movements seeking change, and the sheer magnitude of the tasks.

What can the young person (of whatever age) do? The psychic energy of most of us will have to be channelled into our relationships and maintaining subsistence. Still, despite the dispiriting implications of this book, pessimism, or denial, can be balanced by a type of hope. Vaclav Havel said in his inaugural statement as president of Czechoslovakia in 1990: 'The kind of hope that I often think about...I understand above all as a state of mind, not a state of the world. Either we have hope within us or we don't; it is a dimension of the soul, and it is not essentially dependent on some particular observation of the world or estimate of the situation. [Hope] is not the conviction that something will turn out well, but the certainty that something makes sense, regardless of how it turns out.'[372]

But that should be considered alongside the admonition of the 19-year-old Swedish environmentalist, Greta Thunberg: 'Hope is not something that is given to you. It is something you have to earn, to create. It cannot be gained by standing by passively and waiting for someone else to do something. It is taking action. It is stepping outside your comfort zone.'[373]

Derrick Jensen of the Deep Green Resistance movement says the same thing, slightly differently: 'In the seventeenth century the Zen poet Bunan wrote, "Die while you're alive and be absolutely dead. Then do whatever you want: it's all good."' Jensen continues: 'We are, of course, already dead. There is no hope. The machine is too powerful, the damage too severe. There are too many child abusers, too many rapists, too many corporations, too many tanks and guns and airplanes. And I'm just one person; I can't do anything. You're dead right, so what the hell are you waiting for?...Give up. Capitulate. Realize there's no hope, then have it. If you're dead, you have nothing to lose and a world to gain.'[374]

# Endnotes

Regarding dates I have used the following conventions
BP Before the Present (used for large time periods of thousands of years)
BCE Before the Christian era (formerly BC)
CE Christian era (formerly AD)

1 Books in English providing overview coverage of the entire history and characteristics of our species are rarer than one might imagine. These include David Christian, *Maps of Time: An Introduction to Big History* (2004); and Yuval Noah Harari, *Sapiens: A Brief History of Humankind* (2014). Clive Ponting, *A New Green History of the World: The Environment and the Collapse of Great Civilizations* (2007 edition); and Jared Diamond, *Collapse: How Societies Choose to Fail or Survive* (2005), are both important.

2 As this book was going to press in April 2023 I went on Google to check if the title had previously been used for a book or newspaper article. It hadn't. But I discovered that the British Labour Party leader, Sir Keir Starmer, had used exactly these words in a speech in Liverpool on 25 July 2022: 'What Britain needs is three things: growth, growth and growth'. In October, at the Conservative Party conference, the British prime minister, Liz Truss – repeating Starmer – stressed: 'I have three priorities for our economy: growth, growth and growth.' Greenpeace protesters, who she pilloried as 'the anti-growth coalition', were removed from the hall. Truss may have been swept away by history, but for the great majority of politicians on the planet, the goal of growth remains sacrosanct.

3 Wittgenstein said: 'What a Copernicus or a Darwin really achieved was not the discovery of a true theory but of a fertile new point of view.' See Ludwig Wittgenstein, *Culture and Value* (1980), p.18.

4 Theodore Roszak, *The Voice of the Earth: An Exploration of Ecopsychology* (1992), p.155; Stephen Jay Gould et al, *The Book of Life. An Illustrated History of the Evolution of Life on Earth* (2001 [originally 1993]), p.7.

5 Quoted in Richard Welford, *Hijacking Environmentalism: Corporate Responses to Sustainable Development* (1997), Frontispiece. Chief Seattle is often referred to as Chief Sealth. The quote, collected by Ted Perry in the 1850s, is also the Frontispiece to Fritjof Capra, *The Web of Life: A New Synthesis of Mind and Matter (1996)*, discussed on p.338 of Roszak, *The Voice of the Earth*, and repeated at the end of chapter 17.

6 See Jo Ellen Barnett, *Time's Pendulum* (1998) for the chronologies.

7 James Lovelock, *Gaia: A New Look at Life on Earth* (1979); James Lovelock, *The Ages of Gaia. A Biography of our Living Planet* (1988); James Lovelock,

*Healing Gaia: Practical Medicine for the Planet* (1991); Lynn Margulis and Dorian Sagan, *Microcosmos* (1986); Lynn Margulis, *The Symbiotic Planet. A New Look at Evolution* (1988).

8 Fred Hoyle, *The Intelligent Universe* (1984).

9 Margulis and Sagan, *Microcosmos*, p.77.

10 Margulis and Sagan, *Microcosmos*, p.78.

11 Margulis and Sagan, *Microcosmos*, pp.101-11.

12 Margulis and Sagan, *Microcosmos*, p.92.

13 Capra, *The Web of Life*, p.238.

14 Margulis and Sagan, *Microcosmos*, p.29.

15 Margulis and Sagan, *Microcosmos*, p.67.

16 Margulis, *Symbiotic Planet* [quoted Harvard Course].

17 Lovelock, *Healing Gaia*, chapter 1.

18 Capra, *The Web of Life*, p.98.

19 See Margulis and Sagan, *Microcosmos*, and Lovelock, *Healing Gaia*, for detail.

20 Margulis and Sagan, *Microcosmos*, pp.93-94.

21 See Margulis and Sagan, *Microcosmos*, chapter 12.

22 Lovelock, *Healing Gaia*, p.12.

23 Jean Baudrillard, *The Transparency of Evil: Essays on Extreme Phenomena* (1993), p.3.

24 Lovelock, *Healing Gaia*, p.20.

25 Margulis, *Symbiotic Planet*, pp.160-61.

26 Gould et al, *The Book of Life*, p.21.

27 See the relevant sections in Christian, *Maps of Time*; Jared Diamond, *The Rise and Fall of the Third Chimpanzee* (1991); Richard Leakey, *The Origin of Humankind* (1994); Steven Mithen, *The Prehistory of the Mind: The Search for the Origins of Art, Religion and Science* (1996). The views on central issues of our origins as a species are in constant flux, partly because of the scarcity of evidence.

28 Thomas Berry, *The Dream of the Earth* (1988), p.209. On our driving innumerable species into extinction, see chapter 20.

29 For example Robert L. O'Connell, *Of Arms and Men: A History of War, Weapons, and Aggression* (1989), p.26: 'Only with the coming of agriculture, and later politics, would true warfare become part of human experience. Then there would be something to steal and governments to organise the theft.'

30 The possession of consciousness, however one defines it, separates us from other animals and hurls us into history. The Spanish philosopher Miguel de Unamuno was of the view: 'Man, because he is a man, because he possesses consciousness, is already, in comparison to the jackass or crab, a sick animal. Consciousness is a disease.' The Romanian philosopher E.M. Cioran echoes Unamuno: 'If we want to know happiness in life, it's not to do anything, to live

and nothing more. I feel that man should not have thrown himself into this amazing adventure that is history. Everything that he does turns against him because he wasn't made to do something, he was made solely to live as the animals and trees do. And I'll go even further, man should not have existed. He should have remained a species like any other and not have separated from the whole creation.' See Sebastian Faulkes, *Engelby* (2007), p.256, for the Unamuno quote; and E.M. Cioran, interviewed by James Weiss (1983).

31 Gary Snyder, *The Real Work. Interviews and Talks 1964-79* (1969); pp.107-08.

32 Peter Matthiessen, *The Snow Leopard* (1979), p.60.

33 A visit to the British Museum will verify this quote. BCE means 'before the Common Era', which used to be expressed as BC ('Before Christ'). Where less precise dates are known, especially for approximate dates in the distant past, I have used BP ('Before the Present').

34 Richard Heinberg, *The Party's Over: Oil, War and the Fate of Industrial Societies* (2003), p.9, quoting from Leslie A White, *The Science of Culture: A Study of Man and Civilization* (1949).

35 Marshall McLuhan, *Understanding Media. The Extensions of Man* (1964; references here to the 2002 edition), p.90.

36 McLuhan, *Understanding Media*, pp.134-35.

37 McLuhan, *Understanding Media*, p.93.

38 Joseph A. Tainter, *The Collapse of Complex Societies* (1988), p.196.

39 Richard Manning, 'The Oil We Eat: Following the Food Chain Back to Iraq', *Harpers*, February 2004, p.40.

40 Despite its title, Jared Diamond's *Guns, Germs and Steel* (1997) says little about guns or steel.

41 The basic facts about Europe's history are wonderfully overviewed in Mortimer Chambers et al, *The Western Experience* (originally 1974,10th edition).

42 See Elizabeth L. Eisenstein, *The Printing Revolution in Early Modern Europe* (1979).

43 McLuhan, *Understanding Media*, p.19.

44 McLuhan, *Understanding Media*, chapter 1.

45 McLuhan, *Understanding Media*, p.194.

46 Speech given to German Information Society by Neil Postman, quoted by Michel Pireu in the [South African] *Business Day*, 28 September 2007.

47 McLuhan, *Understanding Media*, p.168.

48 Quoted in Barnett, *Time's Pendulum*, p.65 (from Lewis Mumford, T*echnics and Civilization* (1934), chapter 1, section 2).

49 Barnett, *Time's Pendulum*, pp.102-112.

50 Yes, Chinese ships reached the east coast of Africa in the 1420s, and the Chinese invented gunpowder. But they did not begin industrialisation, which is what we are trying to explain here.

51 The word 'imperialism' only became common after the 1870s. In this book I use the term to indicate the extraction of resources without adequate compensation – by force or contrivance – from one people by another. See also endnote 59 for a definition of the English as imperialists.

52 For a good introductory account see Chambers et al, *The Western Experience.*

53 Alfred W. Crosby, *Ecological Imperialism. The Biological Expansion of Europe, 900-1900* (1986), pp. 7,131.

54 See Sheldon Watts, *Epidemics and History: Disease, Power and History* (1997). Watts argues (p.134) that syphilis, caused by *Treponema pallidum*, was brought back to Europe by Columbus's men who had been raping Hispaniolan women, having mutated from *Treponema pertenne* that causes yaws. Syphilis was then spread into Italy after 1494 by the armies of Charles VIII. Watts refers humorously to 'the discovery of Europe by *Treponema pallidum*'.

55 Quoted in Titus Alexander, *Unravelling Global Apartheid* (1996), p.59. Lattimore was a US adviser to Chiang Kai-shek 1941-42.

56 '[A] single acre (0.4 hectares) of the crop, plus a cow, could feed a family for much of the year. Therein lay its popularity, and its threat.' L.T. Evans, *Feeding the 10 Million: Plants and Population Growth* (1998), p.80.

57 Quoted in Paul Kennedy, *Preparing for the 21st Century* (1993), p.9.

58 McLuhan, *Understanding Media*, pp.134-35.

59 'If Empire, as Francis Xavier said, was little more than to "conjugate the verb to rob in all its moods and tenses", the English were the purest of imperialists.' Quoted by N. Rodger in Nicholas Canny (ed), *The Oxford History of the British Empire, Vol 1: The Origins of Empire* (1998), p.97. Francis Xavier was a sixteenth century Spanish Catholic missionary, one of the founders of the Jesuit order.

60 A good introductory text is E.H. Hobsbawm, *The Age of Revolution*, 1789-1840 (1962).

61 England and Scotland were separate until 1707, when the two monarchies joined and formed Great Britain. Ireland joined in 1801, so forming the United Kingdom of Great Britain and Ireland. The bulk of Ireland became independent in 1922, so that the full name of the UK became The United Kingdom of Great Britain and Northern Ireland.

62 Roszak, *Voice of the Earth*, pp.218-19.

63 Barnett, *Time's Pendulum*, p.129.

64 See Hobsbawm, *Age of Revolution*. For events from the 1840s to 1914 see Hobsbawm's two sequels: *The Age of Capital* (1985) and *The Age of Empire* (1987).

65 Brilliantly caricatured in W.C. Sellar and R.J. Yeatman, *1066 and All That* (1930).

66 See Heinberg, *The Party's Over* for the material in this chapter,

67 Jeremy Rifkin, *Time Wars* (1987), pp.127-32. Rifkin (p.127) said of Frederick W. Taylor: 'He has probably had a greater effect on the private and public lives of the men and women of the twentieth-century than any other single individual'. See also endnote 184.

68 Timothy Leary, *Chaos and the Cyber Culture* (1994), p.38.

69 See Evans, *Feeding the 10 Billion.*

70 McLuhan, *Understanding Media*, pp.273-4, 278.

71 F.T. Marinetti, *Manifesto of Futurism* [*Manifesto di Futurismo*] (1909).

72 Among the myriad books on capitalism I recommend Thomas Piketty, *Capital in the Twenty-First Century* (2013), and J. Anthony Boeckh, *The Great Reflation: How Investors Can Profit from the New World of Money* (2010).

73 Quoted in Philip Brown and Hugh Lander, *Capitalism and Social Progress: The Future of Society in a Global Economy* (2001), p.1.

74 Mumford, *Technics and Civilization*, p.311. Mumford seemingly refers to the disruptions caused by the 'machine'.

75 Meghnad Desai, *Marx's Revenge: The Resurgence of Capitalism and the Death of Statist Socialism* (2002), p.303.

76 Derrick Jensen, *A Language Older Than Words* (2000), p.105.

77 See Erich Maria Remarque, *All Quiet on the Western Front* (1928) for a German boy's experiences of schoolmaster and sergeant-major in pre-1914 Germany.

78 See the Teddy Lester books by John Finnemore, written between 1907 and his death in 1915.

79 Eric Hobsbawm, *Age of Extremes: The Short Twentieth-Century 1914-1991* (1994), Part One.

80 In January 1914 Winston Churchill wrote a Memo to the British cabinet: 'We are not a young people with an innocent record and a scanty inheritance. We have engrossed to ourselves... an altogether disproportionate share of the wealth and traffic of the world. We have got all we want in territory, and our claim to be left in the unmolested enjoyment of vast and splendid possessions, mainly acquired by violence, largely maintained by force, often seems less reasonable to others than to us.' The words underlined were omitted when this was published in Churchill's book *The World Crisis* in the 1920s. Quoted by Noam Chomsky, *The New Military Humanism. Lessons from Kosovo* (1999), p.78, who footnotes Clive Ponting, *Churchill* (1994), p.132.

81 Martin van Creveld, *The Transformation of War* (1991), p.227. Van Creveld precedes this with: 'War is life written large. Among the things that move between two poles, war alone permits and demands *all* man's faculties, the highest as well as the lowest. The brutality and the ruthlessness, the courage and the determination, the sheer power that strategy considers necessary for the conduct of armed conflict are at the same time its causes. Literature, art, games, and history all bear eloquent testimony to the same elemental fact.'

82 In a letter to his mother in October 1914, quoted in Neil Hollander, *Elusive Dove: The Search for Peace During World War I* (2013), p,191.

83 See Michael Howard, *The Franco-Prussian War: The German Invasion of France* (1961).

84 See Joseph Schumpeter, *Capitalism, Socialism and Democracy* (1942), as well as Werner Sombart, *War and Capitalism* (1913).

85 Quoted in Roger Chickering, *Imperial Germany and a World Without War: The Peace Movement and German Society, 1892-1914* (1988), pp.392-93.

86 See Alistair Horne, *The Price of Glory: Verdun 1916* (1962).

87 David Roberts, *Minds at War: The Poetry and Experience of the First World War* (1996), p.10.

88 Vera Brittain, *Testament of Youth* (1933). Vera Brittain lost in the war her fiancé, brother, and two good male friends.

89 See Leni Riefenstahl's propaganda film of the 1934 Nuremberg Rally, *The Triumph of the Will* (1935).

90 Iris Chang, *The Rape of Nanking* (1991).

91 The atrocities of the Stalin era in the Soviet Union tended to be downplayed by historians before Robert Conquest's 1968 book *The Great Terror: Stalin's Purges of the Thirties.*

92 From a speech to Industrial Managers, February 1931, printed in *Problems of Leninism* (1953), pp.454-58.

93 There is a still ongoing debate amongst specialists as to whether the famine can be categorised as a genocide.

94 Ryszard Kapuscinski, *Imperium* (1993), p.99.

95 For the Stalinist terror see Robert Conquest, *The Great Terror: A Reassessment* (1990); Ryszard Kapuscinski, *Imperium*; Adam Hochschild, *Unquiet Ghost: Russians Remember Stalin* (2003); Varlam Shalamov, *Kolyma Tales* (1980); Anne Appelbaum, *Gulag: A History* (2003).

96 Robert Conquest, *The Great Terror. A Reassessment*, p.287. Conquest quotes the Russian poet Anna Akhmatova, who wrote of this era in Russian history:

> But your spine has been smashed,
> My beautiful pitiful era,
> And with an inane smile,
> You look back, cruel and weak,
> Like a beast that has been supple,
> At the tracks of your own paws.

97 Alexander Solzhenitsyn, *The Gulag Archipelago* (1974 translation), p.93.

98 Nadezhda Mandelstam, *Hope Against Hope* (1989 edition) and *Hope Abandoned* (various editions).

99 Available in English editions respectively 1967 and 1982.

100 Nadezhda Mandelstam, *Hope Against Hope*, p.13.

101 Nadezhda Mandelstam, *Hope Against Hope*, p.146.

102 Nadezhda Mandelstam, *Hope Against Hope*, pp.316-17.

103 See Eugenia Ginzburg, *Into The Whirlwind* for the account of her arrest, imprisonment, and sending to Magadan; and *Within the Whirlwind* for her experiences in the Gulag until her eventual release. Both were made available in English in 1967.

104 Kapuscinski, *Imperium*, p.216.

105 Tzvetan Todorov, *Facing the Extreme: Moral Life in the Concentration Camps* (1996), p.28.

106 Hannah Arendt, *The Origins of Totalitarianism* (English edition, 1951).

107 Olivier Razak, *Barbed Wire: A Political History* (2000), p.5.

108 Quoted Brian Ladd, *The Ghosts of Berlin: Confronting German History in the Urban Landscape* (1997), p.82.

109 See Victor Klemperer, *I Shall Bear Witness: The Diaries of Victor Klemperer 1933-41* (1998) for one family's agonising over whether to leave Germany or not. Klemperer, although Jewish, saw himself first as a German. He had fought with the Kaiser's armies in the First World War.

110 Klemperer, *I Shall Bear Witness*, p.374.

111 For the killing of the sick in Germany after November 1939 see Michael Burleigh, *Death and Deliverance: 'Euthanasia' in Germany c. 1900-1945* (1994).

112 Klemperer, *I Shall Bear Witness*, p.469.

113 For the killing of Jews in German-occupied Europe after Barbarossa, see Christopher Browning, *Ordinary Men: Reserve Police Battalion 101 and the Final Solution in Poland* (1992); for an individual prisoner's experience at Auschwitz see Tadeusz Borowski, *This Way For the Gas, Ladies and Gentlemen* (1946; English translation 1967).

114 For this debate see, amidst a growing literature, Browning, *Ordinary Men*; and David Cesarani, *Final Solution: The Fate of the Jews, 1933-1949* (2016). Browning believes the decision for the 'final solution' was taken as the German armies appeared to be on the verge of an easy victory during July-September 1941, whereas Cesarani believes the final decision was not made until after the United States and Germany were at war in December. If Cesarani is correct, the fate of the Jews resulted from the growing likelihood of Germany's defeat.

115 Cesarani, *Final Solution*, p. xxxvi. On p. xxxv he writes that German military shortcomings produced 'a military disaster in the autumn and winter of 1941 that condemned Germany to a war it could never win. The Jews paid the price for German military failure.'

116 Browning, *Ordinary Men*, pp.188-89.

117 Yitzhak Arad et al (eds), *Documents on the Holocaust* (1981).

118 Primo Levi, *If This Is a Man* (1958). See also Levi, *The Drowned and the Saved* (1988).

119 Quoted in Eric Hobsbawm, *Age of Extremes*, p.1.

120 Gerald Reitlinger, *The SS: Alibi of a Nation,1922-45* (1956), p.288.

121 Robert Oppenheimer quoted in Allan M. Winkler, *Life Under a Cloud: American Anxiety about the Atom* (1993), p.75; Edward Teller quoted in Peter Wyden, *Day One: Before Hiroshima and After* (1984), p.355.

122 Wislawa Szymborska, *View With a Grain of Sand. Selected Poems* (1996), pp.77-78.

123 Much of the material for this chapter is from the magnificent account by Richard Rhodes, *The Making of the Atomic Bomb* (1986).

124 For Chadwick see Alan Brown, *The Neutron and the Bomb* (1997).

125 Rhodes, *The Making of the Atomic Bomb*, pp.230-32.

126 Rhodes, *The Making of the Atomic Bomb*, p.203.

127 Rhodes, *The Making of the Atomic Bomb*, pp.256-64.

128 Rhodes, *The Making of the Atomic Bomb*, pp.303-08.

129 Rhodes, *The Making of the Atomic Bomb*, p.325.

130 Rhodes, *The Making of the Atomic Bomb*, p.355.

131 Rhodes, *The Making of the Atomic Bomb*, p.356.

132 Rhodes, *The Making of the Atomic Bomb*, p.673.

133 Quoted in Rhodes, *The Making of the Atomic Bomb*, p.310.

134 For the Hamburg bombing see Rhodes, *The Making of the Atomic Bomb*, pp.471-75.

135 WG Sebald, *On The Natural History of Destruction* (Penguin edition, 2004), pp.28-9.

136 Rhodes, *The Making of the Atomic Bomb*, p.593.

137 Rhodes, *The Making of the Atomic Bomb*, p.649.

138 For the Lewis and Caron quotes see Rhodes, *The Making of the Atomic Bomb*, p.711.

139 Richard Minear, *Hiroshima: Three Witnesses* (1990); Michihiko Hachiya, *Hiroshima Diary: The Journal of a Japanese Physician, August 6-September 30,1945*, (1955).

140 Rhodes, *The Making of the Atomic Bomb*, pp.724-25.

141 Rhodes, *The Making of the Atomic Bomb*, p.747.

142 Rhodes, *The Making of the Atomic Bomb*, p.733.

143 Rhodes, *The Making of the Atomic Bomb*, pp.735-36.

144 See chapter 21 below for the hydrogen bomb.

145 Hobsbawm, *Age of Extremes*, is an excellent introductory overview.

146 Harold Evans, *The American Century* (1998), p.314.

147 A successful part of today's United States and British neoliberal political propaganda has been to label social-democrat policies after the 1940s as 'socialist', implying that they were 'communist'.

148 Heinberg, *The Party's Over*, p.70.

149 Remember 'White's Law': see endnote 34.

150 Hobsbawm, *Age of Extremes*, p.236. President Eisenhower's farewell radio and television address to the American people of 17 January 1961 included the following: 'Until the latest of our world conflicts, the United States had no armaments industry. American makers of plowshares could, with time and as required, make swords as well. But now we can no longer risk emergency improvisation of national defense; we have been compelled to create a permanent arms industry of vast proportions [...] This conjunction of an immense military establishment and a large arms industry is new in the American experience. The total influence – economic, political, even spiritual – is felt in every city, every State house, every office of the Federal Government. We recognise the imperative need for this development. Yet we must not fail to comprehend its grave implications. Our toil, resources and livelihood are all involved; so is the very structure of our society. In the councils of government, we must guard against the acquisition of unwarranted influence, whether sought or unsought, by the military-industrial complex. The potential for the disastrous rise of misplaced power exists and will persist. We must never let the weight of this combination endanger our liberties or democratic processes. We should take nothing for granted. Only an alert and knowledgeable citizenry can compel the proper meshing of the huge industrial and military machinery of defence with our peaceful methods and goals, so that security and liberty can prosper together.' Quoted in Stephen I. Schwartz (ed.), *Atomic Audit* (1998), pp.519-20.

151 Quoted by Mary Blume in her introduction to *After the War was Over: 168 Masterpieces by Magnum Photographers* (1985).

152 Betty Friedan, *The Feminine Mystique* (1963).

153 Michel Houellebecq, *Atomised* (1999), pp.135-36.

154 Herbert Marcuse, *Eros and Civilization* (1955), p.79.

155 Quoted in Tod Gitlin, *The Sixties: Years of Hope, Days of Rage* (1987), p.291.

156 See Allen Ginsberg, *Howl and Other Poems* (1956).

157 Quoted Gitlin, *The Sixties*, p.9.

158 From their album *Beggars Banquet*, released 1968.

159 Timothy Leary, *Chaos and Cyber Culture* (1994), pp.57-58.

160 Boeckh, *The Great Reflation*, pp.189, 208. Nixon's floating of the dollar in August 1971 was the main cause of the inflation of the 1970s. It resulted partly from overspending by the United States on the Vietnam war.

161 See for example, Hobsbawm, *Age of Extremes*; and William Greider, *One World, Ready or Not: The Manic Logic of Global Capitalism* (1997).

162 It is worth remembering that von Mises had written in 1927: 'It cannot be denied that Fascism and similar movements aimed at the establishment of dictatorships are full of the best intentions and that their intervention has

for the moment saved European civilization.' Quoted in Noam Chomsky, *The Precipice. Neoliberalism, the Pandemic and the Urgent Need for Radical Change* (2021), p.253.

163 A very large literature. I used, inter alia, Greider, *One World Ready or Not*; William Greider, *Who Will Tell the People: The Betrayal of American Democracy* (1992); Amory Starr, *Naming the Enemy: Anti-Corporate Movements Confront Globalization* (2000); Joseph E. Stiglitz, *The Roaring Nineties: A New History of the World's Most Prosperous Decade* (2004); David C. Korten, *When Corporations Rule the World* (1995).

164 Sharon Beder, *Suiting Themselves: How Corporations Drive the Global Agenda* (2006), p.102.

165 Hobsbawm, *Age of Extremes*, p.414.

166 Quoted in John Lanchester, 'The Robots are Coming', *London Review of Books*, 5 March 2015, p.5. Norbert Wiener, the inventor of cybernetics, had written at the turn of the 1950s: 'The automatic machine...is the precise economic equivalent of slave labor. Any labor which competes with slave labor must accept the economic conditions of slave labor.' Quoted David Brown, *Cybertrends: Chaos, Power and Accountability in the Information Age* (1997), p.41.

167 Francis Fukuyama, *The End of History and the Last Man* (1992). Today Fukuyama's argument that in the early 1990s history was at an end 'that is, the end point of man's ideological evolution and the universalization of Western liberal democracy', seems premature.

168 See John Stauber and Sheldon Rampton, *Toxic Sludge is Good for You: Lies, Damned Lies and the Public Relations Industry* (1995).

169 Stauber and Rampton, *Toxic Sludge is Good for You*, p.205.

170 Noam Chomsky wrote in *Class Warfare* (1996), p.153: 'The [modern business] corporations are just as totalitarian as Bolshevism and fascism. They come out of the same intellectual roots, in the early twentieth-century.'

171 Korten, *When Corporations Rule the World*, p.121.

172 Starr, *Naming the Enemy*, p.17.

173 For GATS and TRIPS see Vandana Shiva, *Protect or Plunder: Understanding Intellectual Property Rights* (2001).

174 Beder, *Suiting Themselves*, p.118.

175 Beder, *Suiting Themselves*, p.220. On p.218 she writes: 'The idea that governments should protect citizens against the excesses of free enterprise has been replaced with the idea that governments should protect business activities against the excesses of democratic regulation.'

176 Quoted in Alexander, *Unravelling Global Apartheid*, p.86.

177 See York W. Bradshaw and Michael Wallace, *Global Inequalities* (1996); Alexander, *Unravelling Global Apartheid*; John Clark, *Worlds Apart: Civil Society and the Battle for Ethical Globalisation* (2003); Thom Hartmann,

*Unequal Protection: The Rise of Corporate Domination and the Theft of Human Rights* (2004).

178 Mentioned in South Africa's *Finweek*, 27 July 2006.

179 Bradshaw and Wallace, *Global Inequalities*, pp.4-6.

180 As for example in the United Kingdom today.

181 John McMurtry, *Value Wars. The Global Market versus the Life Economy* (2002), p.88. The italics are McMurtry's.

182 Edward S. Herman and Noam Chomsky, *Manufacturing Consent. The Political Economy of the Mass Media* (1988), p.94.

183 McMurtry, *Value Wars*, p.81.

184 Noam Chomsky, *Imperial Ambitions: Conversations with Noam Chomsky on the Post-9/11 World*, edited David Barsamian (2005), p.21. The 'philosophy of futility' is part of Chomsky's wider thought: 'It's interesting to look back at the 1920s, when the public relations industry began. This was the period of Taylorism in industry, when workers were being trained to become robots and every single motion was controlled and regulated. Taylorism created highly efficient industry, with human beings turned into automata. The Bolsheviks were very impressed with Taylorism, too, and tried to duplicate it, as did others throughout the world. But the thought-control experts soon realized that you could have not only what was called "on-job control" but also "off-job control". It's a fine phrase. Off-job control means turning people into robots in every part of their lives by inducing a "philosophy of futility", focussing people on "the superficial things of life, like fashion consumption". Let the people who are supposed to run the show do so without any interference from the mass of the population, who have no business in the public arena. And from that idea grew enormous industries, ranging from advertising to universities, all very consciously committed to the belief that you must control attitudes and opinions, because the people are otherwise just too dangerous.' Chomsky for his quotations refers the reader to Michael Dawson, *The Consumer Trap* (2003); and Stewart Ewan, *Captains of Consciousness* (1976), p.85.

185 For some of the problems see for example Andreas Malm, *How to Blow Up a Pipeline: Learning to Fight in a World on Fire* (2021).

186 *Mail & Guardian*, 27 May 2005.

187 John Vidal, *McLibel: Burger Culture on Trial* (1997).

188 It is worth pondering the words of Michael Mansfield QC, who represented Steel and Morris, who said, at the end of the trial: 'What this case has demonstrated, through all the verbiage, the statistics, the claims and the counter-claims, is that capitulation is not a political inevitability. Additionally, Steel and Morris have provided inspiration to a generation which has witnessed a relentless descent into moral bankruptcy.' See Vidal, *McLibel*, p.318.

189 See Eric Schlosser, *Fast Food Nation: The Dark Side of the All-American Meal* (2002), p.5.
190 Korten, *When Corporations Rule the World*, p.206.
191 Greider, *Who Will Tell the People*, p.11.
192 John Berger, 'Written in the Night: The Pain of Living in the Present World', *Le Monde Diplomatique*, 18 February 2003.
193 See chapter 4.
194 Edward Goldsmith and Jerry Mander (eds), *The Case Against the Global Economy and for a Turn Towards Localization* (2000), p.54.
195 Brett Scott, *Cloud Money: Cash, Cards, Crypto and the War for our Wallets* (2022), p. 180.
196 Quoted in the UK *Sunday Independent*, 17 October 1999.
197 McLuhan, *Understanding Media*, p.354.
198 Explored in Carl Sagan, *The Demon-Haunted World: Science as a Candle in the Dark* (1996).
199 Lewis Mumford, *Pentagon of Power: The Myth of the Machine*, Vol.2 (1964), p.294.
200 Timothy Snyder, *The Road To Unfreedom: Russia, Europe, America* (2018), p.281.
201 Hobsbawm, *Age of Extremes*, p.3.
202 Martin Amis, *Einstein's Monsters* (1987), p.17.
203 Asoka Bandarage, *Women, Population and Global Crisis* (1997), p.158.
204 Neil Postman, *The Disappearance of Childhood* (1994), p.118.
205 Robert Bly, *The Sibling Society* (1997), p.132.
206 Zygmunt Bauman, *Liquid Love: On the Frailty of Human Bonds* (2000), p.49 (Bauman's emphases).
207 Alan Durning, *How Much Is Enough? The Consumer Society and the Future of the Earth* (1992), p.125.
208 Richard Wilkinson, *Unhealthy Societies: The Afflictions of Inequality* (1996), p.226.
209 Bly, *The Sibling Society*, p.130.
210 See endnote 153.
211 Quoted in Majid Rahnema (ed), *The Post-Development Reader* (1997), p.350.
212 William Kilpatrick, *Why Johnny Can't Tell Right from Wrong* (1992).
213 Luciana Bohne, 'Review/Arts', in *This Day*, p.3, 21 November 2003.
214 See Snyder, *The Road to Unfreedom*.
215 Sagan, *Demon-Haunted World*, p.26.
216 See photo 122 in Rhodes, *The Making of the Atomic Bomb*.
217 Baudrillard, *The Transparency of Evil*, p.81.
218 Bly, *The Sibling Society*, pp.169-70.
219 A very good overview is Evans, *Feeding the Ten Billion*. See also Paul Ehrlich, *The Population Explosion* (1989 edition). In 1955, when global population

was around 2.5 billion, Julian Huxley stressed the dangers of compounded expansion; at the time the daily increase of population was 95 million, and the hourly increase 4,000. See Thomas Malthus, Julian Huxley and Frederick Osborn, *On Population: Three Essays* (1960), p.64.

220 Colin Mason, *The 2030 Spike: Countdown to Global Catastrophe* (2003), p.9.

221 Thomas Homer-Dixon, *The Ingenuity Gap: How Can We Solve the Problems of the Future?* (2000), p.67. Homer-Dixon adds: 'Put another way, nearly two and a half billion people are alive today because the proteins in their bodies are built with nitrogen that comes from a factory using the Haber-Bosch process.'

222 See Lester R. Brown, *Outgrowing the Earth: The Food Security Challenge in an Age of Falling Water Tables and Rising Temperatures* (2005).

223 United Nations media brief: The Human Right to Water and Sanitation (2010).

224 See Larbi Bouguerra, *Water Under Threat* (2006).

225 Germaine Greer, *Sex and Destiny: The Politics of Human Fertility* (1984).

226 Greer comments: 'It seems obvious that people who do not care to reproduce do not actually care whether they die out or not.' Greer, *Sex and Destiny*, p.381.

227 Greer, *Sex and Destiny*, p.376.

228 Greer, *Sex and Destiny*, p.409.

229 For deforestation see the relevant sections in Lester R. Brown, *Plan B 2.0: Rescuing a Planet Under Stress and a Civilization in Trouble* (2006); Jared Diamond, *Collapse: How Societies Choose to Fail or Survive* (2005); Edward Wilson, *The Future of Life* (2005). According to Wilson (p.58): 'Over 60 percent of temperate hardwood and mixed forest has been lost, as well as 30 percent of conifer forest, 45 percent of tropical rain forest, and 70 percent of tropical dry forest.' And that by 2005. For today's rate of loss see pp.203-04 301, 307.

230 See chapter 19.

231 George B. Schaller, 'Gold or Flowers: One View of the State of the World', in Wildlife Conservation Society, *State of the Wild 2006: A Global Portrait of Wildlife, Wildlands, and Oceans* (2005), p.8.

232 Ellen K. Pikitch, 'The Gathering Wave of Ocean Extinctions', in Wildlife Conservation Society, *State of the Wild 2006*, pp.197-99.

233 Kapuscinski, *Imperium*, pp.254-64. Characteristically, Soviet administrators began working on the idea of how to divert the north flowing rivers of Siberia towards the south so as to permit continued growing of cotton.

234 Alan Weisman, *The World Without Us* (2007), ch.7, 'Polymers Are Forever'.

235 Rachel Carson, *Silent Spring* (1962), p.6.

236 DDT had first been synthesised in Germany in 1874. The first to appreciate its potency for killing insects was Paul Müller of Switzerland, who received

the 1948 Nobel Prize for Medicine for the discovery.

237 Carson, *Silent Spring*, p.25.

238 Carson, *Silent Spring*, pp.46-50.

239 Deborah Cadbury, *The Feminization of Nature: Our Future At Risk* (1997).

240 For the 'Living Planet Index' and the 'Ecological Footprint' see the World Wildlife Fund, *Living Planet Report*, annually. I encouraged my history students to calculate their own personal ecological footprints. I could not get mine much below 3, however much I cheated.

241 Quoted in Richard Douthwaite, *The Growth Illusion: How Economic Growth has Enriched the Few, Impoverished the Many and Endangered the Planet* (updated and revised edition 1999 [originally 1992]), p.201. In 1991 Larry Summers was chief economist at the World Bank.

242 Thomas Berry, *Befriending the Earth* (1991), pp.106-07.

243 Berry, *Befriending the Earth*, p.20. Berry wrote in *The Dream of the Earth*, p.209: 'The day of reckoning has come. In this disintegrating phase of our industrial society, we now see ourselves not as the splendor of creation, but as the most pernicious mode of earthly being. We are the termination, not the fulfillment of the earth process.'

244 Carson, *Silent Spring*, quoted frontispiece of Jacklyn Cock, *The War against Ourselves: Nature, Power and Justice* (2007),

245 For chief Sealth, or Seattle, see endnote 5 for reference.

246 Lovelock, *Healing Gaia*, p.18.

247 George Monbiot, *Mail & Guardian*, 5-11 December 2003, p.17.

248 For overviews see Heinberg, *The Party's Over*; and Jeremy Leggett, *Half Gone: Oil, Gas, Hot Air and the Global Energy Crisis* (2005).

249 For Hubbert see Heinberg, *The Party's Over*, pp.87-88, 90-92, 96.

250 In March 2022 oil reached US$ 139 a barrel.

251 Ponting, *A New Green History of the World*, p.388. One of the first to refer to Arrhenius was John Gribbin, *Hothouse Earth: The Greenhouse Effect and Gaia* (1991).

252 Jim Hansen's cautious views of the late 1980s had hardened by the early 2000s. See his review on global warming in *The New York Review of Books*, 13 July 2006, pp.12-16.

253 Though, note that in August 2022 the United States Congress passed the 'Inflation Reduction Act' which, it is estimated, could cut US carbon emissions 40% by 2030.

254 For detail see Ponting, *A New Green History of the World*, pp.388-408, and Flannery, *The Weather Makers*.

255 Flannery, *The Weather Makers*, p.147.

256 The South African examples are discussed in Leonie S. Joubert, *Scorched: South Africa's Changing Climate* (2006).

257 Quoted in Ponting, *A New Green History of the World*, p.407.

258 See the most recent book by Bill McGuire, *Hothouse Earth* (2022). He writes that there is now no prospect of avoiding a runaway warming, and that climate experts in private conversation accept that, whatever they may say in public.

259 For an overview see Franz Broswimmer, *Ecocide: A Short History of the Mass Extinction of Species* (2002).

260 Margulis and Sagan, *Microcosmos*, pp.196, 237.

261 Edward O. Wilson, *The Future of Life* (2002), pp.98-99.

262 Wilson, *The Future of Life*, p.50, summarises the forces at work as HIPPO, which stands for Habitat destruction; Invasive Species; Pollution; Population; and Overharvesting.

263 Jared Diamond, *The Rise and Fall of the Third Chimpanzee: How our Animal Heritage Affects the Way We Live* (1991), ch.17.

264 Wilson, *The Future of Life*, p.92.

265 Diamond, *Rise and Fall of the Third Chimpanzee*, p.289.

266 For the Hawaiian extinctions see Wilson, *The Future of Life*, Ch.3; and Diamond, *Rise and Fall of the Third Chimpanzee*, p.291.

267 Wilson, *The Future of Life*, p.95.

268 Diamond, *Rise and Fall of the Third Chimpanzee*, p.292.

269 Diamond, *Rise and Fall of the Third Chimpanzee*, pp.294-95.

270 Wilson, *The Future of Life*, p.77. Wilson suggests on pp.77-78 a message to our descendants: 'We bequeath to you the synthetic jungles of Hawaii and a scrubland where once thrived the prodigious Amazon forest, along with some remnants of wild environments here and there we chose not to lay waste. Your challenge is to create new kinds of plants and animals by genetic engineering and somehow fit them together into free-living artificial ecosystems. We understand that this feat may prove impossible. We are certain that for many of you even the thought of doing so will be repugnant. We wish you luck. And if you go ahead and succeed in the attempt, we regret that what you manufacture can never be as satisfying as the original creation. Accept our apologies and this audiovisual library that illustrates the wondrous world that used to be.'

271 See J. del Hoyo, A. Elliott and J. Sargatal (eds), *Handbook of the Birds of the World.* Vol.7 (2002), Jacamars to Woodpeckers, Foreword: Extinct Birds, pp.32-34.

272 *Handbook of the Birds of the World*, Vol.7, Extinct Birds, pp.30-31.

273 *Handbook of the Birds of the World*, Vol.7, Extinct Birds, pp.12, 34-36.

274 *Handbook of the Birds of the World*, Vol.7, Family PICIDAE (Woodpeckers), p.418. See too *The Daily Despatch*, 30 April 2005 (referring to an article in the London *Daily Telegraph*), reporting a sighting of the ivory-billed woodpecker in Arkansas.

275 For the cranes see Peter Matthiessen, *The Birds of Heaven. Travels with Cranes*

(2001); and J. del Hoyo, A. Elliott and J. Sargatal (eds), *Handbook of the Birds of the World*, Vol.1 (1992), *Ostrich to Ducks*, pp.198-215.

276 For the Sumatran Rhino see Wilson, *The Future of Life*, 79-88.

277 Graham Spence, *Saving the Last Rhinos: The Life of a Frontline Conservationist* (2019).

278 Richard Leakey and Roger Lewis, *The Sixth Extinction: Biodiversity and Its Survival* (1995), pp.201-02.

279 Leakey and Lewis, *The Sixth Extinction*, pp.203-17. For elephant numbers see the Wikipedia article on the 'great elephant count of 2016'. It is estimated that before Europeans entered with firearms there were about twenty million elephants in Africa.

280 For the massacre of gorillas and chimpanzees see Dale Petersen, *Eating Apes* (2003).

281 Diamond, *The Rise and Fall of the Third Chimpanzee*, p.25.

282 Ellen K. Pikitch, 'The Gathering Wave of Ocean Extinctions', *State of the Wild 2006*, p.195.

283 Diamond, *Collapse*, p.480.

284 Pikitch, 'The Gathering Wave of Ocean Extinctions', *State of the Wild 2006*, p.199.

285 Wilson, *The Future of Life*, p.77.

286 Jensen, *A Language Older Than Words*, p. ix.

287 Raphael Lemkin first defined the concept of 'genocide' in his 1944 work *Axis Rule in Occupied Europe: Laws of Occupation, Analysis of Government, Proposals for Redress.*

288 Martin Shaw, *War and Genocide: Organised Killing in Modern Society* (2003); Jonathan Glover, *Humanity: A Moral History of the Twentieth Century* (1999).

289 See chapter 11.

290 This comes out in Klemperer, *I Shall Bear Witness.*

291 Browning, *Ordinary Men*, p.189.

292 This is a summary of the Wikipedia article 'Indonesian Mass Killings of 1965-66'.

293 Sir Andrew Gilchrist to foreign office, 5 October 1965.

294 This is a summary of the Wikipedia article '1971 Bangladesh Genocide'.

295 The quotes are from the relevant Wikipedia article.

296 For the Cambodian mass killings I have used Ben Kiernan, *The Pol Pot Regime* (1996); Karl Jackson (ed), *Cambodia 1975-78: Rendezvous With Death* (1989); Haing S. Ngor, *Surviving the Killing Fields* (1988); and Glover, *Humanity* (1996).

297 The emptying out of Phnom Penh comes out frighteningly in the 1984 film *The Killing Fields.*

298 'In short, Pol Pot was implementing Mao's plan with Stalin's methods.' See Jackson (ed), *Cambodia 1975-78*, p.236.

299 See Jackson (ed), *Cambodia 1975-78*, p.185

300 See Jackson (ed), *Cambodia 1975-78*; Kiernan, *The Pol Pot Regime*; and Haing Ngor, *Surviving the Killing Fields*, for detail.

301 For Uganda see Phares Mutiba, *Uganda Since Independence* (1996); and Mark Leopold, *Idi Amin: The Story of Africa's Icon of Evil* (2021).

302 For the Rwandan genocide I recommend Gérard Prunier, *The Rwandan Crisis 1959-1994: History of a Genocide* (1995); Philip Gourevitch, *We Wish to Inform You that Tomorrow We Will Be Killed with Our Families* (1998); and Diamond, *Collapse*, chapter 10: 'Malthus in Africa: Rwanda's Genocide'.

303 Quoted in the Wikipedia article on *Kangura*.

304 Prunier, *The Rwandan Crisis*, p.238.

305 Diamond, *Collapse*, pp.320-28.

306 Diamond, *Collapse*, p.323.

307 Diamond, *Collapse*, pp.327-28.

308 See chapter 12.

309 Rhodes, T*he Making of the Atomic Bomb*, p.649.

310 Diamond, *The Rise and Fall of the Third Chimpanzee*, p.266. Note his bracketing of Dresden and Hiroshima with Auschwitz and Treblinka as genocides.

311 Gerard J. DeGroot, *The Bomb. A Life* (2004), p.102.

312 DeGroot, *The Bomb*, pp.109-10.

313 DeGroot, *The Bomb*, p.109.

314 For the development of the Soviet atomic and hydrogen bombs see David Holloway, *Stalin and the Bomb: The Soviet Union and Atomic Energy 1939-1956* (1994).

315 Holloway, *Stalin and the Bomb*, chapters 6 and 10.

316 DeGroot, *The Bomb*, pp.145-46. Another member of the Soviet atomic team, Iulii Khariton, said: 'when we succeeded in solving this problem, we felt relief, even happiness – for in possessing such a weapon we had removed the possibility of its being used against the USSR with impunity.' See Holloway, *Stalin and the Bomb*, p.216.

317 For the US development of their first hydrogen bomb, see Richard Rhodes, *Dark Sun: The Making of the Hydrogen Bomb* (1995).

318 Amis, *Einstein's Monsters*, p.17.

319 DeGroot, *The Bomb*, p.182.

320 DeGroot, *The Bomb*, p.194.

321 DeGroot, *The Bomb*, p.208.

322 At the Flamingo Hotel guests could get an 'atomic hairdo' and dance the 'Atomic Bomb Bounce'. DeGroot, *The Bomb*, p.250.

323 On the Cuban missile crisis see Max Hastings, *The Abyss: Nuclear Crisis Cuba 1962* (2022).

324 Arkhipov's vetoing of the missile launch saved humans from a fatal nuclear

exchange.

325 Jonathan Schell, *The Fate of the Earth* (1982), p.148. Schell continued: 'In the long run, if we are dull and cold towards life in its entirety we will become dull and cold towards life in its particulars – towards the events of our daily lives – but if we are alert and passionate about life in its entirety we will also be alert and passionate about it in its dailiness.'

326 For the numbers, types and costs of the US missile collections see Stephen I. Schwartz (ed), *Atomic Audit: The Costs and Consequences of US Nuclear Weapons Since 1940* (1998).

327 Charles Perrow, *Normal Accidents: Living with High-Risk Technologies* (1984).

328 For the Chernobyl disaster see Svetlana Alexievich, *Voices from Chernobyl: The Oral History of a Nuclear Disaster* (1997).

329 Svetlana Alexievich, *Chernobyl Prayer. A Chronicle of the Future* (1997), p.27.

330 James Lovelock, *The Revenge of Gaia: Why the Earth is Fighting Back – and How we Can Still Save Humanity* (2006), p.153.

331 *Financial Times* review of James Lovelock, *Novacene: The Coming Age of Hyperintelligence* (2019), by Stephen Cave, July 16 2019.

332 John Cirincione, *Bomb Scare: The History and Future of Nuclear Weapons* (2005), p.89.

333 Cirincione, *Bomb Scare*, p.96.

334 See Amis, *Einstein's Monsters*, pp.22-23, where the rival nuclear powers are compared to children at a tea party: 'The party has not been going on for very long and lasts until the end of time.'

335 For the post-1928 financial crisis see Robert S. McElvaine, *The Great Depression: America,1929-41* (2nd edition 1993).

336 See chapter 14.

337 Boeckh, *The Great Reflation*, chapter 1: 'The Age of Inflation'.

338 For the financial crash of 2007-09 see Mark Zondi, *Financial Shock: A 360° Look at the Subprime Mortgage Implosion, and How to Avoid the Next Financial Crisis* (2009); and Martin Wolf, *The Shifts and the Shocks: What we Have Learned and Still Have to Learn From the Financial Crisis* (2015).

339 Matt Taibbi wrote on 13 July 2009: 'The first thing you need to know about Goldman Sachs is that it's everywhere. The world's most powerful investment bank is a great vampire squid wrapped around the face of humanity, relentlessly jamming its blood funnel into anything that smells like money. In fact, the history of the recent financial crisis, which doubles as a history of the rapid decline and fall of the suddenly swindled dry American empire, reads like a Who's Who of Goldman Sachs graduates.' See Matt Taibbi, *The Great American Bubble Machine* (2009), p.1.

340 See Anat Admati and Martin Hellwig, *The Bankers' New Clothes; What's Wrong with Banking and What to Do about it* (2013).

341 For a critique of the EU's handling of the Greek debt crisis, and of the

structures of the European Union, see Yanis Varoufakis, *And the Weak Suffer What They Must: Europe, Austerity and the Threat to Global Stability* (2016).

342 See two *Guardian* essays by Nouriel Roubini of 29 June and 9 August 2022, respectively 'A Stagflationary Debt Crisis Now Looms', and 'From Great Moderation to Stagflation'.

343 Svetlana Alexievich, *Second-Hand Time: The Last of the Soviets* (2016), p.166.

344 Burgis, *Kleptopia*, p.157.

345 For Putin's rise to power see Snyder, T*he Road to Unfreedom*, chapter 2.

346 Bovis Kagarlitsky, quoted in John Pilger, *The New Rulers of the World* (2002), p.5.

347 See Snyder, *The Road to Unfreedom* and Burgis, *Kleptopia*.

348 Snyder, *The Road to Unfreedom*, p.194.

349 Snyder, *The Road to Unfreedom*, p.261.

350 Snyder, *The Road to Unfreedom*, chapter 6.

351 It took until mid-2023 before Trump and other top level politicians were charged for a crime after instigating what was an attempted coup. Political support for Trump remained high, and he was the front-runner Republican candidate for the 2024 presidential elections.

352 Including nuclear fissile material, particularly plutonium.

353 Manuel Castells, *The Information Age: Economy, Society and Culture, Vol.3 End Of Millennium* (1998), p.166.

354 Snyder, *The Road to Unfreedom*, p.246.

355 Hannah Arendt, *Crisis of the Republic: Lying in Politics* (1972), p. 11. I am indebted to Rebecca Hodes for this reference.

356 For the 'Spanish flu' epidemic of 1918-19 see Catharine Arnold, *Pandemic 1918* (2018).

357 See Ponting, *A New Green History of the World*, chapter 8.

358 Leakey and Lewin, *The Sixth Extinction*; and see chapter 19.

359 David Quammen, 'We Made the Coronavirus Epidemic', *The New York Times*, 5 February 2020.

360 For the North Pacific Gyre, and for nurdles, see Weisman, *The World Without Us*, chapter 9: 'Polymers Are Forever', pp.146-61.

361 Flannery, *The Weather Makers*, pp.105-106.

362 Inevitably the latest examples of climate news cited will be out of date as soon as this book is printed. Thus London experienced a temperature of over 40°C in August 2022. And rivers throughout Europe such as the Po, Elbe, Loire and Rhine are drying up, revealing dead bodies and abandoned settlements. Sections of the Yangtze in China are also dry, restricting navigation.

363 Peter Kalmus, *The Guardian*, August 2021.

364 Diamond, *Collapse*, p.521.

365 Ponting, *A New Green History of the World*, p.423.

366 Hochschild, *The Unique Ghost. Russians Remember the Past*, pp.276-77.

367 Lovelock, *Healing Gaia*, p.16.

368 Andrew Harvey (with Mark Matousek), *Dialogues with a Modern Mystic* (1994), pp.27-28.

369 Hobsbawm, *Age of Extremes*, pp.584-85.

370 Tony Wood, reviewing *Klimat: Russia in the Age of Climate Change* by Thane Gustafson. *London Review of Books*, 6 October 2022, p.18.

371 Malm, *How to Blow Up a Pipeline*, pp.156-57. Malm takes aim at movements, such as Deep Green Resistance, which aim to 'induce widespread industrial collapse, beyond any economic or political systems'. Whilst stressing this was a route he would not consider going down, he warns that this 'should be read as a symptom of a hardening despair and deadlock...Perhaps there will be more fever dreams of this kind on a burning planet.'

372 Quoted by Fritjof Capra, *The Hidden Connections: A Science for Sustainable Living* (2003), pp.233-34.

373 Greta Thunberg, in a speech on day four of the Glastonbury Festival, 2022.

374 Jensen, *A Language Older than Words*, p.371.

## Postscript to the 2026 edition

In the two and a half years since *Growth, Growth, Growth* was first published by Mvusi Books, the planet's human population has increased by 250 million, there is 60 billion more tons of $CO_2$ in the air, and 300 thousand sq km less forest cover. Atmospheric temperatures were on average 1,5 degrees centigrade higher over 2023–25 compared to the 1850s, resulting in more frequent and more devastating fires and floods. The President of the USA claimed that global heating was a hoax, and advocated for greater reliance on coal and oil.

Given the world's current political instability, with undemocratic trends in China, Russia and the USA, and an increasingly impotent and disunited Europe, a change of vision and course of action is unlikely. The attack on the natural world will accelerate.

## Acknowledgements

This book originated from a first year lecture series given at Rhodes University, South Africa, between 1997 and 2012. It was an overview of the entire history of the human species, with a focus on the crises that confront us today and how they came about. I am grateful to Professor Paul Maylam for giving the idea his support, and to the several thousand students who attended over the years.

Special thanks to Ali Conn and Adam Sadian for prodding me to get it written up, and to aMan Bloom for coffee talks. Thank you too to my editor and publisher, Robert Berold, for substantial improvements of earlier drafts; and to proofreader Mindy Stanford for further sandpapering. Thank you also to Jessica Powers of Catalyst Press for republishing my book in the USA.

And a big thank you to Cathy Gorham for being a critical soundboard and for very much additional help.

www.ingramcontent.com/pod-product-compliance
Lightning Source LLC
LaVergne TN
LVHW091033080826
845145LV00002B/478

* 9 7 8 1 9 6 7 6 7 3 0 0 1 *